Economics
for Cambridge IGCSE®

Robert Dransfield
David Needham
Terry Cook

Nelson Thornes

Contents

How to use the practice exam questions   iv

Unit 1 The basic economic problem: choice and the allocation of resources

	Unit introduction	1
1.1	The economic problem	2
1.2	Factors of production	4
1.3	Opportunity cost	6
1.4	Opportunity cost in action	8
	Practice exam questions	10

Unit 2 Allocating resources: the market at work and market failure

	Unit introduction	13
2.1	Allocating resources in an economy	14
2.2	Demand	16
2.3	Supply	18
2.4	Equilibrium price	20
2.5	Causes of changes in demand and the effect on the market	22
2.6	Causes of changes in supply and the effect on the market	24
2.7	Price elasticity of demand	26
2.8	Price elasticity of supply	28
2.9	Usefulness of price elasticity of demand	30
2.10	Merits of the market system	32
2.11	Market failure	34
2.12	Private and social costs and benefits	36
2.13	Conflict between private and social interests	38
	Practice exam questions	40

Unit 3 The individual as producer, consumer and borrower

	Unit introduction	43
3.1	The functions of money	44
3.2	Commercial banks	46
3.3	Central banks	48
3.4	Stock exchanges	50
3.5	Choice of occupation	52
3.6	Changes in earnings over time for an individual	54
3.7	Differences in earnings between occupations 1	56
	Differences in earnings between occupations 2	58
3.8	Trade unions	60
3.9	Specialisation	62
3.10	Motives for spending, saving and borrowing	64
3.11	Income and expenditure patterns	66
	Practice exam questions	68

Unit 4 The private firm

	Unit introduction	71
4.1	Sole proprietors and partnerships	72
4.2	Private companies	74
4.3	Public companies	76
4.4	Multinationals	78
4.5	Cooperatives	80
4.6	Public corporations	82
4.7	Effects of changes on business growth	84
4.8	The demand for factors of production	86
4.9	Fixed and variable costs	88
4.10	Total and average costs	90
4.11	Output and costs	92
4.12	Total and average revenue	94
4.13	Profit maximisation	96
4.14	Price and output in perfect competition	98
4.15	Pricing and output policies in monopoly	100
4.16	Different sizes of firms	102
4.17	Different forms of integration	104
4.18	Economies and diseconomies of scale	106
4.19	Advantages and disadvantages of monopoly	108
	Practice exam questions	110

Unit 5 The role of government in an economy

	Unit introduction	113
5.1	The government as a producer and employer	114
5.2	Government policy: full employment	116
5.3	Government policy: price stability	118
5.4	Government policy: economic growth	120
5.5	Government policy: redistribution of income	122
5.6	Government policy: balance of payments stability	124
5.7	Conflicts between government aims	126
5.8	Types of taxation	128
5.9	Government influence on private producers: regulation	130

Contents

5.10	Government influence on private producers: subsidy	132
5.11	Government influence on private producers: taxes	134
	Practice exam questions	136

Unit 6 Economic indicators

	Unit introduction	139
6.1	The Retail Price Index	140
6.2	Causes of inflation	144
6.3	Consequences of inflation	146
6.4	Patterns and levels of employment	148
6.5	Causes of unemployment	152
6.6	Consequences of unemployment	154
6.7	Gross Domestic Product	156
6.8	Comparing living standards	158
	Practice exam questions	162

Unit 7 Developed and developing economies

	Unit introduction	165
7.1	What is development?	166
7.2	Policies to reduce poverty	168
7.3	Factors that affect population growth	170
7.4	Reasons for different rates of population growth	172
7.5	Problems of population change	174
7.6	The effect of changing size of population on an economy	176
7.7	Changes in population structure and its effect on an economy	178
7.8	Living standards	180
	Practice exam questions	182

Unit 8 International aspects

	Unit introduction	185
8.1	Benefits and disadvantages of specialisation	186
8.2	The current account of the balance of payments	188
8.3	Exchange rates	190
8.4	Causes of exchange rate fluctuations	192
8.5	Consequences of exchange rate fluctuations	194
8.6	Methods of protection	196
8.7	The merits of free trade	198
8.8	The merits of protection	200
	Practice exam questions	202
	Glossary	205
	Index	210

How to use the practice exam questions

You will find three pages of exam-style questions at the end of each unit in the book. These will help you practise your examination technique and you should be able to answer them after completing all the work in the unit. You should answer them without referring to the information in the book or your notes.

The *short-answer questions* in Section 2 test your knowledge and understanding of what you have learnt. Generally, these will ask you to state, identify, define, discuss and explain one or a number of factors, differences or meanings. Your answers will be fairly brief, perhaps bullet points, but avoid single-word 'lists', especially where an explanation is required. Do not spend too long or write too much – usually you will be allocated a space in the examination of two to four lines. Where an example is required, give one from your own experience, either as a consumer or as an observer of your local economic environment.

The *questions for analysis and critical examination* in Section 3 provide practice in interpreting and analysing data presented in a passage, similar to what you will meet in Paper 3. Read the material carefully, because this will help you to give an answer that is appropriate to the question. Marks will not be awarded where answers do not 'fit' the case.

Most 4- and 6-mark questions include some marks for Application, so make sure you refer to the circumstances of the business or company, rather than just mentioning them by name. Analysis and Evaluation marks will be gained by considering both sides of an issue and coming to a supported conclusion.

Command words explained

The instruction in the question is given by the *command* word: as the word suggests, this tells you what is required. The following is a list of the command words you are likely to see in your examination.

Analyse, e.g. 'Analyse the consequences of the merger between the two companies.' When asked to 'analyse', state or calculate the answer, use a linking word, such as 'because' before developing your response, using business theory concepts.

Calculate, e.g. 'Calculate the price elasticity of demand.' You need to do some mathematics to produce an answer. Always show your workings.

Consider, e.g. 'Consider the two options given in the case study.' You need to weigh up the merits of a situation or decision and give the opposing view as well.

Define, e.g. 'Define *effective demand*.' State the exact meaning of the term; this will be a short answer, sometimes including an example to illustrate it.

Describe, e.g. 'Describe the economy of country A.' Give an account of something.

Discuss, e.g. 'Discuss the consequences for the business of increasing the price of their product.' This term requires you to put forward various points of view, advantages and disadvantages or benefits and costs.

Explain, e.g. 'Explain what is meant by a price-elastic demand.' This term enables you to show your understanding of a term or topic. You can do this by including an example or a descriptive development.

Give, e.g. 'Give an example of a fixed cost.' This is a short-answer command, requiring you to state a fact or provide an example to demonstrate your understanding.

Identify, e.g. 'Identify two factors a company should consider before deciding to issue more shares.' 'Identify' (or 'State') requires you to select from a number of possibilities. Only a brief answer is necessary, so a list may be fine, but if you are unsure, include a sentence of clarification or an example.

Justify, e.g. 'Should company X buy more machinery? Justify your answer.' This requires a longer answer which you should support with reasons.

Outline, e.g. 'Outline the main features of a business partnership.' You should give a short description of (in this example) the main features of the partnership.

Recommend, e.g. 'Recommend which option the company should take.' You should make a positive suggestion, usually with reasons that support your ideas.

State, e.g. 'State two features of a sole trader business.' Provide a short answer; this is usually intended for you to show your knowledge. See also the notes for 'Identify'.

Why, e.g. 'Why has the population of the country fallen?' You should give reasons for an event or outcome and provide some development of the points you make in your answer.

1 The basic economic problem: choice and the allocation of resources

The basic economic problem

Unit 1 introduces the basic economic problem: insufficient resources to meet all our needs and the choices that have to be made as a result. It is explained that while the earth is a very rich source of raw materials that support human life, most of these resources, in particular, oil, gas and fertile agricultural land, are limited.

The unit looks at how the resources of land, labour, capital and enterprise are used to become factors of production. The example of a successful entrepreneur illustrates how factors can be combined to generate wealth and opportunity for growth in an economy.

The unit develops the idea of choice with the introduction of the concept of opportunity cost. Explanations are given of how every economic decision involves a choice, and that when choices are made, the sacrificed alternative becomes the opportunity cost.

> **LEARNING OUTCOMES**
>
> With regard to the **economic problem**, candidates should be able to:
>
> - define the nature of the economic problem (finite resources and unlimited wants)
> - define the factors of production (land, labour, capital, enterprise)
> - define opportunity cost and analyse particular circumstances to illustrate the concept
> - evaluate the implications of particular courses of action in terms of opportunity cost.

1.1 The economic problem

LEARNING OUTCOMES

Candidates should be able to:
- define the nature of the economic problem.

Gathering fuelwood in Tanzania – fuelwood provides 90 per cent of domestic energy supplies in Tanzania, but is becoming increasingly scarce

EXAM TIP

Every country faces the economic problem. You will come across this in various places throughout this book and you should be able to work it into many examination answers.

DID YOU KNOW?

Sustainable use of resources means using them today in such a way that future supplies of these resources are not reduced.

The economic problem

We cannot have everything that we want because there are not enough resources to produce it all. Everything produced comes from a resource. There are a number of types of resource (Figure 1.1.1).

Natural resources	Man-made resources	Human resources
soil, climate, water, minerals, forests and fisheries	machinery, buildings and equipment	people and their skills

Figure 1.1.1 Types of resource

If society had all the land, labour, raw materials and other resources it needed, we could produce all the goods we wanted without making sacrifices. In reality resources are **scarce**. When we use resources to produce an item, we are taking away these resources from producing something else. This is a major problem for all societies.

Decision-making over the use of resources involves:

- making a **choice** (we can do one thing *or* the other)
- making a **sacrifice** (if we choose to do this with a resource, we cannot also do the other).

CASE STUDY | Fuelwood scarcity in Tanzania

In Tanzania fuelwood is gathered for household use from nearby forests. Some of it is gathered in a sustainable way: branches are cut and the trees regrow them. However, some wood is used for village industries, including tobacco curing, burning bricks, fish smoking, baking and tea drying. Some of the fuel for these purposes comes from charcoal and often involves cutting down whole trees and the destruction of forest areas.

Various studies have shown that annual firewood consumption in Tanzania is higher than the supply of new trees, resulting in deforestation. Fuelwood provides about 90 per cent of the energy supply and many people in Tanzania spend over 30 per cent of their income on it. As it becomes more scarce, the price goes up, and people also have to travel further to collect it.

Questions

1 What is meant by *scarcity*?

2 Why is fuelwood becoming more scarce in Tanzania?

3 How might this scarcity affect future choices that people make?

Making choices

Gathering fuelwood is an important activity in Tanzania, particularly for people in rural areas. People have to decide whether to buy the wood or collect it themselves, in which case they need to decide how long to spend gathering it and then how to cut it. Having to make choices like this is a result of the **economic problem**. Domestic energy is not provided freely to households – people have to gather fuel themselves or pay for it.

Our daily lives involve thousands of choices that we have to make that involve how we spend our time and our money.

- Time is a scarce resource – there are only 24 hours in a day.
- Money is a scarce resource – we only have a limited amount.

So daily life involves solving many economic problems where choices have to be made. Imagine that you have to decide whether to buy a book or borrow it from a library. If you buy the book, you 'sacrifice' the opportunity to buy something else with the money you would have saved by borrowing it. If you borrow it, you sacrifice the opportunity to own the book. In Units 1.3 and 1.4 we will explore this further in terms of the *cost* of the sacrifice – the **opportunity cost**.

ACTIVITY

Use your local and national papers or the internet to find a story about scarcity in your region or country. What is it that is scarce? Who is affected by the scarcity? What sorts of choices are people having to make as a result of this scarcity? Share your findings with your group.

EXAM TIP

Another way of thinking about choice and sacrifice is in terms of time. For example, what are you going to do this evening: stay in and do your homework or go out with friends? You cannot do both. You will need to show that you fully understand the implications of making a choice in terms of what has to be given up.

KEY POINTS

1. The economic problem is one of scarcity and choice.
2. Resources are scarce; this requires societies and individuals to make choices.
3. Making a choice involves a sacrifice.

SUMMARY QUESTIONS

1 What resources can you think of that are particularly scarce in your country?

2 Give an example of a situation in which you have had to make a choice because you have not had access to enough resources.

3 In what situations do your school and community make choices because of a scarcity of available resources? Give reasons for each in your answers.

1.2 Factors of production

LEARNING OUTCOMES

Candidates should be able to:

- define the factors of production (land, labour, capital and enterprise).

A canning factory brings together land, labour, capital (machinery and buildings) and enterprise to create the finished product

EXAM TIP

The concept of capital in economics can sometimes appear confusing. In some senses, it can mean money, but in relation to the factors of production, it means any man-made aid to production.

Imagine that you are visiting a modern food-processing plant. It is processing vegetables to put into cans. What do you see?

The most obvious sight will be large areas of land and factory buildings. Inside, you will see machinery, equipment and employees. Some workers will be looking after the equipment. In the production area you will see people preparing the vegetables. Other workers will be loading and unloading supplies and finished goods.

The **factors of production** are what make the business work: **land**, **labour**, **capital** and **enterprise**.

- In the vegetable-processing plant, the land includes the site on which the factory is built.
- The labour is the factory employees.
- The capital is the buildings and machinery that are used to make the canned vegetables.
- Finally, enterprise is the factor that takes the risk in bringing the factors together to produce goods in order to make profits.

ACTIVITY

Talk to the owner of a small local business. Find out how the business uses its land and capital, the type of labour employed and the enterprise skills needed to ensure that the enterprise is successful.

Definitions

Over the years the four factors of production have come to mean more than the examples used above:

- **Land** is now used to refer to all natural resources, e.g. farmland, water, coal.
- **Labour** is used to refer to all the physical and mental contributions of an employee. So it is more than just the physical effort of digging coal or making car parts. It also includes the mental effort of an accountant or the services provided by a bank clerk.
- **Capital** includes all those items that go into producing other things, e.g. a machine manufactures products, tools contribute to this process, and so on.

    Machines, tools and buildings are all examples of physical capital.

- **Enterprise** is the factor that brings the other factors together to produce goods in order to make profits.

CASE STUDY | Combining the factors of production

Lakshmi Mittal is a well-known entrepreneur. He founded the Mittal Steel company in India (now part of Arcelor Mittal). The company has expanded to take over a network of steel producers from across the world. Today it has steel works in 14 countries. Mittal brings together factors of production in effective combinations to create the only truly global steel company. To run his enterprise Lakshmi Mittal rewards certain features.

Lakshmi Mittal

- **Labour with wages**: attractive salaries and wages have to be paid to workers in each of the 14 countries.
- **Land with rent**: Arcelor Mittal has to pay rent on some of the sites on which its factories are located.
- **Capital with interest**: like most other businesses, Arcelor Mittal borrows money from banks to fund its activities. Interest must be paid at regular intervals on the loans.
- **Enterprise with profits**: profits are a reward for enterprise. The profits of Arcelor Mittal are shared out among shareholders (or reinvested in the business).

Questions

1 Which factor is responsible for bringing together the other factors of production?

2 Why is labour so important to a giant steel company?

EXAM TIP

Textbooks used to leave out 'enterprise' and refer to only three factors of production. Don't make that mistake; if a question asks about the factors of production, make sure that you refer to all four!

DID YOU KNOW?

Arcelor Mittal was created in 2006 by the merger (joining together) of Luxembourg-based Arcelor with Lakshmi Mittal's global steel business. The company employs about 300,000 people.

ACTIVITY

Think of an entrepreneur in your own country who brings together the factors of production in a particular company. Research and write a short report about your chosen person.

KEY POINTS

1 Factors of production are combined to produce goods.
2 Enterprise is responsible for bringing together land, labour and capital.
3 Factors are rewarded in the form of incomes, e.g. wages for employees.

SUMMARY QUESTIONS

1 Choose a familiar product and describe how factors of production are brought together to produce it.

2 What are entrepreneurs? What do they do?

3 What type of capital do the following work with?
   a farm workers
   b factory workers
   c teachers.

1.3 Opportunity cost

LEARNING OUTCOMES

Candidates should be able to:
- define opportunity cost and analyse particular circumstances to illustrate the concept.

Opportunity cost

We may often ask someone with a new purchase, 'How much did it cost?' In this sense we are asking how much was paid. However, in economics we employ a slightly different meaning of 'cost', which we refer to as the 'opportunity cost'. Economists believe that 'opportunity cost' reveals the 'real cost' of making a choice.

Opportunity cost refers to the next best alternative that we give up when we make a particular choice. For example, when you choose to buy a new pen, the sacrifice that you are making is the next best thing that you could have spent the money on. The real cost of any choice is therefore the alternative that is sacrificed.

Two examples of opportunity cost

You may have thought about buying an expensive pen to help you with your studies. However, there are alternatives that you could also consider. You could spend the money on a new top and maybe a trip to the cinema as well. Or you could buy the MP3 player that you have been planning to buy for a long time. When you think carefully about the alternatives, the choice may come down to the player or the pen. So when you go into the shop and pay for the pen, the real sacrifice that you are making is the MP3 player that you have given up. This is the 'real' cost.

People will often spend a lot of time making choices, particularly when they buy items like clothes. What they are often doing is weighing up the opportunity cost: if I buy this top, how am I going to feel about not being able to buy another one that I like almost as much? Here they are thinking about the sacrifice made – that is, the next best alternative that they are giving up.

EXAM TIP

Remember that opportunity cost is not just in terms of a number of possible alternatives that have been forgone. It is specifically in terms of the next best alternative that has been given up. This is one of the most significant ideas in economics.

The opportunity cost to you of buying an expensive pen may be the MP3 player that you were also thinking of buying

Another decision that we make frequently is how to make use of our time. Sometimes it is difficult to decide whether to stay in to study or go round to a friend's house. When you choose to carry out a leisure activity and the next best alternative is time spent studying, the study time that you sacrifice is the opportunity cost.

Opportunity cost is a particularly important economic concept. Economists argue that many decisions taken do not take account of alternatives that are sacrificed when using resources in a particular way. This can lead to undervaluing and, consequently, overuse of important resources.

ACTIVITY

Identify two situations where you have recently had to make a decision about how to use your time. Explain how opportunity cost was involved in the choice you made.

Then think of another situation in which you had a choice about how to spend your money. Explain how opportunity cost was involved in the choice.

KEY POINTS

1 Opportunity cost is the next best alternative that is sacrificed in making an economic choice.

2 The opportunity cost is the real cost of any economic decision.

3 Purchasing decisions and decisions about how to make use of time involve an opportunity cost.

SUMMARY QUESTIONS

1 Dalvinder has saved up US$10 to spend on clothes. She has set out a wish list of what she would like and ranked the items from 1 to 3, with 1 being the most desirable.

	What I want to buy this week	Shop price
1	Two T-shirts	US$9.50
2	Bracelet	US$10.00
3	Skirt	US$10.00

If she purchases the T-shirts, what is the opportunity cost of making this decision?

2 Why should opportunity cost be considered when making economic choices?

3 In what way is time significant in making economic decisions?

DID YOU KNOW?

One of the most important choices an individual makes is how much time to spend studying. Research shows that spending more time at school, college and university leads to better-paid jobs in the long term. The opportunity cost of choosing not to study might be the loss of earnings resulting from a lower-paid job.

EXAM TIP

Decisions in economics involve opportunity costs – in other words choosing a particular course of action always involves making a sacrifice. Try to identify the next best course of action that could have been taken – this is the opportunity cost.

1.4 Opportunity cost in action

LEARNING OUTCOMES

Candidates should be able to:
- evaluate the implications of a particular course of action in terms of opportunity cost.

Opportunity cost – the next best alternative to the Chinese government spending on hospitals could be spending more on primary schools

ACTIVITY

Think of some of your most recent purchases. Did all of them involve thinking about the sacrifices involved in making your choice? Were there some purchases in which you gave greater consideration to opportunity cost than others?

Volkswagen switches production plant from Europe to Brazil

Government increases spending on education – defence cuts likely

More shoppers buying luxury brands

Newspaper headlines illustrating choices involving an opportunity cost

Economic actions

Economic choices are made every day: an employer may choose to hire a young apprentice or a more experienced worker; a consumer may choose to spend part of their income on rice rather than on potatoes.

The main groups that make up the economy are:

- consumers (people who buy goods and services)
- producers (people who make and sell goods and services)
- the government (which acts both as a producer and consumer, and as lawmaker).

You need to understand how the actions of each of these groups involve an opportunity cost. You also need to evaluate the implications of the choice – in other words, understand any effects of the choice of one alternative over another.

Consumers

Everyone is a consumer, whether they are an individual or part of a household that uses goods or services produced in the economy.

The opportunity cost of making any decision about consumption is the next best alternative that is sacrificed. When you buy a cup of coffee, the opportunity that you are giving up is the next best alternative that you could have spent your money on. This might be a cup of coffee from an alternative supplier, or it might be another drink that you could have bought.

Producers

Decisions made by a producer include:

- what to produce
- where to produce, e.g. whether to set up a bottling plant in Germany or Brazil.

Each of the following decisions involves an opportunity cost.

- When a farmer decides to grow maize in a particular field, the opportunity cost is the next best crop that could be grown, e.g. onions.
- One of the most important decisions is where to locate production. Key considerations are wage costs and whether there is a suitable pool of labour with the right skills. The opportunity cost of setting up in one location is the advantage sacrificed from setting up elsewhere.

Business activity is often criticised for failing to consider some elements of the opportunity cost of its activities that affect others. For example, the opportunity cost of creating pollution and waste is the cleaner environment that would otherwise exist.

Government

Governments receive income in the form of taxes and other revenues. Led by the finance minister, a government must then decide how to spend the money. The finance minister works with the various government ministries – for example, health, education, defence and transport – to allocate government funds. There will be a minister in charge of each key area, and each will make a case for more spending for their department.

In each case it is necessary to identify the opportunity cost: if US$100 million extra is spent on education, that money cannot also be spent on health or road building. You can see how detailed discussion is necessary to make choices about how best to spend government money.

> **EXAM TIP**
>
> The concept of opportunity cost is important. In terms of pollution and its effect on the environment, you would need to demonstrate that you understand that cleaning up the effects of pollution costs money, and could possibly lead to an increase in prices charged by a firm.

> **EXAM TIP**
>
> Government spending decisions involve opportunity cost – for example, the implication of spending less on defence and more on education. You need to be able to apply the concept of opportunity cost to such decisions.

KEY POINTS

1. The main groups in the economy consist of consumers, producers, government and financial institutions.
2. Decisions made by these organisations involve an opportunity cost.
3. Taking into account the opportunity cost of decisions means that the real cost of economic activity can be assessed.

SUMMARY QUESTIONS

1. Describe a choice made by:
   a. a consumer
   b. a producer
   c. a government.

   Explain the opportunity cost.

2. Why is it important to consider opportunity costs in economic decision-making?

3. Outline the implications to a government in terms of opportunity cost of deciding to build more schools.

Unit 1 — Practice exam questions

SECTION 1: Multiple-choice questions

Each question has ONE correct answer.

1 Which of the following BEST describes the basic economic problem?
   a Limited needs and unlimited resources
   b Unlimited wants and scarce resources
   c Limited incomes and spending power
   d Unlimited choices of consumer goods

2 Which of the following is a *man-made* resource?
   a A production worker
   b A forest
   c A field of wheat
   d A factory

3 Which of the following is an opportunity cost of using farmland to allow animals to graze?
   a The cost of animal feed
   b The price that the animals can be sold for
   c The use of the land to grow crops
   d The cost of preparing the land for grazing

4 Which of the following is NOT a *factor of production*?
   a Labour
   b Money
   c Enterprise
   d Capital

5 Which of the following is the reward to an entrepreneur?
   a Profit
   b Wages
   c Revenue
   d Employment

6 Which of the following illustrates sustainable use of resources?
   a Discovering new sources of oil for fuel
   b Recycling soft drink bottles
   c Burying rubbish in landfill
   d Replanting trees following use for fuelwood

7 Which of the following is an example of opportunity cost as applied to consumers?
   a The cost of an item bought regularly
   b The ability to buy more when prices are lower
   c The decision to buy a book instead of a CD
   d The cost of a present bought for a friend

8 Which of the following is NOT a decision made by producers?
   a Which goods or services to produce
   b Where to locate a factory
   c How to produce the goods or services
   d How much of the good or service will be bought

9 Why must a government consider the opportunity cost of spending decisions?
   a To get the best value for money
   b Because the money comes from taxation
   c Because a choice must be made between alternative uses
   d To meet all the people's needs

10 Which of the following is NOT a scarce resource?
   a Air
   b Land
   c Money
   d Oil

SECTION 2: Structured questions

1. Country A is a small island nation in Asia, whose native population is growing at 5 per cent a year. The main town is situated in the south of the island and is growing fast, as many jobs are based there. The country is a popular tourist destination and beach resorts are located in the coastal areas. Several big hotel chains have built hotels and there are others that would like to buy land to build all-inclusive leisure resorts, with numerous facilities for guests. Apart from tourism, the main industry is fish canning and a large factory is situated in the west of the island. The fishing boats bring their catch into the small port and much of the canned produce is exported to Europe and the US.

   a Explain why the resources of the island need to support more people than just the native population. (4)

   b Identify and explain TWO examples of scarce resources mentioned above. (6)

   c Using the information given, identify and explain TWO examples of natural resources that are being used by the people of Country A. (4)

   d Discuss what sacrifices, in terms of resource use, may need to be made if the government of Country A wants to increase tourism. (6)

2. Fishing and tourism are the main industries in Country A. The government would like to welcome more tourists to the island.

   a Identify the four *factors of production* as used in the fishing industry in Country A. (4)

   b Choose THREE of the factors you have identified in A and explain the likely rewards to the owners of these. (6)

   c Identify the four *factors of production* as used in the hotel industry in Country A. (4)

   d Discuss how the proposed increase in tourism may affect the fishing industry and those employed within it. (6)

3. The main town on the island is becoming very busy and congested with traffic, which is also causing air pollution. For business, it is virtually impossible to find a shop or office to rent and many local residents are moving to quieter areas outside town, where new apartments are being built. They then need to spend time and money to travel into town by bus or car to work.

   a According to the extract, what has been the opportunity cost of using more buildings in the town for offices and shops? (4)

   b Describe TWO opportunity costs to local residents who choose to move out of town. (6)

   c Describe TWO possible opportunity costs to the owners of the land where the new apartments are being built of the choice to provide homes for local residents. (4)

   d Discuss how the government of Country A might use its resources to reduce congestion and pollution in the town. (6)

4. Two large international holiday companies have been planning to build hotel and leisure facilities for tourists on one of the island's beaches, which is also a popular day-trip destination for local families. The government tourism minister is keen to encourage these new developments in order to 'make best use of our resources'. He also believes that if the hotel companies take their money elsewhere, this could lead to a loss of tourists coming to Country A.

   a Explain what is meant by 'our resources' in this instance. (3)

   b Explain the minister's view that more hotels will 'make best use of our resources'. (3)

   c State TWO possible opportunity costs to the island of a decision in favour of the hotel developments. (6)

   d Using the concepts of scarce resources and opportunity cost, discuss whether increased tourism may be the best use of the island's resources in the long term. (8)

Total: 80 marks

SECTION 3: Analysis and critical evaluation

Country B is a developing nation, whose economy has been growing at an average of 7 per cent a year for the last four years. The older industries are in the manufacturing sector, mainly based on cotton textiles and related products. Newer industries include computer games software development and customer call centre facilities for multinational banks. These organisations are owned and run by a growing group of 'new entrepreneurs'. There is a big demand for wood and other building materials throughout Country B, and this is leading to the loss of many square kilometres of forest. Generally the forest is not replanted, but used for farmland.

- The population is growing at approximately 4 per cent a year, although this is hard to measure as there is no formal census.
- The unemployment rate is very low, with jobs available for anyone who wants one. Wages are increasing as employers try to attract workers to their businesses.
- The average price level is also increasing as firms raise prices in order to pay higher wages. People on a fixed income are having to think very carefully about how they spend their limited money as prices rise.
- The government of Country B has recently raised the age of compulsory schooling to 14 and is investing in new school buildings in rural areas.

1 a Explain what is meant by *human resources* and give an example from the text. (2)

   b Explain what is meant by *man-made resources* and give an example from the text. (2)

2 a Give ONE example of *scarce resources* from the text. (2)

   b Suggest ONE likely reason for the increased demand for resources in Country B. (2)

3 Discuss whether the use of labour in the new call centre industry in Country B may benefit the economy more than the established textiles factory jobs. (5)

4 a Explain why increased payments for labour are leading to rising prices. (2)

   b Discuss the possible opportunity cost of the use of wood from forests in country B for building materials. (5)

5 Using the example of a new call centre business, explain how the FOUR factors of production may be used. (5)

6 Using the concept of opportunity cost and information in the text, discuss whether the government of Country B is wise to spend money on increasing education provision for the population. (7)

Total: 32 marks

2 Allocating resources: the market at work and market failure

Unit 2 looks at how markets work. The market brings together buyers (who demand goods and services) and producers and sellers (who supply goods and services). It explains how the market helps to decide how scarce resources, such as 'land' and 'labour', will be used. Demand is the quantity that buyers are willing to buy at different prices and supply is the quantity that suppliers are prepared to sell at these prices.

Unit 2 also shows how price elasticity affects market prices. Elasticity is a measure of how quantities demanded and supplied in the market are affected by changes in price.

The notion of market failure is also introduced. This shows how markets may not always be efficient in meeting the needs of all members of a society.

Throughout Unit 2, graphs and diagrams illustrate the points under discussion.

LEARNING OUTCOMES

With regard to **allocating resources**, candidates should be able to:

- describe the allocation of resources in market and mixed economic systems
- demonstrate the principle of equilibrium price and analyse simple market situations with changes in demand and supply
- describe the causes of changes in demand and supply conditions and analyse such changes to show effects in the market
- define price elasticity of demand and supply and perform simple calculations
- demonstrate the usefulness of price elasticity in particular situations, such as revenue changes and consumer expenditure
- describe the concept of market failure and explain the reasons for its occurrence
- evaluate the merits of the market system
- define private and social costs and benefits and discuss conflicts of interest in relation to these costs and benefits in the short term and long term through studies of the following issues:
  – conserving resources versus using resources
  – public expenditure versus private expenditure.

2.1 Allocating resources in an economy

LEARNING OUTCOMES

Candidates should be able to:
- describe the allocation of resources in market and mixed economic systems.

Allocation of resources

Resources can be used to make goods. Some – for example, timber or water – are provided by nature. Others, such as tools and equipment, are man-made.

The table indicates some of the decisions that have to be made in an economy about allocating resources – that is, deciding how they will be used to produce goods and services.

Decisions involving allocation of resources	Examples
What resources will be used to produce goods and services	Type of energy (nuclear, coal, wind, solar) to use to power industry and homes
How the resources will be used	For example, whether energy supplies will be available for industrial production (e.g. in factories) or for private use (in homes)
Who decides how the resources will be used	Whether government-owned or private businesses will generate energy
Who benefits from the use of the resources	Whether the energy resources are available for just a few people or for all

Government influence on economic decision-making

In some countries the government plays a major role in decision-making. In North Korea, for example, industries are government-owned and officials working for the government decide what will be produced, the methods of producing goods and the prices charged. In contrast, the government in most other countries plays a smaller part in this type of decision-making. Figure 2.1.1 gives some examples of countries and the different levels of **government interference** in their markets.

EXAM TIP

You need to be able to show that you understand how government intervention in an economy can change according to economic conditions; in recent years intervention has increased as a result of the 'credit crunch'.

Figure 2.1.1 Levels of government involvement

The market and economic decision-making

In a **market economy** goods and services are freely exchanged and **prices** are decided by individual suppliers. Buying and selling decisions are made by buyers and sellers. Prices act as a guide:

- If prices are high enough, suppliers will be willing to supply to the market. High prices create profit and increased supply.
- If buyers think that prices give good value for money, they will buy goods. The lower the price, the more customers will buy.

Supporters of the market system argue that it is decentralised and automatic. The allocation of resources is determined by the wishes of individual consumers and suppliers.

A mixed economy

In most countries, decisions are made by a combination of government decision-making and the market. This is a **mixed economy**.

CASE STUDY | Mauritius

Mauritius is an island economy in the south-west Indian Ocean. The market is an important part of economic life in Mauritius. Mauritius is a trading economy that imports and exports large quantities of textiles. Companies on the island produce T-shirts and designer clothes for famous brand names such as Lacoste and Nike. Other industries include sugar cane and tea plantations owned by private companies. There are also thousands of small businesses producing household goods.

Most economic decisions are made by businesses and consumers. However, the government does play a part. One example is the payment of subsidies (sums of money) to encourage 'derocking': rocks are taken from the land to increase the quantity of fertile soil for growing sugar cane. Another example is management of the island's water shortage in the form of a government limit on water use at certain times of the year.

Questions

1 What economic decisions will be made by private businesses?

2 Why do you think that the government gets involved in the economy of Mauritius?

3 Does Mauritius have a mixed economy? Give a reason for your answer.

EXAM TIP

Adam Smith was one of the earliest economists, and he described the price system as an 'invisible hand'. His theory was that if consumers and producers are allowed to choose what to buy and sell, prices will settle at a level that benefits individuals and their community. You might get the opportunity to refer to this in an examination question.

In a mixed economy like that of Mauritius, most decisions are made by the market. However, the government does intervene by subsidising 'derocking' to help farmers increase sugar cane production

KEY POINTS

1 In a market economy buyers and sellers interact and this decides how resources are allocated.

2 Prices act as signals to buyers and sellers.

3 In a mixed economy the government makes some of the decisions about how resources will be used.

ACTIVITY

What types of goods and services are provided by government businesses in your country? Which ones are provided by private businesses?

SUMMARY QUESTIONS

1 Who are the main participants in a mixed economy?

2 What are economic resources?

3 Who decides on the use and allocation of resources in a market economy?

2.2 Demand

LEARNING OUTCOMES

Candidates should be able to:
- define and explain the term *demand*.

The lower the price of roasted nuts sold from a stall, the higher demand for them will be

DID YOU KNOW?

When price falls and demand increases, this is referred to as an extension in demand. When price rises and demand falls, this is referred to as a contraction in demand.

EXAM TIP

It is important to understand that a movement along a demand curve (either an extension or contraction in demand) is caused by changes in the price of a product with everything else held constant.

Demand for goods and services

The **effective demand** for a good or service is a want, supported by the money to purchase it. If a good is in great demand, there will be a lot of people wanting to buy it at the current price.

Business organisations try to predict how much the demand for their products will be at different prices. They can then decide how much to make in order to meet demand.

Recording demand

The demand for a product can be recorded in a table which shows how many items would be demanded at given prices. It is also useful to record the demand for a product on a graph. A **demand graph** shows that larger quantities of any good will be bought at lower prices, and lower quantities at higher prices. Common sense and personal experience help to explain this: when goods are sold at a lower price, more people can afford to buy them. Existing purchasers will be tempted to buy more because they have to give up less of their income to make the purchase.

The table below shows the demand for bananas at different prices per kilo. Figure 2.2.1 shows the same figures transferred onto a **demand curve**.

Price per kg	Quantity demanded
45 cents	1,000 kg
35 cents	3,000 kg
25 cents	4,500 kg
15 cents	6,500 kg

Figure 2.2.1 Demand for bananas at different prices per kilo

The demand curve is constructed by showing prices on the vertical axis and quantities demanded along the horizontal axis. You can see that:

- higher prices lead to lower quantities being bought
- lower prices lead to higher quantities being bought.

CASE STUDY | Market demand

Demand for a product can be found by adding together the demand of all the consumers in the marketplace.

Rajesh sells small packets of roasted nuts from a stall in his village. It costs him 10 cents to grow the nuts that go into each packet. He sells the nuts to the other villagers, who come from five families. He has calculated the demand by asking the families how many packets they would buy from him per week at different prices.

Price per packet	Demand from the families					
	Family Panwar	Family Singh	Family Patel	Family Rai	Family Jain	TOTAL
10 cents	15	15	20	20	15	85
15 cents	12	12	20	15	11	70
20 cents	8	8	15	10	9	50
25 cents	7	7	12	9	5	40
30 cents	6	6	9	7	2	30
35 cents	5	4	6	5	–	20
40 cents	–	2	3	–	–	5
45 cents	–	–	–	–	–	–

Questions

1. Illustrate the information provided in the table in the form of a graph.
2. What is the relationship between price and quantity illustrated in the table and the graph?
3. How would you explain this relationship?
4. Why might it be more sensible for Rajesh to charge 25 cents per packet of nuts rather than 10 cents or 40 cents? Work out how much revenue (price × quantity sold) Rajesh will make at each price level.

Straight-line demand curves

Although in reality demand curves have a curved or irregular shape, economists find it convenient to draw them as a straight line (Figure 2.2.2) – it is quick and easy to draw. They are still referred to, however, as demand 'curves'. Price is shown on the vertical (x-axis) and quantity demanded on the horizontal (y-axis).

KEY POINTS

1. Effective demand is a want or need backed up by the ability to make a purchase.
2. At lower prices greater quantities will be demanded than at higher prices.
3. A demand curve usually slopes down from left to right.

EXAM TIP

Make sure that any diagrams you use in the examination are clearly drawn and labelled. Marks will be awarded for correct labelling of the horizontal and vertical axes.

ACTIVITY

Identify one good that you or your family have recently bought more of because its price has fallen. Identify another good that you have bought less of because its price has risen. Compare your findings with others in your group.

DID YOU KNOW?

Demand for products in a mixed economy is made up of demand from individuals, businesses and the government.

Figure 2.2.2 Straight-line demand curve

SUMMARY QUESTIONS

1. What is the difference between *want* and *demand*?
2. How would you illustrate a demand curve for pencils?
3. How does knowledge of demand help businesses?

17

2.3 Supply

LEARNING OUTCOMES

Candidates should be able to:
- define and explain the term *supply*.

The **supply** of a product is the quantity that a supplier is willing to provide at different prices. Typically suppliers will supply more at higher prices than at lower prices. Higher prices enable producers to cover costs and make increasing profits.

For example, every year large numbers of pilgrims fly from Delhi to Mecca for the annual pilgrimage, the Haj, an important festival in the Islamic calendar. Groups from the various mosques in India charter flights – that is, they hire airlines to provide special flights.

A charter airline might run six flights a day between Delhi and Mecca when pilgrims are prepared to pay US$200 for the return journey. However, if pilgrims are willing to pay US$300 each, the airline might buy more planes and run nine planes a day. At US$400 they might run 12 planes.

Supply of flights by the airline can then be illustrated on a **supply curve**, as shown in Figure 2.3.1.

The higher the price an airline can charge people wishing to fly, the greater the number of flights it will be willing to supply

EXAM TIP

Make sure that when you are drawing a demand and supply diagram, you clearly label these. The demand curve will usually slope downwards from left to right and the supply curve will ususally slope upwards from left to right.

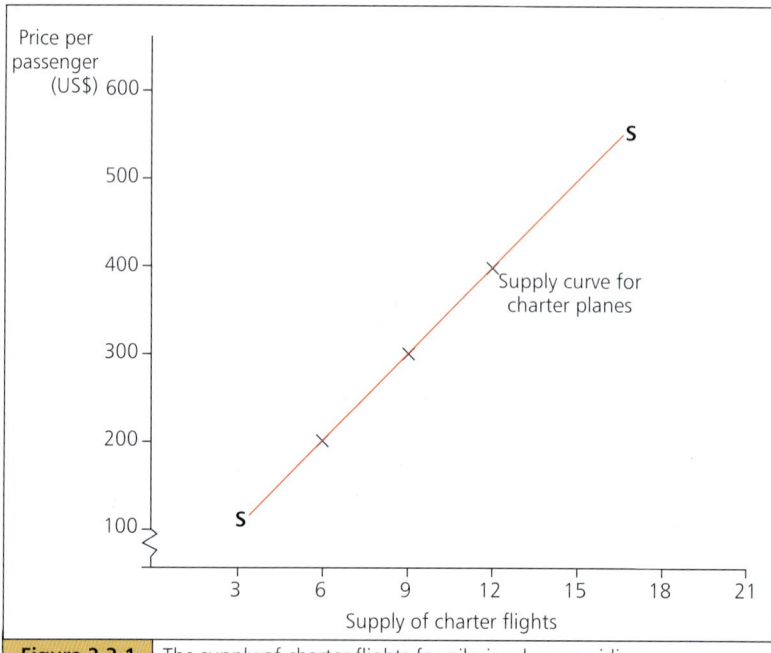

Figure 2.3.1 The supply of charter flights for pilgrims by one airline

Individual and market supply

Figure 2.3.1 illustrates the supply curve in an individual airline. To find out the **market** supply curve we need to add the individual supply curves of all the airlines supplying flights to Mecca. The same principle applies to the supply of any product to its market.

If there are three airlines supplying charter flights, the individual and market supply curves might look like those in Figure 2.3.2.

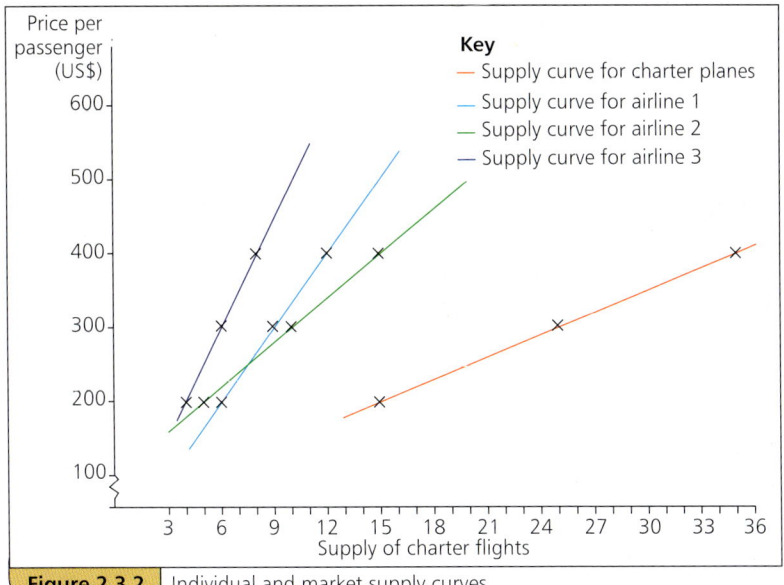

Figure 2.3.2 Individual and market supply curves

Price per seat (US$)	Supply by airline 1 (flights/day)	Supply by airline 2 (flights/day)	Supply by airline 3 (flights/day)	Market supply (flights/day)
200	6	5	4	15
300	9	10	6	25
400	12	15	8	35

Extensions and contractions in supply

In the example above we looked at how the supply of a product changes as a result of an increase in its price. This is referred to as an **extension in supply**. Should the price that pilgrims are prepared to pay rise from US$200 to US$400, this would lead to an increase in flights from 15 to 35 per day. In Figure 2.3.3 this is illustrated by the movement from Q to Q1. Supply extends from Q to Q1. In contrast, a fall in the price of charter flights would lead to a **contraction in supply**.

DID YOU KNOW?

Extension and contraction can also be used to refer to extensions in demand and contractions in demand. This relates to changes in quantity demanded resulting from changes in the price of a good.

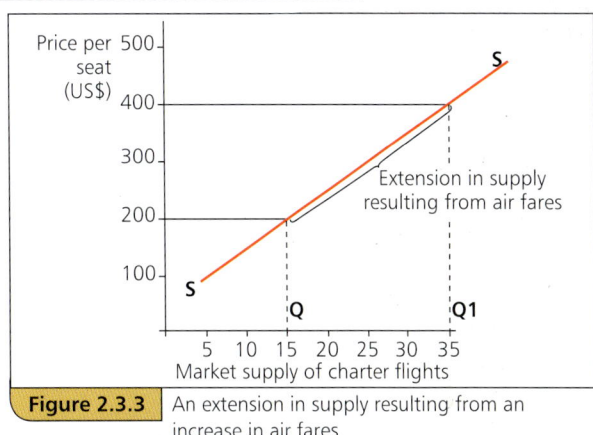

Figure 2.3.3 An extension in supply resulting from an increase in air fares

KEY POINTS

1. Supply is the quantity that producers provide to the market at different prices.
2. Producers supply more at higher prices than at lower ones.
3. The supply curve slopes up from left to right on a supply diagram.
4. Extensions and contractions in supply result from changes in the price of a product.

SUMMARY QUESTIONS

1. Describe the relationship between quantity supplied and price.
2. How does a rise in price lead to an extension in supply?
3. How does a fall in price lead to a contraction in supply?

19

2.4 Equilibrium price

LEARNING OUTCOMES

Candidates should be able to:
- demonstrate the principle of equilibrium price.

Equilibrium price

Equilibrium means a state of balance. **Equilibrium price** occurs when there is a balance between demand and supply: the quantity demanded by consumers is equal to the amount that suppliers are willing to provide. For example, Ramesh and his family collect fresh coconuts in a plantation that they own. They sell them at a local holiday beach. The higher the price they can get, the more they will supply. The lower the price that Ramesh charges, the more customers will buy his coconuts (they can always buy from rival sellers).

The table of demand and supply schedules shows the weekly demand and supply for Ramesh's coconuts:

Price of Ramesh's coconuts (US$)	Supply per week	Demand per week
2.50	500	200
2.00	400	400
1.50	300	600
1.00	200	800

These demand and supply curves can be illustrated on a single drawing, as in Figure 2.4.1.

The price that the coconut seller charges is determined by demand and supply. The higher the price, the more the supplier will bring to market. The lower the price, the more consumers will want to buy

EXAM TIP

The equilibrium position in a market will be where demand and supply intersect. When you draw this in a diagram, you will need to make sure that you clearly show the equilibrium price as the vertical axis and the equilibrium quantity on the horizontal.

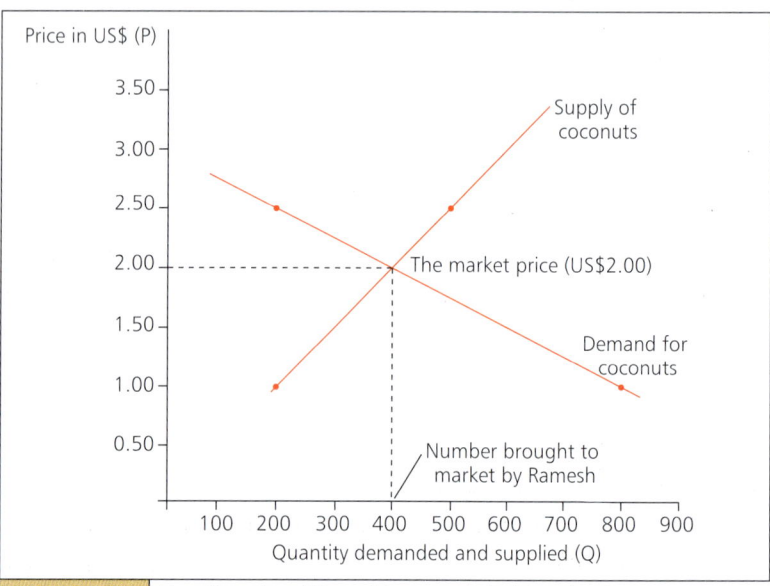

Figure 2.4.1 How the price of Ramesh's coconuts is determined

You can now see that, at a price of US$2.00 per coconut, 400 would be bought each week. At this price Ramesh's customers would be happy to buy all 400 and Ramesh would be happy to supply this quantity. This is the equilibrium price, as both seller and buyer are happy with the price.

You can see why this point is an equilibrium one by considering non-equilibrium points. For example, at US$2.50 Ramesh would be prepared to supply 500 coconuts, but buyers would only be prepared to purchase 200 (leaving 300 unsold). Alternatively, if we examine a price below the market one (US$1.00), customers would be willing to buy 800 coconuts, but Ramesh would only be prepared to bring 200 to sell. Customers would soon bid the price back up to the equilibrium price.

The market price is often referred to as the **market clearing price**, because demand matches the quantity supplied. Therefore the market would be 'cleared', with no coconuts remaining and no dissatisfied customers.

> **ACTIVITY**
>
> Identify some food items in a local shop or market that are being sold off at the end of the day. It is possible that the prices that had been charged were above the equilibrium price. Try to identify food items that have run out as well – it may be that the price charged was too low.

CASE STUDY: Demand and supply for Sweet Pastilles

Sweet Pastilles is a popular type of sweet sold from a variety of shops and small kiosks. The following table sets out the demand and supply schedules for different prices of Sweet Pastilles.

Price per packet (cents)	Demand (million packets per year)	Supply (million packets per year)
10	320	0
20	240	80
30	160	160
40	80	240

Questions

1 Set out the figures in the form of a graph.

2 a What is the equilibrium price?

   b Why is this the equilibrium price?

3 What volume of sweets will be supplied at the equilibrium price?

4 Explain why neither 10 cents nor 40 cents is the equilibrium price.

> **EXAM TIP**
>
> The idea of a market clearing price is very important. You need to show that you understand that this will bring demand and supply together at a particular price without any need for government intervention.

KEY POINTS

1 At the equilibrium price demand and supply are in balance.

2 The equilibrium price is also known as the market clearing price.

3 The market clearing price can be illustrated by demand and supply curves.

SUMMARY QUESTIONS

1 Why is the equilibrium price the best price for suppliers to charge?

2 What would happen if the price were higher than the equilibrium price?

3 What would happen if the price were lower than the equilibrium price?

2.5 Causes of change in demand and the effect on the market

LEARNING OUTCOMES

Candidates should be able to:
- describe the causes of changes in demand conditions
- analyse changes in demand to show effects in the market.

Movement along the demand curve

A demand curve shows the relationship between demand and price, all other factors remaining the same. When the price of a good rises or falls there is a movement **along** the curve. The movement is **down** the curve (contraction) for a rise in price, and **up** the curve (expansion) for a fall in price.

Changes in the conditions of demand

In addition to price, there are a number of factors that influence the demand for a product. If one of these factors alters, the conditions of demand are said to have changed. These factors include:

- popularity or fashion
- income
- the age distribution of the population
- the price of substitute and complementary goods (**complements**).

Changes in one (or a combination) of these factors will cause a **shift in the demand curve**. The demand curve will shift to the left if smaller quantities are wanted than before at given prices. A shift to the right indicates that larger quantities are wanted than before at given prices.

Popularity

Figure 2.5.1 shows that originally a quantity of 600 highlighter pens would be bought per month at 80 cents. However, if the pens become more popular with students, more will be demanded at all prices, so that, for example, at 80 cents perhaps 800 will be bought each month.

If the use of highlighter pens becomes more popular among students, the demand curve for them will shift upwards to the right – this will lead to a rise in price

EXAM TIP

You need to make sure that you clearly show in a diagram which direction a demand or supply curve is shifting. This can be done through arrows and through clear labelling, such as: a shift from DD to D1D1.

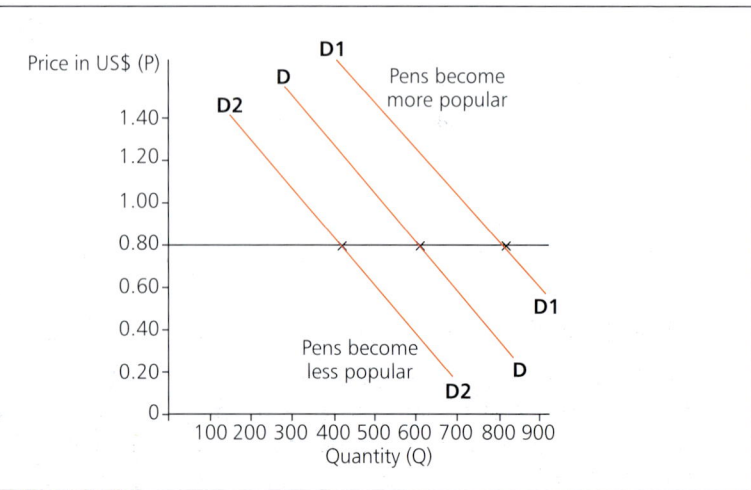

Figure 2.5.1 Changing the demand for highlighter pens

22

Alternatively, if the highlighters become less popular, fewer will be bought at all prices so that at 80 cents 400 highlighters will now be demanded.

Income

It is obviously easier to buy goods if you have money to spend. The amount of income people have to spend on goods is known as their **disposable income**. Average incomes tend to rise over time, which leads to a general increase in demand for most goods, noticeably expensive branded goods. An increase in incomes leads to a shift in the demand curve to the right.

However, some products may become less popular as income rises: they may be regarded as inferior as spending power increases. So a bicycle may be replaced by a motor scooter or car. In the case of inferior goods, demand shifts to the left when incomes rise.

Age distribution

The **age distribution** of the population can affect demand. Many products appeal to certain age groups. For example, trainers or sneakers are particularly popular among young people across the world. The rising number of young people in many countries such as Brazil, China and Saudi Arabia has led to an increase in demand for trainers.

Price of other products

The demand for products that have close **substitutes** will often be strongly influenced by the price of the substitutes. This would be the case, for example, with different brands of tinned fruit or different brands of petrol, because there are many different brand names from which consumers can choose.

The demand curve for a product is likely to shift to the right if a substitute product rises in price. The demand curve for a product is likely to shift to the left if a substitute product falls in price.

Some products are used together (**complementary goods**) so that the demand for one is linked to the price of another. An example of this might be cars and car radios: if the price of cars falls, this is likely to lead to an increase in demand for car radios.

KEY POINTS

1. Movements along a demand curve result from changes in price.
2. Shifts in demand result from changes in factors other than price.
3. Shifts in demand result from changes in the popularity of goods, in disposable incomes, changes in age distribution of the population, and changes in the prices of complements and substitutes.

ACTIVITY

Identify two goods that you use that are complements. How does this affect your demand for both goods when the price of one of them falls?

EXAM TIP

You need to show that you understand that a shift of a demand curve takes place when something happens in a market other than a change in the price of a product. A common error in examinations is confusion between movements along a demand curve and a shift of a demand curve to the right or left.

SUMMARY QUESTIONS

1. Give three examples of situations in which the demand curve for mobile phones would shift to the right.
2. What is an inferior good? Give an example. What would happen to demand for this good if incomes rise?
3. Give three examples of competing substitute products. What would happen to the demand for one of these as a result of a fall in the price of a substitute?

2.6 Causes of changes in supply and the effect on the market

LEARNING OUTCOMES

Candidates should be able to:

- describe the causes of changes in supply conditions
- analyse changes in supply to identify effects in the market.

Factory robots in the Czech Republic: improvements in technology reduce costs of production, leading to a shift to the right in the supply curve

EXAM TIP

Oil is a vitally important resource in most countries. It would be useful to know whether the general price of oil is going up or down, and to demonstrate that you are up to date with current events.

Shifts in the supply curve

The cost of producing an item is determined by the price of the various inputs, including the raw materials and machinery used to make it. Rises in the prices of some of these resource inputs will increase production costs, which in turn results in a reduction in supply at each price rise (see Figure 2.6.1).

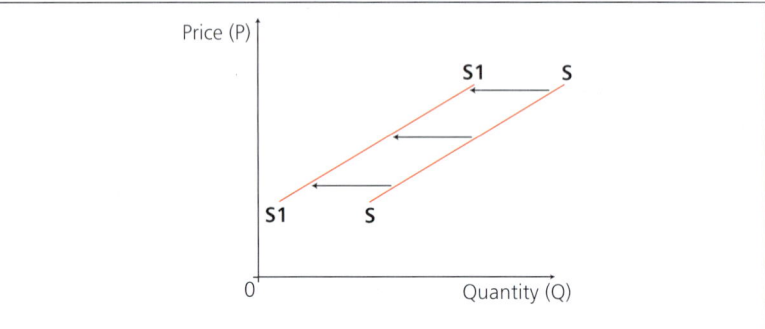

Figure 2.6.1 Effect of a shift in the supply curve

The supply curve shifts to the left when, at any given price, fewer items are produced and offered for sale.

Causes of changes in supply conditions

There are several factors that can cause **changes in supply**:

- rising or falling production costs
- changes in physical conditions
- taxation and subsidies
- joint supply.

Rising or falling production costs

A rise in production costs pushes the supply curve to the left (it will cost more to produce each level of output), and a fall in production costs pushes the supply curve to the right.

Production costs fall when the price of resources falls. So when the price of oil falls, for example, energy costs for all industries are reduced. Rising resource prices lead to rising production costs. Wars and conflicts can restrict the supply of important resources such as oil, and can lead to rapid increases in production costs. In recent years economic growth in China has led to price rises on global markets of many important industrial metals.

The development of new technology in the form of computer-based processing systems and computer-controlled machinery has reduced production costs in many industries.

Physical conditions

Changes in the weather, the quality of soil and natural disasters such as flooding and drought can have a major impact, particularly on agricultural products. Global warming (the rise in temperature) means that it is increasingly difficult to grow crops in drier areas of the planet.

Taxation and subsidies

Rises in taxation and **subsidies** pull in opposite directions on the supply curve. A production tax of 10 cents per unit on a good would increase the cost of its production by 10 cents per unit. In contrast, a subsidy would reduce the costs of production. Supply will therefore shift to the left as a result of rising taxes on a product, and to the right as a result of a subsidy (see Figure 2.6.2).

Joint supply

Some production processes create more than one product (**joint supply**): when oil is refined the process creates by-products that can be used to manufacture goods such as synthetic carpets and soap. Increases in oil supply will therefore drive down the price of these by-products as more of them are supplied to the market.

> **ACTIVITY**
>
> The following headlines have appeared in newspapers. State in each case the likely impact on supply in the relevant industries or areas.
>
> - Wages fall in printing industry
> - South Africa – good wine-growing conditions reported
> - High-tech start-up businesses – new subsidies announced
> - Brazil – poor coffee harvest
> - South East Asia earthquake – latest news
> - Wages fall in printing industry

Effect of changes in supply on the market

An increase in supply results in a fall in the price of a product. This leads to a movement along the demand curve (more is bought in response to the lower price).

A decrease in supply results in a rise in the price of a product. This leads to a movement along the demand curve (less is bought in response to the higher price).

> **KEY POINTS**
>
> 1. The supply curve shifts to the right as a result of increases in supply at each price.
> 2. The supply curve shifts to the left as a result of a fall in supply at each price.
> 3. Shifts in supply result from changes in costs of production, physical conditions and changes in joint supply.

> **DID YOU KNOW?**
>
> In the Middle East and North Africa (MENA) area, an increasingly scarce resource is water (Yemen is the country most affected). There are 300 million people here with a desperate need for water. In many areas water is delivered in tankers or sold in bottles. Increasing scarcity for businesses drives up this important cost of production.

> **DID YOU KNOW?**
>
> A subsidy is a sum of money given by the government to support a particular purpose or activity. For example, a subsidy might be 10 cents per unit produced.

Figure 2.6.2 The impact of taxes and subsidies on the supply of a product

> **SUMMARY QUESTIONS**
>
> 1. Explain and illustrate the effect of the use of improved manufacturing technology in the car industry.
> 2. How might a fall in the supply of oil have a multiple effect in many markets?
> 3. Explain joint supply by giving an example of a locally produced product.

2.7 Price elasticity of demand

LEARNING OUTCOMES

Candidates should be able to:
- define price elasticity of demand
- perform simple calculations.

By cutting the price of rail fares, Indian Railways has substantially increased revenues, because demand is elastic

DID YOU KNOW?

Price elasticity measures how much the demand for a product alters in response to a change in its price. Demand for a product is elastic when it alters by a larger proportion than the change in price. Demand is *in*elastic when it alters by a smaller proportion than the change in price.

What is price elasticity of demand?

A restaurant owner who is considering increasing prices will first want to know what effect this will have on the customers. Will there be no effect, a small fall in customers or a large fall? If the number of customers remains the same or falls by a smaller percentage than the price change, the business will make more revenue and profit. The calculation used to estimate this is **price elasticity of demand**, which measures how demand for a product responds to a change in its price. Anyone wishing to raise or lower prices should first estimate the price elasticity.

It is useful for a government to know the effect of raising taxes on particular goods. If it raises taxes a little and customers continue to buy as many goods as before, tax revenue will rise without harming the demand. However, if the tax leads to a substantial fall in demand this could lead to:

- a fall in tax revenues
- a substantial fall in sales for makers of the taxed goods.

CASE STUDY | Indian Railways lowers prices

Railways in India are government-owned. Indian Railways is India's largest employer.

In July 2001 an expert declared that India's railway network was on the edge of bankruptcy. The cost of running the railway was 107 per cent of revenue, a loss-making position. By 2005 costs had been cut to 84 per cent of revenues, a surplus position, and in 2007 costs were 78 per cent of revenues. By 2007 the railways had become the second largest cash generator in India's public sector.

Instead of raising fares, the Railway Board cut them. This led to much higher passenger numbers. At the same time the trains were lengthened. Because each train pulls more carriages the cost per passenger has fallen.

Questions

1. Why do you think that it was decided to cut rail fares?
2. What would have been the effect on revenues and profit of cutting rail fares? (Note that revenue refers to the money received by Indian Railways principally from the sale of rail tickets.)

Measuring price elasticity

Where falls in price have a more than proportional effect on demand, as in the Indian Railways case, demand is said to be **elastic**. If instead demand changes by a smaller proportion than the change in price, it is said to be **inelastic**. Price elasticity of demand is calculated as follows:

$$\text{Price elasticity of demand} = \frac{\text{\% change in quantity demanded}}{\text{\% change in price}}$$

Making simple calculations

1. First calculate the percentage change in quantity demanded (the demand would be an estimate). This is the change in demand as a percentage of the quantity originally demanded (before the price change).
2. Next calculate the percentage change in price. This is the change in price as a percentage of the original price (before the price change).
3. Divide the percentage change in demand by the percentage change in price.
4. Remember to include the minus sign.
5. If the figure is less than −1, demand is relatively elastic. If it is greater than −1, demand is relatively inelastic.

Example 1: A railway company reduces rail fares from US$1 to 90 cents. Daily demand for tickets rises from 100,000 to 120,000.

Price elasticity is therefore −2 (elastic demand)

$$\frac{20 \text{ per cent}}{-10 \text{ per cent}} = -2$$

Example 2: A bus company reduces bus fares from US$1 to 90 cents. Daily demand for tickets rises from 10,000 to 10,500.

Price elasticity is therefore −0.5 (inelastic demand)

$$\frac{5 \text{ per cent}}{-10 \text{ per cent}} = -0.5$$

SUMMARY QUESTIONS

1. Why should a business estimate elasticity of demand before changing its prices?
2. Calculate the price elasticity of demand for melons sold from a fruit store: the owner reduces prices from 20 cents to 15 cents per melon, and daily demand increases from 100 to 150.
3. Why is price elasticity of demand represented by a minus figure?

DID YOU KNOW?

Price elasticity of demand is always a minus figure. This is because an increase in price (+) leads to a fall in demand (−). A fall in price (−) leads to a rise in demand (+). Another way of putting this is that there is an *inverse relationship*.

EXAM TIP

A common mistake is to write that a particular good is elastic – for example, a CD. You need to show that you realise that it is not the CD that is elastic, but the demand for it.

KEY POINTS

1. Price elasticity of demand measures the responsiveness of demand to price changes.
2. Price elasticity of demand is calculated by dividing the percentage change in quantity demanded by the percentage change in price.

2.8 Price elasticity of supply

LEARNING OUTCOMES

Candidates should be able to:
- define price elasticity of supply
- perform simple calculations.

For goods that cannot be stored for long, such as these fresh fruits and vegetables in a market in Dominica, price elasticity of supply is reduced

DID YOU KNOW?

The term *perfectly inelastic supply* refers to a situation in which, however much price increases, it is impossible to increase supply by a single unit.

Changes in supply

When the price of a good rises or falls, this leads to an **extension in supply** – that is, a movement up or down the supply curve. The extent to which supply responds to a change in price is determined by how elastic supply is.

Price elasticity of supply

Price elasticity of supply is the extent to which supply alters in response to a change in price. It is measured by the formula:

$$\text{Price elasticity of supply} = \frac{\%\text{ change in quantity supplied}}{\%\text{ change in price}}$$

In the case of supply there is a positive relationship between the two variables. As a result price elasticity of supply will typically be represented by a + sign.

Elastic supply occurs when the percentage change in quantity supplied is greater than the percentage change in price – for example, if supply increased by 10 per cent as a result of a 5 per cent drop in price.

Factors influencing price elasticity of supply

The main factor influencing price elasticity of supply is time. At a particular moment in time it may be impossible to increase supply – for example, reprinting a popular book – however much price increases. Supply in this instance is perfectly inelastic. In the short term it may be possible to increase supply using existing equipment and machinery. In the longer term it may be possible to increase supply further by acquiring more machinery and equipment. The longer the period of time, the more elastic supply is in response to a price change (see Figure 2.8.1).

Figure 2.8.1 Price elasticity of supply and time

In Figure 2.8.1, S1 shows **perfectly inelastic supply** at a moment in time, S2 shows relatively inelastic supply in the short period, and S3 represents relatively elastic supply in the longer period.

Other factors affecting price elasticity of supply are:

- The ease with which a product can be stored. If stores of a product can be kept easily, supply will be more elastic. Coffee can be stored in jars (making supply elastic), but fresh strawberries go off very quickly (making supply more inelastic).
- The cost of increasing supply. The less costly it is to increase supply, the more elastic supply will be.

Making simple calculations

Example 1: A rise in the price of rice in a country from US$1 per bag to US$1.20 per bag leads to an increase in supply by farmers from 1,000 bags per month to 1,300 bags per month.

$$\text{Price elasticity of supply} = \frac{30 \text{ per cent}}{20 \text{ per cent}}$$

$$= 1.5 \text{ (relatively elastic supply)}$$

Example 2: There is a shortage of flour in a country. A rise in the price of bread from 50 cents to 60 cents a loaf leads to an increase in supply by bakers from 1,000 loaves per month to 1,100 loaves per month.

$$\text{Price elasticity of supply} = \frac{10 \text{ per cent}}{20 \text{ per cent}}$$

$$= 0.5 \text{ (relatively inelastic supply)}$$

> **DID YOU KNOW?**
>
> We use the term 'price elasticity of supply' because quantities supplied are responding to changes in the price of a good. The raised price gives an incentive to, or encourages, producers to supply more.

> **EXAM TIP**
>
> Remember that when producers are not manufacturing at full capacity, they could always produce a little more if the price increased. So when businesses have unused capacity, supply tends to be more elastic than if they are producing at full capacity. In a period of recession supply can be quite elastic, in that producers have the ability to supply more.

> **KEY POINTS**
>
> 1. Price elasticity of supply measures the responsiveness of supply to changes in price.
> 2. Price elasticity of supply is a positive number.
> 3. Price elasticity of supply is calculated by dividing the percentage change in quantity supplied by the percentage change in price.

> **SUMMARY QUESTIONS**
>
> 1. If rail services are suddenly cancelled on a particular day, why might the supply of bus journeys be inelastic in supply?
> 2. If the rail service remains closed, why might the supply of bus journeys become increasingly elastic over time?
> 3. Increasing demand for melons in a city pushes up the price from 20 cents to 25 cents per melon. This leads to an increase in supply of melons per day from 2,000 to 2,500. Calculate the price elasticity of supply.

2.9 Usefulness of price elasticity of demand

LEARNING OUTCOMES

Candidates should be able to:

- demonstrate the usefulness of price elasticity of demand.

Knowledge of elasticity enables governments to decide how much tax can be levied on products like petrol to maximise tax revenues

Illustrating price elasticity of demand

In Unit 2.7 we saw that price elasticity of demand measures the responsiveness of changes in the quantity demanded to changes in price. Where demand for a product is elastic this is represented by a shallow sloping demand curve. Where demand is inelastic the demand curve will be steeper (see Figure 2.9.1).

Comparing the same price change – a fall from P to P1 on the graph – the change in quantity from Q to Q1 is much larger for the good with the elastic demand than for the one with the inelastic demand (Q to Q2).

Revenue implications

The **revenue** of a business is the sum of money that it receives from sales of goods.

Revenue = Quantity sold × Price per item

For example, if a business sells 5,000 items at US$30 per item, its sales revenue will be US$150,000.

Knowledge of price elasticity enables sellers to calculate revenues at different prices. For example, Yin Qiang is going to import radios and is deciding on a price to charge. He has carried out research that reveals the following:

Price US$	Demand per month	Sales revenue
50	1,000	50,000
40	2,000	80,000
30	5,000	150,000
20	6,000	120,000

Using this information he will be encouraged to charge a price of US$30, because this will yield the most revenue.

The price elasticity of demand is particularly elastic between US$40 and US$30. The price elasticity is −10. When price is reduced from US$40 to US$30 (a price change of 25 per cent), quantity demanded increases by 250 per cent (from 2,000 to 5,000).

$$\frac{250 \text{ per cent}}{-25 \text{ per cent}} = -10$$

(a reduction in price from $40 to $30 is 25 per cent)

Yin Qiang would also need to take into consideration the cost of importing the radios before deciding on the price to charge.

Figure 2.9.1 Illustrating price elasticity of demand

Factors that influence the price elasticity of demand for products include:

- whether consumers see the product as essential or as a luxury: demand for necessities – for example, basic foodstuffs such as rice, noodles and potatoes – is relatively inelastic
- how much consumers spend on the item: if they spend only a tiny fraction of their income on an item, demand may be more inelastic than for goods they spend a lot on, such as matches (relatively inelastic) or luxury foods (relatively elastic).

Tax decisions

Knowledge of price elasticity is also important for a government when it levies taxes on goods. As we shall see in Unit 5, a government has a number of objectives in raising taxes. One of these is to bring in revenue to finance government spending. Taxes need to be levied at rates that maximise these revenues. A number of goods taxed by governments have inelastic demand: the demand for petrol in the UK, for example, is unaffected by a price that includes tax of more than 70 per cent. The government therefore needs to be careful not to overtax items to the point at which they become so expensive that demand for them becomes relatively elastic.

Exchange rate changes

In Unit 8 we explain the importance of the exchange rate. The **exchange rate** is the rate at which the currency of one country will exchange for the currency of another country. When the exchange rate of a currency rises or falls this affects prices for firms that buy and sell internationally. In Unit 8 we explain how price elasticity of demand affects the revenues as a result of changes in exchange rates.

KEY POINTS

1. Knowledge of price elasticity of demand helps decision-making.
2. Businesses should identify price elasticity of demand in order to maximise revenues.
3. Governments can use knowledge of price elasticity to set tax rates on goods.

SUMMARY QUESTIONS

1. Describe two situations in which knowledge of price elasticity would help a decision-maker to set prices.
2. If a business raised the price of a product with an inelastic demand, what would be the effect on sales revenue?
3. How would knowledge of price elasticity of demand for petrol help a government in deciding how much tax to levy on it?

EXAM TIP

You may well need to show that you understand why knowledge of price elasticity of demand is useful to a business. If demand is price elastic, a business should lower the price to increase revenue. If, however, demand is price _inelastic_, a business should raise the price to increase revenue.

ACTIVITY

Interview someone who has a small business to find out how knowledge of consumer demand influences the prices charged for products.

DID YOU KNOW?

An important factor affecting price elasticity of demand is whether there is a substitute for a product. If there are no substitutes, the product is likely to have an inelastic demand (and a high price). This is the case with a number of important medicines developed by pharmaceutical companies. The companies take out legal protection in the form of a patent. A **patent** is a licence granted to an inventor preventing others from copying the idea.

2.10 Merits of the market system

LEARNING OUTCOMES

Candidates should be able to:
- evaluate the merits of the market system.

The market

In this unit we have been looking at how the market works. We have explained how the forces of demand and supply determine market price. Changes in demand and supply lead to changes in the market price. The main groups involved in the market system are consumers, the government and other businesses.

Markets such as this one in Kingston, Jamaica bring together buyers and sellers. Through demand buyers are able to show their preferences for goods they want to be supplied

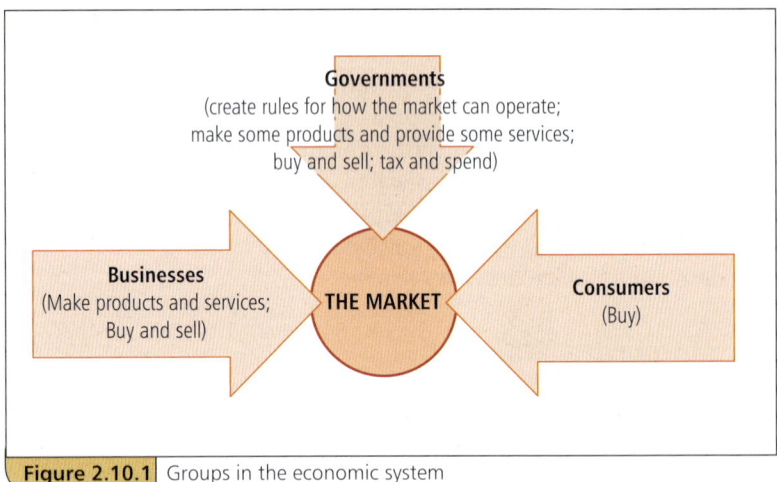

Figure 2.10.1 Groups in the economic system

Bringing together buyers and sellers

The **market** brings together buyers and sellers. This might be in a traditional market, where buyers and sellers come together to trade for vegetables, meat, clothing and other items. The term 'market' also describes any other situation where buyers and sellers contact each other. They might do this over the telephone or on the internet.

The price the seller sets helps buyers to decide what and how much they want to purchase. Buyers show what they prefer by their choice of purchase. This is **effective demand**.

Allocating resources to goods in demand

Every day millions of buying and selling decisions are made. When you go shopping you may make a decision (a choice) to buy, say, a particular type of canned drink.

If many consumers decide to buy a new type of drink, then a manufacturer will react by switching resources (such as labour, machinery and materials) into making that type of drink. Figure 2.10.2 shows how, as the demand for the new drink continues to rise, suppliers are willing to increase supply – a movement up the supply curve from Q to Q1 and then to Q2, and then Q3.

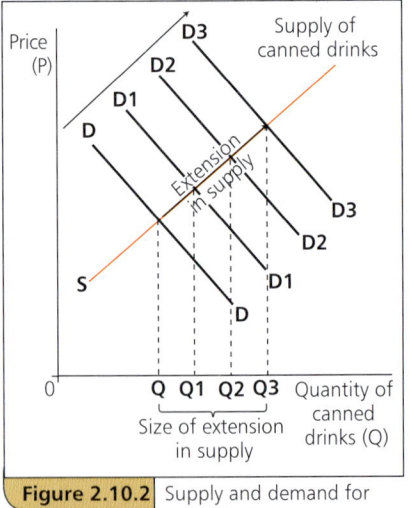

Figure 2.10.2 Supply and demand for canned drink

Coordinating decision-making

One of the greatest efficiencies of the market system is that it coordinates billions of decisions. Across the world, every second, billions of consumers are making purchasing decisions. They may be persuaded by fashion or advertisements, but the decision is ultimately theirs. They then make their decisions known through the purchases that they make. Sellers then make their own decisions about what to produce and sell based on what is selling well.

Providing plenty of choice

In a market that is working well, customers have **choices**: there will be plenty of competing rivals providing goods. For example, in most countries there are rival companies providing different mobile phone services, and there are rival firms producing household goods such as soap, washing powder and cooking oil.

Keeping prices down

Competition in the market helps to keep prices down. Rival businesses will seek to beat the competition by providing lower prices than those offered by rivals.

> **EXAM TIP**
>
> Make sure you understand that in a pure market system, there would be no need for a government to intervene to allocate resources.

ACTIVITY

Identify a product market where you have lots of choice of goods and prices are competitive. Compare this with a market in which there is less choice and prices seem high. How could the uncompetitive market become more like the competitive one?

KEY POINTS

1. The marketplace is any situation in which buyers and sellers come into contact.
2. Producers and sellers supply the market provided they can make a profit.
3. The market allocates resources, coordinates buyer and seller decisions, provides choice and helps to keep prices down.

DID YOU KNOW?

A country with a fast-growing competitive telecoms market is Pakistan, with 100 million mobile phone subscribers and 6 million landlines. There is plenty of choice for consumers, with five major competitors in the mobile market: Mobilink; Ufone; Telenor; Warid; and Zong. The market is regulated by the government's Pakistan Telecom Authority, which makes sure that consumers get a fair deal. Prices are low because there is so much competition.

SUMMARY QUESTIONS

1. How does the market help both consumers and producers/sellers?
2. How does the market help to channel resources into goods where demand is increasing?
3. What would the features be of a smooth working market?

2.11 Market failure

Market failure

Markets are said to fail when they are inefficient. This would arise if:

- they fail to produce goods that consumers want
- they fail to produce the quantities of goods required
- they fail to produce goods at acceptably low prices.

A good example of **market failure** is in the provision of treatment for children for HIV and AIDS. Large numbers of children in poorer countries are born with HIV/AIDS that they contract from their mother. These children are in desperate need of the drugs required to protect them. However, the prices of these medicines is very high so most families cannot afford them. The market therefore fails these children.

Inoculating children against harmful diseases not only benefits the children, but the whole community too

It is important to identify some of the failures of the market system. Criticisms can be levelled in two main ways:

- The market system does not always produce 'desirable' outputs. For example, it could be argued that cigarettes and fast or junk food, such as fatty burgers, are bad for health.
- The market system does not always work. Some of the worst failures of the market system are outlined in the following paragraphs, and in Unit 2.12.

Not producing public or merit goods

A **public good** is one that must be provided to the whole of a community or not at all – for example, a police force. Individuals would be reluctant to pay for such a service because people who chose not to pay (free-riders) would still benefit from the service. Public goods are therefore provided by the government, which usually funds them by means of taxes.

LEARNING OUTCOMES

Candidates should be able to:
- describe the concept of market failure
- explain the reasons for its occurrence.

DID YOU KNOW?

There is no automatic mechanism in the market system for protecting the environment. Environmental resources such as rivers and lakes are often used for dumping industrial and household waste. Government regulation, taxes and fines are therefore required to prevent pollution, because the market often fails to protect the natural world.

EXAM TIP

The terms 'public good' and 'merit good' do not actually appear in the syllabus. You can, therefore, gain maximum marks in an answer without referring to them. However, they are useful terms for conveying the idea of market failure.

A **merit good** is one with substantial benefits (sometimes referred to as positive external effects or externalities) for society as a whole rather than being restricted to individuals – for example, inoculation against a particular disease. Everyone benefits if these are provided at low cost.

> **CASE STUDY** — Providing vaccinations and family planning services
>
> Many illnesses can have severe effects across wide populations. Some diseases can spread rapidly across the globe. Many of the inoculations required to protect against these diseases are very expensive and many people cannot afford them. On its own the market would fail to provide for the poorest sectors of the community.
>
> Governments and international bodies can help to combat market failure. The international body responsible for looking after the health of people worldwide is the World Health Organisation (WHO). The WHO provides funds and supports governments across the globe by providing free inoculation against serious diseases. International efforts have helped to eradicate smallpox and polio from most countries.
>
> The WHO also supports programmes of family planning across the world. Families are given advice and support to limit the number of children they have. Both of these initiatives provide benefits to the wider community.
>
> **Questions**
>
> 1 Why does the market fail to meet the health needs of the poor in many situations?
>
> 2 In what ways are inoculation against smallpox and free family planning merit goods?
>
> 3 Why does the government sometimes need to step in when the market is failing?

The market system will often fail to provide essential goods and services that benefit the wider public, such as street lighting, good roads, a police force and fire service. The market often does not provide these goods because it is very difficult to get the people who benefit to pay for them.

> **KEY POINTS**
>
> 1 Market failure involves inefficiency in producing goods that consumers want at prices they can afford.
>
> 2 The market may produce 'undesirable' goods.
>
> 3 Public goods and merit goods require government provision.

> **DID YOU KNOW?**
>
> Some people think that persuading consumers to buy goods that they do not really need does not always benefit the market. Large businesses can also restrict competition by undercutting the prices of smaller rivals and forcing them out of business.

> **ACTIVITY**
>
> Create a poster with the heading 'Market Failure'. On the poster illustrate market failure by providing examples from your local area.

> **SUMMARY QUESTIONS**
>
> 1 Define *market failure*. Illustrate your answer with two recent examples.
>
> 2 State which of the following are public goods: street lighting, soap, motor cars, flood defence systems, police services, chocolate.
>
> 3 In what circumstances might the market system be unstable?
>
> 4 Why is the market not a good protector of:
>   a the environment
>   b poorer people?

2.12 Private and social costs and benefits

LEARNING OUTCOMES

Candidates should be able to:
- define private and social costs and benefits.

Building a new factory in Thailand has both private and social costs and benefits – it is not just the factory owners who will benefit or make a loss from the new venture

Private costs and benefits

When a business, small or large, makes a decision, it will first consider the **private costs** and **private benefits** – in other words, the financial advantages and disadvantages. In the table below the example of a business owner in Thailand considering whether to set up a new factory is used to show the costs and benefits that help the owner to make a decision.

DID YOU KNOW?

Some practices, such as industrial activities that create a lot of pollution, would be stopped if the social costs were taken into consideration.

Private costs of building and operating a factory in Thailand	Private benefits of building and operating a factory in Thailand
Cost of borrowing the necessary finance to build the factory	The revenues earned by the factory
Cost of building the factory and equipping it with machinery	The savings to the business resulting from operating in Thailand rather than at a higher-cost location
Cost of labour	
Cost of raw materials	

To work out the profit from running the factory, an accountant will calculate the net financial return in the following way:

Private benefits – private costs = Net private benefit or profit

This method does not take into account social costs and benefits and is a very narrow way of looking at the impact of the decision. It does not consider **externalities**.

EXAM TIP

The term 'externalities' is not explicitly referred to in the syllabus, but you should refer to the distinction between private and social costs and benefits.

Externalities

An externality is the result of economic activity, such as building a new factory, that is not taken into account by the individuals who make a decision. In other words, it is the external, or 'outside', effect of a decision. For example, the new factory may provide local jobs, but it may force an existing local factory to close down, with the loss of some jobs. The favourable effect is a **positive externality**. The effect on the rival factory is a **negative externality**.

Social costs and benefits

Social benefits include the private and other positive benefits that result from a particular business activity or decision. **Social costs** are the private costs to the company, say of building a factory, plus all the other costs resulting from this, such as traffic noise affecting local residents. The overall net benefit of an economic activity can be calculated by:

(private benefits + external benefits) − (private costs + external costs)

The table below illustrates some of the major costs and benefits of setting up a factory in Thailand.

Private costs of building and operating the factory	Private benefits of building and operating the factory
As set out in table opposite	As set out in table opposite
Social costs of building and operating the factory	**Social benefits of building and operating the factory**
Jobs lost in a rival factory that is forced to close – the wages lost	Jobs created in the factory – the wages earned
Loss of profit by owners of the rival factory that closes, and loss of taxes by the government	Rise in tax revenue for the government of Thailand from profits of the company
Increased traffic and noise pollution created by the new factory	New products that come onto the market in Thailand that are produced by the new factory

Activities should only be carried out if the social benefits are greater than the social costs. It is not always easy to calculate social costs and benefits and give a monetary value to factors such as noise pollution or the benefit of reduced journey times.

SUMMARY QUESTIONS

1 What is the difference between a private cost of an activity and the social cost of that activity?

2 Give an example of an activity that involves private costs and benefits and social costs and benefits. Suggest examples of these costs and benefits.

3 Why might it be difficult to measure costs and benefits?

EXAM TIP

Candidates are sometimes confused about the precise meaning of 'social costs' and 'social benefits'. Make sure that you fully understand that social costs are equal to the sum of private costs and external costs. Social benefits are equal to the sum of private benefits and external benefits.

ACTIVITY

Imagine that a large retail outlet or factory is to be built close to your school. New access roads will need to be built. Who is likely to be affected? In each case, outline one social benefit and one social cost to each of these groups. Have a class debate, with some pointing out the benefits and some the costs.

KEY POINTS

1 Private costs and benefits are monetary calculations of the effect of economic activity for individuals or businesses.

2 Private costs and benefits are only part of wider social costs and benefits.

3 To find out the true net benefits of economic activity, both private and social costs and benefits should be considered.

2.13 Conflict between private and social interests

LEARNING OUTCOMES

Candidates should be able to:
- discuss conflicts of interest in relation to costs and benefits in the short and long term.

Conflicts of interest

Decisions made by individuals, businesses and governments have an effect on **third parties**. These are **stakeholders** with an interest in activities and decisions. Conflicts of interest occur between stakeholders likely to receive positive benefits from an activity and stakeholders who will suffer from negative externalities. These conflicts of interest can be illustrated by the issues of:

- **conserving**, as opposed to using, resources
- public expenditure versus private expenditure.

Commercial logging in the Amazon creates timber that can be sold, but can destroy the livelihoods and environments of people who live in the forests

Conserving resources versus using resources

In Unit 1.3 we saw that economic actions involve an opportunity cost – the next best alternative that was not chosen. A major opportunity cost for society is that when resources are used for a particular purpose, they are not available for other uses. Many people argue that it is important to conserve resources for the future. For example, if we cut down timber in the rainforests we destroy forest habitats that provide for people, plants and animals today and in the future.

Conservation involves taking a long-term rather than a short-term view. Conservationists argue that this generation should pass on to future generations at least as many resources as our own generation has inherited. As a society we inherit:

- **natural capital** – in the form of lakes, rivers, clean air and other gifts of nature

ACTIVITY

Using your local newspaper, identify a dispute about the conservation of local resources. What is the issue? Who are the groups concerned? How much influence does each group have in the decisions that are being made? Share your findings with your group.

EXAM TIP

A one-sided answer that only looks at one aspect will not be able to gain full marks; make sure that you consider both the use and the conservation of resources.

- **man-made capital** – in the form of roads, bridges, factories and offices
- **social capital** – in the form of relationships between members of society such as family and community.

Producing more man-made capital in the form of factories and other production units may come at the expense of sacrificing other forms of capital, such as the natural environment.

Conflicts often arise between businesses seeking to develop new mines, factories and roads, and environmentalists, local communities and other groups seeking to conserve natural capital.

Public expenditure versus private expenditure

Public expenditure is carried out by national and local government and public sector enterprises (see Unit 4). **Private expenditure** is carried out by individuals and businesses that are not government-owned.

In a mixed economy there is considerable debate about how much expenditure should be public and how much private. Those in favour of most being private argue that:

1. Individuals are best placed to choose how to spend their own money. If we give our money to the government in the form of taxes, the government can only guess how we would like it to be spent.
2. When the government spends money it can be wasteful.

Those in favour of more public expenditure argue that:

1. The government can provide public goods and merit goods that the market would not produce in sufficient quantities for everyone.
2. Public sector workers may be more likely to spend money in a way that is fair to all; narrow interest groups are less likely to do that.

ACTIVITY

Working in small groups, make a list of the key items of capital in your neighbourhood: natural, man-made and social. Discuss in your group which of these types of capital are most important for the well-being of members of your community.

DID YOU KNOW?

The economist Milton Friedman believed that the government should play a minimum role in spending money in the economy. One of his best-known books was *Free to Choose*, in which he argued that allowing individuals and firms to manage their own buying decisions led to an efficient market system.

KEY POINTS

1. Conflicts arise between private and social interests.
2. Resources can be used up now or conserved for the future.
3. Another conflict is between whether the use of resources should be decided by private expenditure or whether the government should make more of the spending decisions.

SUMMARY QUESTIONS

1. Give three examples of resources where more conservation could be carried out for the future. Explain the benefit of conserving these resources.
2. What are the arguments for more public expenditure?
3. Would you be in favour of more public or more private expenditure in your national economy?

Unit 2 — Practice exam questions

SECTION 1: Multiple-choice questions

Each question has ONE correct answer.

1 Which of the following describes a country with a mixed economy?
 a Goods and services are provided by private companies
 b Goods and services are provided by the government
 c Goods and services are provided by private companies and by the government
 d Goods and services are provided by individuals and by companies

2 Which of the following describes the economic aim of sellers of goods and services?
 a A wide range of goods on offer
 b A product made from best-quality materials
 c A high-cost advertising campaign
 d A high price to provide profit for the business

3 What is *effective demand* for a good or service?
 a A want, backed up by money to purchase the item
 b A need, by all consumers desiring the item
 c A demand depending on level of income
 d A demand by one group of consumers

4 What does a typical supply curve show about the relationship between the amount supplied of a product and its price?
 a Firms will supply more at a lower price
 b Consumers will buy more at a higher price
 c Firms will supply more at a higher price
 d Consumers will buy more at a lower price

5 Which one of the following pairs of products are in joint supply?
 a Potatoes and maize
 b Beef and leather
 c CDs and CD players
 d Cars and tyres

6 What does the *equilibrium price* in a market show?
 a The price at which a company will get the highest number of sales
 b The price at which quantity supplied is equal to quantity demanded
 c The price at which the most profit will be made
 d The price at which all production costs will be covered

7 Which of the following would cause the demand curve for chocolate bars to shift to the right?
 a A decrease in the price of the chocolate bars
 b A decrease in the price of cocoa beans
 c A 'chocolate is good for your health' advertising campaign
 d A health scare about the dangers of eating too much sweet food

8 The price elasticity of demand (PED) for a product is estimated at −1.5. The current level of sales is 1,000 per week. If the PED estimate is correct and the price of the product increases from £2 to £2.40, what will be the new weekly level of sales?
 a 700
 b 1,300
 c 800
 d 900

9 Which of the following is NOT an example of a merit good?
 a Literacy education
 b Mobile telephone
 c Family planning advice
 d Mosquito net

10 Which of the following is an example of a social cost?
 a Provision of essential medicines
 b Recycling plastic bottles
 c Building community facilities
 d Pollution from a factory

SECTION 2: Structured questions

Country A is a developing country, with a growing market for consumer products. The political environment has changed recently and the economy is in the process of moving away from a planned system, where all production was controlled by the government. The economy is now moving towards a mixed system, where an increasing number of goods and services are produced by private companies, whose aim is to make as much profit as possible.

The consumers in Country A now have the opportunity to choose from a much wider range of products and services. This choice means that the sellers now need to be much more aware of what consumers are looking for. Many of the older companies, who relied on their products being the only ones available, have gone out of business.

However, it is not all good news for the population, as the decline of many of the older companies has led to unemployment for workers who had relied on a 'job for life'. There is talk of a widening gap between rich and poor under the new system.

1 a Explain what is meant by a *mixed* economy. (4)
   b Identify and explain TWO reasons why 'a growing market for consumer products' will lead to more choice for individuals. (6)
   c Using the information given, identify and explain why sellers need to be more aware of the needs and wants of consumers. (4)
   d Discuss what may be the advantages and disadvantages of the changing economic environment for the population of Country A. (6)

2 One of the new retailers in Country A is importing clothing and shoes from the US and selling these products in big new shops in the larger towns. They also stock traditional styles that are made in local factories.
   a Draw and label a demand and supply diagram for traditional-style clothing before the new products arrived from the US. (4)
   b Draw a new demand and supply diagram illustrating the likely changes in this market following the introduction of imported goods. Explain what your diagram shows. (6)
   c Analyse the impact that the change in demand will have on how the retailer uses his resources. (4)
   d Discuss how the increase in imported products may affect local consumers and workers in Country A. (6)

3 Large wheat farms are major suppliers of food in Country A. Traditionally, they have received large subsidies from the government to produce basic foodstuffs, for sale at low prices to the population. Now these subsidies are being taken away and the market opened to competition.
   a Suggest ONE reason why the government in Country A might have chosen to subsidise wheat production. (4)
   b Draw a supply and demand diagram that illustrates the removal of subsidies to wheat farmers in Country A. (4)
   c Using your diagram, explain the likely effects of the removal of the subsidy and opening the market to competition. (6)
   d With reference to the 'widening gap between rich and poor', discuss whether the removal of these subsidies and opening the market to competition will benefit the population and economy of Country A in the long term. (6)

4 Under the new economic system, the government of Country A is continuing to provide education, health and public transport services by bus and rail. However, air services are being provided by a new low-cost airline, which is offering very low fares between the major cities and to major overseas destinations.
   a Explain why the government of Country A may have decided to continue education provision. (3)
   b Explain the view that free health services lead to a more productive population. (3)
   c Explain why vaccination programmes and family planning services may provide social benefits to the population of Country A. (6)
   d Discuss whether the increased use of air services of the new low-cost airline may lead to market failure. (8)

Total: 80 marks

SECTION 3: Analysis and critical evaluation

Sui Toys is a major manufacturing company with five factories, based in a large developing country. It is a public limited company, with shares quoted on stock markets worldwide, including London, Hong Kong and New York. Sui Toys manufactures for many of the major toy companies throughout the world and its product range is very diverse, from traditional toys and games to computer games and consoles. With a share of around 30 per cent of this highly competitive market, the company enjoys considerable monopoly power and other toy manufacturers keep a close watch on Sui's prices and product range.

The worldwide recession has hit the company hard, with demand in many countries decreasing. Consumers are still buying the lower-priced products, but demand at the luxury end has declined considerably. Sui's share price has declined by 20 per cent and the company's managing director is concerned that the dividend this year may be low.

Sui also needs to make a major investment in the business, both on the manufacturing side and to improve communication between different parts of the company. As the company has grown, raw materials have become cheaper due to buying in bulk, but communication between the factories and management is very poor, leading to mistakes and delays on orders.

1 a Explain the difference between a *public limited company* and a *public sector organisation*. (2)

  b Explain who owns a public limited company. (2)

2 a Explain what is meant by 'monopoly power' in the case of Sui Toys. (2)

  b The management team of Sui Toys has set *profit maximisation* as a major business objective. Explain what this means. (2)

3 Discuss the extent to which Sui Toys may be able to charge high prices for its toys in this market situation. (5)

4 a Explain what is meant by the statement 'Sui's share price has declined by 20 per cent'. (2)

  b If the Sui Company decides to pay a low dividend this year in order to invest in the business, discuss the possible effects on the share price, using an appropriate diagram. (5)

5 Using the extract above and the theory of economies and diseconomies of scale, explain and give examples of both within Sui Toys. (5)

6 Using all the information given, discuss how Sui Toys may increase efficiency and profitability. (7)

Total: 32 marks

3 The individual as producer, consumer and borrower

This unit considers the parts played by money in the modern world, beginning with the evolution of currency systems from early exchange and barter systems. The role of commercial and central banks, and their importance to individuals and businesses, is discussed.

The individual as producer is considered through factors that might affect the choice of occupation. The unit looks at how people may choose to earn less in favour of job satisfaction, and the various reasons that earnings vary over time.

Individuals as consumers and borrowers are discussed through the examples of spending, saving and borrowing, and how motives differ according to both individual circumstances and the economic situation in the wider world.

> **LEARNING OUTCOMES**
>
> With regard to **money and financial institutions**, candidates should be able to:
> - describe the functions of money and the need for exchange
> - describe the functions of central banks, stock exchanges and commercial banks.
>
> With regard to the **individual as producer**, candidates should be able to:
> - identify the factors affecting an individual's choice of occupation
> - describe likely changes in earnings over time for an individual
> - describe the differences in earnings between different occupational groups
> - describe trade unions and their role in the economy
> - describe the benefits and disadvantages of specialisation for the individual.
>
> With regard to the **individual as consumer and borrower**, candidates should be able to:
> - analyse the different motives for spending, saving and borrowing
> - discuss how and why different income groups have different expenditure patterns.

3.1 The functions of money

LEARNING OUTCOMES

Candidates should be able to:
- describe the functions of money and the need for exchange.

What is money?

Money is anything that is widely accepted or used to exchange for goods. Today when we think about money we are typically referring to notes and coins. However, households and businesses also use many other ways of making payments, such as credit and debit cards.

Before money was used, people would **barter** – that is, exchange goods, say a goat for several chickens. This requires the two people who make the trade to want what the other has to offer (a **double coincidence of wants**). The obvious disadvantage is that one partner may not have enough goods to make the exchange fair, or they might not want a whole goat, for example. People realised that small but valuable items, such as cowrie shells, could be used instead.

DID YOU KNOW?

Cowrie shells were valued highly because they were rare. They were widely used as money for several hundred years in parts of China, India and Africa. They were also used as jewellery.

EXAM TIP

You need to be able to explain why money is preferable to barter as a means of exchange.

For centuries cowrie shells were used as money in many areas of the world

Why were cowrie shells used as money so widely? Look at this list of characteristics of the shells:

- Scarcity – shells were valuable because they were relatively scarce.
- Acceptability – people were prepared to accept shells as payment because they knew that they could use them for future trading.
- Portability – the shells could easily be carried for long distances.
- Durability – the shells were hard-wearing and long-lasting.
- Divisible – shells could be supplied in various quantities, to buy purchases of different sizes. Purchases would be possible using a few or, for the wealthy, hundreds of shells. In modern terms, a car can be priced at thousands or millions of dollars. Dollars can be divided into cents for small items like a packet of chewing gum or a piece of fruit.

ACTIVITY

Do some research on the history of money in your own country. Write a report of your findings or make a poster to display in the classroom.

The functions of money

The functions of money are as follows:

1 As a medium of exchange – money is generally accepted as a means of payment for most goods.
2 As a **unit of account** – the price of an item can be measured in terms of how many units of currency it is worth. For example, whereas a low-quality top may cost US$10, a high-quality one may be valued at US$100 or more.
3 As a **store of value** – you can save money because it keeps its value. Saving enables use of the money in the future.
4 As a **standard for deferred payments** – borrowers are able to borrow money and pay it back at a future date.

EXAM TIP

You will need to make sure that you can explain these four functions of money in the examination.

CASE STUDY | The yuan

The yuan is the money in use in China today. The smallest units of currency are the jiao and fen (10 fen = 1 jiao, 10 jiao = 1 yuan). You can buy goods with the yuan in any shop in China. The notes are easy to carry around and store. Individuals can save yuan in their own homes. Alternatively, they can deposit their savings at a bank like China's Industrial and Commercial Bank. The yuan maintains its value over time. As a result a bank can lend yuan to a business knowing that when the time comes for repayment, the value of the currency will be at least as much as when they lent the money.

Questions

1 Explain some of the properties of the yuan that make it such a good currency.
2 Show how the yuan acts as a medium of exchange, a standard for deferred payments and a store of value.

SUMMARY QUESTIONS

1 Are the functions of money today the same as when cowrie shells were used?
2 How useful would the following be in performing the functions of money today: a gold bar, a chocolate bar, paper currency notes produced by the government, gold coins, an antique table, cowrie shells?
3 What is the smallest unit of currency in your country? How useful is it as a medium of exchange?

KEY POINTS

1 Money is anything that is generally accepted for payment.
2 Today money consists of notes and coins, and also bank card payments.
3 The main function of money is as a means of making exchange (payment for goods).

3.2 Commercial banks

LEARNING OUTCOMES

Candidates should be able to:
- describe the functions of commercial banks.

What is a commercial bank?

Commercial banks provide a safe place to keep money and will also lend money. Sometimes they are called retail banks because their lending to businesses and households is relatively small compared with some investment banks which provide large sums of capital to business.

The main activities of commercial banks

The basic functions of a bank are:

1. **Keeping money safe**: a bank's vaults are more secure than a safe deposit box in a private house. Individuals and businesses can open bank accounts. They deposit money in the account. **Savings accounts** pay the depositor a set rate of interest on sums saved. **Current accounts** are for keeping money safe, but sums can be withdrawn to make payments. A current account may pay some interest, but this will be lower than on a savings account. Banks also keep documents and other valuable items in safe deposit boxes.

2. **Lending**: many people and businesses need to borrow money – for example, for expensive purchases such as a car. Businesses may borrow from banks when they want to grow. Borrowing methods include:

   - **Loans** – borrowing a fixed sum (e.g. US$1,000) for a set period of time (e.g. two years). The business will need to pay back the sum borrowed (US$1,000) plus the agreed rate of interest. For example, if the interest rate is 10 per cent, then over the two years the borrower will pay back US$1,100 (US$1,000 + US$100 interest).
   - An **overdraft** – that is, taking out more than has been put into the account. The borrower has an agreed overdraft limit, and will pay interest to the bank if the account is overdrawn.
   - Banks offer customers a **credit card**. This enables users to buy goods and pay for them later. Every month users receive a **statement** showing how much they owe the bank. If they pay the bill by a given date, they will not have to pay interest. However, if they do not pay the bill in full, they are charged a high rate of interest. Many businesses use credit cards to finance short-term cash flow needs. A **debit card** is a means of payment using funds in your own bank account rather than through borrowing.
   - **Mortgages** – banks lend to firms and households to buy office buildings and factories. The legal deeds of ownership of the property are kept by the bank until the mortgage has been repaid. Mortgages are usually for long periods of time, such as 25 years.

Commercial banks look after the money of depositors, lend money and make it possible to make payments

DID YOU KNOW?

Interest is paid by the bank as a reward to savers. It is calculated as a percentage of the sum saved. The bank also charges interest for lending money.

Commercial banks act as financial intermediaries in the way shown in Figure 3.2.1.

Other banking services

Commercial banks also perform a number of other important services that benefit the economy:

- They provide **means of making payment**, such as cheques and banker's drafts. These are slips of paper, printed with the name, address and logo of the bank, and customers write in the name of the person and the amount they wish to pay. The bank then transfers money to the recipients. Banks can also make regular payments in the form of standing orders (set payments of regular sums) into a named account. Banks process payments through automatic electronic payments as well as internet banking. In some countries (e.g. in 2018 in the UK) banks will stop the use of cheques because cards are so much easier to use.
- They provide **foreign currency**. If you visit another country that uses different currency, your local bank may be able to provide you with the currency. However, ATMs (automated teller machines) make it easy for a customer to withdraw money in most urban areas worldwide.

Figure 3.2.1 Banks – linking savers and borrowers

ACTIVITY

Identify a commercial bank that operates in your country. Find out the range of services that it offers and compare these with the functions outlined in this Unit. Make a poster that would advertise the bank and its services.

DID YOU KNOW?

There is a highly competitive commercial banking structure in Pakistan and many different banks. Some banks meet the general needs of business and household customers. Others target specific types of customers, such as First Women Bank, which sets out 'to be the lead bank for women'.

KEY POINTS

1. Commercial banks provide banking services to businesses and households.
2. Their main functions are to lend money, facilitate payment systems and keep money safe.
3. Banks act as intermediaries between borrowers and lenders.

EXAM TIP

You will need to be able to explain why a person might prefer to keep their money in a commercial bank rather than hide it somewhere in their house.

SUMMARY QUESTIONS

1. Why might a customer prefer to have a deposit rather than a current account?
2. How do commercial banks play an intermediary role in the economy?
3. Describe three ways in which commercial banks provide credit for customers.

3.3 Central banks

Central banks

Every country has a **central bank** whose job it is to supervise the banking system in the domestic economy. In Britain the central bank is the Bank of England; in Germany it is the Deutsche Bundesbank; in Mauritius it is the Bank of Mauritius.

The central bank influences the economy in the following way. The head of the central bank holds regular meetings with senior officials from the other banks to outline policy for lending. If there is too much spending in an economy leading to rising prices, the head of the central bank may request that banks reduce lending. If there is too little spending in the economy, leading to **recession** (see Unit 6), banks will be requested to lend more. The central bank also creates rules (**financial regulations**) that affect how other banks can be set up, and, for example, how much they can safely lend.

As well as supervising the financial system, the central bank has additional functions:

- Printing the notes and minting the coins that are **legal tender** (notes and coins that should be accepted as payment). It also destroys torn notes and worn-out coins.
- The central bank plays a major role in setting **interest rates**. The interest rate is the price paid for borrowing money. Setting interest rates gives the central bank considerable power in the economy. Changing interest rates help the central bank to control lending by other banks.

Reduction in interest rates	Borrowers find borrowing cheaper, borrow more, increase spending
Increase in interest rates	Savers save more, borrowers borrow less, spending falls

- The central bank acts as a lender of last resort. If another bank needs cash in a hurry (perhaps because depositors are withdrawing unusually large sums of money), it can borrow from the central bank. In this situation, the central bank may decide to penalise other banks for lending too much and charge them a high rate of interest. Other banks set their interest rates at levels just above the central bank's base rate – that is, the rate set by the central bank on which all other interest rates are based.
- Supervising **monetary policy**: this determines the quantity of money in the economy and the interest rate. The central bank helps the government to create and manage monetary policy.
- Acting as banker for the commercial banks and for the government. By acting as the banker's bank, debts between the commercial banks can be settled through their accounts at the central bank.

LEARNING OUTCOMES

Candidates should be able to:
- describe the functions of central banks.

The Central Bank of Bahrain is responsible for regulating banking in Bahrain, issuing notes and coins and other functions

ACTIVITY

Find out the current base rate charged by the central bank in your country and compare it with the rates charged in each of the previous twelve months. Discuss with your classmates why the central bank may have raised or lowered its base rate over this period.

- Government tax revenue and major spending is carried out through accounts with the central bank.
- The central bank helps the government to borrow money by issuing government bills and bonds. The total amount the government owes to lenders is called the **national debt**. The bonds are official promises to repay money in the future with interest in return for the loan. Rich investors and other financial institutions are happy to lend governments money because in many countries it is a very safe investment.
- Helping to manage the international financial system. On a world scale there needs to be generally acceptable methods of making payment for international transactions. This requires confidence in the international financial system. The **International Monetary Fund (IMF)** was set up to provide supervision for the world's banking system. One of its functions is to lend money to governments to help them in times of financial crisis when investors may have lost confidence in the banking systems of those countries. Central banks work closely with the IMF to create financial stability. Countries deposit gold and their own currency with the IMF. This can then be lent to countries in crisis. Leading central bankers will meet regularly with important government officials and members of the IMF to create better systems of international financial management.

DID YOU KNOW?

The size of national debt is a major concern to governments. If the debt becomes too large, lenders will become reluctant to make further loans and demand higher rates of interest. The higher rates of interest lead to a greater burden of future debt repayments.

In 2010, the government of Greece found that it was difficult to finance the national debt. As the amount of debt was so large, lenders insisted on much higher rates of interest to lend Greece money.

DID YOU KNOW?

The central bank manages the national debt. This involves repaying investors who have lent the government money and paying the interest on this debt. In the UK, the Bank of England was established in 1694 to manage the national debt.

ACTIVITY

Create a poster showing the name of the central bank in your country and setting out some of its main functions.

KEY POINTS

1. The central bank supervises the other banks and has a close link with government monetary policy.
2. The central bank issues notes and coins.
3. The central bank is the government's bank and the banker's bank.

EXAM TIP

You might be asked in the examination to discuss the role of the central bank in a country's economic and financial system.

SUMMARY QUESTIONS

1. Explain the terms *central bank*, *lender of last resort*, and *national debt*.
2. Describe what you consider to be the two main functions of a central bank.
3. The Central Bank of Sri Lanka is responsible for the conduct of monetary policy in the country. What do you think this would involve?

3.4 Stock exchanges

LEARNING OUTCOMES

Candidates should be able to:
- describe the function of the stock exchange.

ACTIVITY

Create a poster showing a world map. Mark on it 25 major world stock exchanges. Include the stock exchange of your own country if it has one.

DID YOU KNOW?

The price of shares depends on how keen buyers are to purchase shares in particular companies. The more popular a share, the higher its price. Investors want to buy shares of companies that make good profits, so that they can take a share of this profit in the form of a dividend and benefit from the rising share price.

The stock exchange

The **stock exchange** was originally a building in which shares in public companies (see Unit 4) were traded. The stock exchange is now a very important institution for raising funds for business, and many countries today have one. Well-known examples include the New York, London, Mumbai and Beijing Stock Exchanges.

The trading floor of the Shanghai Stock Exchange, China, showing the importance of computer networks for share trading

Shares are bought and sold by **traders** who purchase the shares from other traders. In some exchanges trades are still made by verbal bids and offers (e.g. on the New York Stock Exchange). However, on many exchanges (e.g. the Paris Bourse) traders buy and sell shares using computer screens.

Today most share buyers are financial institutions – for example, insurance companies and pension funds. They buy shares as a form of financial investment, calculating that if they purchase shares wisely, their investments will increase in value over time.

The **stock market** is a very efficient market. This is because each trader has instant access through their screens to the prices of all of the shares traded on a particular exchange.

The stock exchange is usually self-regulating – that is, it appoints officials to supervise and set the rules for trading. Regulations set out who can act as brokers, who need to pass special examinations.

Institutions and individuals wishing to sell shares → Traders at the stock exchange → Institutions and individuals wishing to buy shares

Figure 3.4.1 The stock exchange as marketplace

ACTIVITY

Choose a company that operates in your country and find out how much shares cost to purchase. Allocate yourself a set sum, (e.g. US$1,000) to invest in that company. How many shares would you be able to purchase? (*Hint:* US$1,000 divided by the share price.) Now see if you can find a newspaper article about whether that company has made good profits recently. What effect is the profitability of the business going to have on:

a its ability to pay dividends

b changes in the price of the share?

DID YOU KNOW?

Share prices rise when:

a a company is expected to make good profits

b another company wants to take over the business and is prepared to pay more than the existing share price to complete the deal.

The functions of the stock exchange

The main purpose of the stock exchange is to help public companies raise capital. Financial capital is the money that a business raises from selling shares. This finance can then be used to purchase physical capital, such as buildings and machinery.

The existence of a stock exchange gives the public and financial institutions confidence that:

- they can buy new shares
- they can sell their shares when they want to.

A shareholder in a company is a part-owner of that company. The rewards from holding shares are that:

- every 6 or 12 months shareholders will receive a payment known as a dividend, which is their reward, their share of the company profits
- they may also benefit from the rising value of their shares
- some companies offer special concessions to their shareholders – for example, cheap flights for holders of airline shares, or discount vouchers to use in the company's stores.

Shareholders are protected by **limited liability**. This is legal protection so that if a company gets into financial difficulty, the limit that a shareholder may lose is the value of their shareholding in the company. They are not expected to pay any more to cover the debts of the company. Stock exchanges also protect shareholders with strict rules setting out what a company must do for its shares to be listed on the exchange. Listed companies are required to produce an annual report for shareholders and are required to have their accounts checked each year by an independent **auditor**.

The stock exchange also plays an important role in helping the government to raise finance through selling bills and bonds. Institutional and other investors lend the government money knowing that they are almost certain to be paid back. In most countries government bonds are more secure than shares in companies. The return on a government bond may be lower than a dividend on a share in a company.

KEY POINTS

1 Stock exchanges bring together buyers and sellers of shares.

2 They enable businesses to raise financial capital.

3 They also help the government to raise finance.

SUMMARY QUESTIONS

1 What are shares? What are the benefits of holding shares?

2 How do stock exchanges enable shareholders to invest in public companies?

3 Give two other functions of the stock exchange.

3.5 Choice of occupation

LEARNING OUTCOMES

Candidates should be able to:
- identify the factors affecting an individual's choice of occupation.

Different types of occupation

There are thousands of different occupations, each with its own conditions of work. Employees are expected to work under a variety of arrangements, including full-time, part-time and shift work. Some people work indoors and others outdoors, some for large companies and others for **micro-businesses**, some work at night and others during the day. Some people are self-employed and work for themselves. There are many factors that help to determine a person's choice of occupation. Particularly important among these are wage factors and non-wage factors.

Wage factors

An important consideration in choosing a career is the wages paid. For example, doctors and accountants typically earn more than electricians and drivers.

Wages are payments for carrying out work. The higher the wage, the more attractive a job may seem. However, highly paid jobs typically require a lot of training and skill development, which can reduce the supply of qualified applicants. Some dangerous jobs – for example, working on an offshore oil rig – will only attract applicants if wages are relatively high.

In choosing an occupation a potential employee will consider the amount paid, including basic pay and additional incentives such as bonuses and overtime opportunities.

- **Basic pay** is the amount of money that will be received by an employee before any additional increments or deductions are made. For example, the basic pay may be set at US$200 for a 40-hour week.
- **Earnings** relates to the total amount an individual receives when additional payments are added, including overtime, bonuses and commission.
- **Overtime** is hours worked in addition to the basic contracted number of hours. It will be paid at a higher rate – for example, time and a half (150 per cent of the wage rate). The higher rate is often required to encourage people to work 'unsocial' hours.
- A **bonus** is used as an incentive – that is, to persuade employees to work harder (or longer), for example to meet targets such as given production or sales figures.
- **Commission** is a payment made as a percentage of the sales a salesperson makes. In a retail store an employee might receive 10 per cent of each sale made, or may be paid an hourly rate plus 5 per cent commission on each sale.

An offshore oil platform: high wages can encourage people to work in hard and dangerous occupations

Non-wage factors

Non-wage factors can be highly influential in the choice of occupation. They include the following:

- **Job satisfaction**: many people are prepared to work for less if they enjoy the work. Job satisfaction is personal to the individual; a person with the skills to be a successful business executive may choose manual work, say making beautiful objects. Some people prefer to work for a business with regular income; others prefer the freedom of working for themselves.
- **Career prospects**: many people want to work in occupations where there is opportunity for promotion – for example, from junior salesperson to sales supervisor, sales manager, area sales manager, and so on.
- **Fringe benefits**: these are non-financial incentives given to employees. For example:

Type of fringe benefit	Benefits
Subsidised housing	Subsidised or free housing is a strong incentive in city areas where accommodation is expensive and there are long waiting lists
Payment of school fees	Scholarships for education to the children of company employees
Company car or subsidised transport	Provides the benefit of a first car or second car or cheap rail and/or bus transport passes for families of workers
Subsidised company products	Reduced prices for company products

- Other non-wage incentives include length of holidays (e.g. for teachers), good pension schemes (particularly for public sector workers) and job security (again, often in the public sector). Another influencing factor is the location of the job, such as being close to family and friends, or in a desirable area.

> **DID YOU KNOW?**
>
> Employees may be paid by time, or according to a piece rate, performance rate or through profit-sharing. Piece rates are sometimes used in the textile and electronics industries: payment is made for each item that meets a given quality standard. Performance rates are related to meeting given targets. Profit-related pay is an additional reward related to the company's profit.

> **ACTIVITY**
>
> Think of a job that you would like to do when you leave school or college. List the three most important influences that would make the job attractive to you.

> **SUMMARY QUESTIONS**
>
> 1 Divide the following rewards into wage and non-wage factors:
>
>   basic pay   overtime   subsidised meals   company car   bonus   reduced price company products
>
> 2 Explain the difference between basic pay and earnings. Which figure will be higher?
>
> 3 Explain how the following will have an important part to play in influencing a person's choice of occupation:
>   a one wage factor
>   b one non-wage factor.

> **KEY POINTS**
>
> 1 The higher the reward, the bigger the incentive to work in a particular occupation.
>
> 2 Rewards consist of wage rewards and non-wage rewards.
>
> 3 An individual's choice of occupation is determined by a combination of wage and non-wage factors.

3.6 Changes in earnings over time for an individual

LEARNING OUTCOMES

Candidates should be able to:
- describe likely changes in earnings over time for an individual.

In Unit 3.5 we saw how earnings include additional payments such as bonuses as well as basic pay. Over the working life of an individual there will be considerable changes in earnings.

An employee starting work in a particular career, such as nursing, or in a particular industry, say the textile industry, would expect their earnings to rise steadily over their working life as their skills, training and qualifications increase. However, if they lose their job and have to retrain, they may have to start again at a lower grade.

Entry to the workforce

A young employee will receive relatively low earnings. This is largely because of a lack of work skills and experience. There are a number of opportunities to become more skilled. One way is to take an apprenticeship. The apprentice will learn from working with more skilled workers and often be provided with off-the-job training and study opportunities at local skills training facilities or colleges. Another possibility is to join a management training scheme. These typically involve providing a range of work-based experiences relevant to a specific industry. The trainee might be asked to work in different departments for a few months to get a general feel of how an organisation is run. Other young employees will be provided with training opportunities enabling them to acquire several job-related qualifications.

As workers become more skilled they are able to secure higher wages because of the high demand for the scarce skills that they have. NVQ-Js are Jamaican National Vocational Qualifications gained through HEART and other training programmes. Gaining NVQ-Js enables employees to gain higher wages

Skilled workers

The more experience an employee has, the more opportunities there are to increase earnings. Overtime is more likely to be offered, and there is more potential for earning bonuses. The more skilled a worker becomes, the greater the demand: more skilled employees will be in shorter supply and they will be able to command higher earnings. If an employer wishes to attract more highly skilled workers from other companies, higher rewards must be offered.

Figure 3.6.1 shows how the demand for the services of skilled workers helps to push up their wages, from W to W1.

End-of-career employees

If workers keep updating their skills and engaging in more training, they will be able to command higher wages. However, employees who do not keep up to date with changing trends and technologies may find that in their late career they become obsolete – that is, their skills are no longer required or are valued less. These workers may experience a fall in demand and falling wages. This is illustrated in Figure 3.6.2 by a fall in wages from W to W1. Older workers whose wages are relatively high may find themselves vulnerable to redundancy.

Figure 3.6.1 Increasing demand for skilled workers

Figure 3.6.2 Falling wages of late-career employees

CASE STUDY — Training in Jamaica

In Jamaica the HEART (Human Employment and Resource Training) Trust and the National Training Agency set out to provide a Jamaican workforce trained and qualified to international standards. There are 26 training institutions at which trainees can learn industry-related skills such as hospitality and catering, and information technology skills. The programme offers more than 40 qualifications. Anyone over 17 can apply for a HEART training programme. These last from 6 to 12 months, at no cost to the learner. Learners are both trained and assessed. They receive certificates of competence enabling them to work more productively and to earn more money as a result of their higher qualifications.

Questions

1 Why are HEART programmes of benefit both to the trainees and to the Jamaican economy?

2 Draw demand and supply diagrams to illustrate the effect for a young person in Jamaica of completing a HEART programme in hospitality. (*Hint:* Draw two diagrams – one before starting the training and the second after completing the training.)

ACTIVITY

Study a newspaper advertising jobs. Compare the average wages being offered for new starter jobs with those adverts targeted at more experienced workers. Discuss your findings with other students.

EXAM TIP

You need to be able to show in the examination that you understand why a person's earnings could rise and fall over their lifetime.

KEY POINTS

1 When people first start work they have relatively few skills.

2 As employees become better trained and more skilled and their experience increases, they will receive higher wages.

3 Later on wages may fall if an employee fails to update themselves with new skills.

SUMMARY QUESTIONS

1 Identify key points in a person's working life when they are likely to receive increases in wages and earnings.

2 Why are these increases likely to occur?

3 How can training schemes help employees to earn higher wages?

3.7 Differences in earnings between occupations 1

LEARNING OUTCOMES

Candidates should be able to:
- describe the differences in earnings between different groups.

In this Unit we explain why earnings vary between different occupational groups:
- skilled/unskilled
- private sector/public sector
- male/female
- agriculture/manufacturing/services.

A major cause of differences results from demand and supply. However, there is also an element of discrimination that may lead to inequalities.

CASE STUDY: The relative earnings of doctors and hospital porters

Why does a doctor earn more than a hospital porter?
- To reflect the time and skill invested in gaining medical qualifications.
- To reflect the responsibility the doctor carries.
- Because of the greater demand for and limited supply of doctors.

The demand curve for doctors has a steep shape (relatively inelastic demand, see Unit 2.7). The supply of doctors is also steep (relatively inelastic supply) because of the time, and expense that it takes to train them. In contrast, the supply and demand curves for hospital porters are relatively more elastic. A rise in wages of porters will lead to a much more rapid increase in the numbers making themselves available to work in hospitals.

a Doctors' salary

b Porters' wage

Questions

1 Explain why the supply curve for hospital doctors is steeper than that for hospital porters.

2 Explain why the wage rate of doctors is US$40,000, whereas it is only US$20,000 for hospital porters.

In most countries a large proportion of teachers work in the public sector. High levels of job security and relatively good pensions are non-wage factors encouraging people to work in this sector, as well as the love of the job

Skilled and unskilled workers

If labour is in short supply and the demand for that particular type of labour is strong, employers will be prepared to pay higher wages to engage suitable workers.

Another reason for skilled labour being paid more than unskilled is that it is highly productive. A skilled worker contributes far more value to production than an unskilled worker. For example, if a skilled furniture maker can produce five high-quality chairs in a day and an unskilled apprentice only one, the skilled worker is five times more productive than the unskilled one and merits a higher rate of pay.

The public and private sectors

In many countries, workers in the **public sector** earn more than those in the **private sector**. This is the case for example, in the UK, Ireland, the US and India.

This difference is sometimes described as the public sector premium.

> **CASE STUDY** — Public and private sector wages, UK
>
> The table gives comparisons between public and private sector workers in the UK, based on the Annual Survey of Hours and Earnings (2009).
>
> | Year | Private sector | Public sector | Difference in weekly pay |
> |------|----------------|---------------|--------------------------|
> | 1997 | £309 | £349 | +£40 |
> | 2004 | £410 | £452 | +£42 |
> | 2006 | £426 | £483 | +£57 |
> | 2008 | £460 | £522 | +£62 |
>
> In 2009 a public sector worker was paid on average of £23,660, compared with private sector workers at £21,528 a year.
>
> **Questions**
>
> 1 Why do you think wages are higher in the public sector?
>
> 2 What possible reasons could be put forward for the increasing differences in pay?

Differences in pay

There are many economic reasons for the relative differences in pay. Important reasons include the high level of education and professional training required to work in many public sector occupations, such as the civil service and teaching. Other reasons might include the strong bargaining power of **trade unions** in the public sector. Public sector workers may carry out work that is regarded as essential, such as providing medical care.

Some economists argue that in fact public sector workers' wages would be higher if it were not for the job security and relatively high pensions associated with such work.

Male and female workers: the wage gap

In most countries average wages for men are higher than for women.

The term **wage gap** refers to a comparison between the wages of men and women. It can also be used to refer to differences between ethnic groups. The wage gap is expressed as a percentage – for example, women earn 80 per cent as much as men.

The table shows the wage gap in the US for 2004–8 between men and women (figures for 2010 showed that women were still only earning 77 cents for every dollar earned by male wage earners).

> **DID YOU KNOW?**
>
> Private sector wages can give a distorted picture – they may appear lower because non-wage factors, such as a company car, are not considered.

> **ACTIVITY**
>
> Compare a job carried out by two workers in your economy who have similar education and skills, one of whom works in the private sector and the other in the public sector. Which worker receives the greatest range of non-wage benefits?

> **DID YOU KNOW?**
>
> In some countries the **average earnings** of women are broadly similar to those of males (e.g. in Bolivia and Guatemala in South America). In Bahrain, however, women earn 40 per cent more than men, but there are far fewer female than male workers in the labour force.

2004	76.6 per cent
2005	77.0 per cent
2006	76.9 per cent
2007	77.8 per cent
2008	77.1 per cent

Source: US Women's Bureau and the National Committee on Pay Equity

3.7 Differences in earnings between occupations 2

In India wages of agricultural labourers using little capital are low. They are much higher for those in the new industries, such as engineers in wind energy

There are various explanations for the gap. One is that on average women spend a shorter period as part of the full-time labour force. As a result they are less likely to be skilled, leading to lower wage rates. Women are also more likely to be doing part-time jobs, as illustrated by UK figures (2009):

Part-time male	2 million
Part-time female	6 million
Full-time male	14 million
Full-time female	7 million

Another reason for inequalities in wages results from **discrimination**. In the US the Equal Pay Act was signed in 1963, making it illegal for employers to pay unequal wages to men and women who hold the same job and do the same work. This has led to some reductions in inequality. In 1963 the wage gap was 58 per cent; in 2010 it was nearer to 80 per cent. However, in the US and elsewhere the wage gap still persists and part of this may be the result of discrimination. Figure 3.7.1 shows the demand for labour resulting from discrimination leading to a lower wage for a group that is discriminated against.

DID YOU KNOW?

Discrimination at work involves treating one group less favourably than others. The discrimination may be in the form of providing poorer working conditions and lower wages.

DID YOU KNOW?

Over the last twenty years the percentage of female to male workers in the UK has been steadily increasing. Today roughly half the workforce is female. However, average wages for men are higher, in part because a greater percentage is in full-time (rather than part-time) work.

Figure 3.7.1 The impact of discrimination

Agriculture and manufacturing/services

Wages vary between different industries. In economics we describe the demand for labour as a **derived demand**. Labour is wanted not for its own sake but to produce end products desired by customers. The demand for a farm worker may therefore be derived from the demand for sugar cane, tea or butter. The demand for a manufacturing worker may be derived from the demand for chocolate bars, cars or radios. The demand for a service sector worker may be derived from the demand for transport services, bank accounts, and so on.

Many theories of development show how low wages in agriculture lead to a migration of populations from poor rural areas to higher-wage occupations in cities where people can get jobs in manufacturing. In many countries much more capital (machinery and equipment) is used in manufacturing. Employers in manufacturing are therefore able to tempt workers to transfer from agriculture into manufacturing.

Today it is the new service industries such as banking, insurance, health and education where there is the biggest demand for workers. As a result service sector jobs offer some of the highest wages. In addition, the new information technology sector of the economy has seen booming wages in areas such as computer games design and robotics.

As new industries develop, wages will increase in these industries. For example, there is an increasing demand worldwide for wind energy. Companies in this area, such as the Danish company Vestas, which has 20 per cent of the global wind power market, are thriving, and are thus able to pay higher wages to their engineers.

> **EXAM TIP**
>
> Many candidates offer very descriptive answers to questions on wage differences, but fail to put the differences in a theoretical context. You need to write about demand and supply in order to get a high mark.

KEY POINTS

1. There are several factors leading to differences in wages.
2. These include the level of skill, the nature of the industry, public or private sector and male/female differences.
3. Sometimes discrimination may distort wages determined by market forces of demand and supply.

SUMMARY QUESTIONS

1. What is meant by derived demand? Using an example of a particular job, show how the demand for it, and hence the wage paid, is derived.
2. Are the differences in pay between males and females simply a result of discrimination?
3. What is meant by the wage gap? How is it measured? Is there an obvious wage gap in your country?

3.8 Trade unions

LEARNING OUTCOMES

Candidates should be able to:
- describe trade unions and their role in the economy.

Workers in Bangladesh demanding better conditions in textile factories: an important function of trade unions is to negotiate better conditions for all their members

What is a trade union?

A trade union is an association of employees formed to protect and promote the interests of its members. Trade unions are formed, financed and run by their members, who pay an annual subscription. The unions try to influence some of the decisions made by the owners and managers of businesses. Public sector unions bargain with government-appointed public sector employers.

In Bangladesh the National Garment Workers Federation, with about 25,000 members, represents textile workers. In some countries, such as Germany, there are very large trade unions that represent all the workers in the same industry. In New Zealand, the Council of Trade Unions (CTU) consists of 19 unions with over 200,000 members, ranging from professional footballers and nurses to building tradesmen and dairy workers.

Figure 3.8.1 shows some of the aims of trade unions. You can see that the main aim is to secure the best possible conditions of work for members. Unions know that the decisions a firm makes will affect the livelihoods of workers and their families.

Figure 3.8.1 The aims of trade unions

- Better working conditions
- Shorter working hours
- Health and safety
- Benefits for members
- Better pay
- Influence over decisions at work
- Training
- Equal opportunities

EXAM TIP

Some trade unions are more powerful than others. You need to show that you understand the various factors that could lead to this.

Negotiation

One of the purposes of a trade union is to negotiate – that is, discuss with employers. Talks take place between the representatives of the employees (union officials) and representatives of the employer. Both sides try to reach agreement on issues such as conditions of employment (e.g. hours worked, safety of the workplace) or wage levels. This negotiation takes place at a local level (e.g. within a factory) or at national level, where the union represents all the members of the trade union in the country.

Figure 3.8.2 illustrates the bargaining range.

Figure 3.8.2 The bargaining range

Trade union membership: the benefit to individuals

Typical benefits of belonging to a trade union include:

- knowing that you are part of a group that represents you and fellow workers
- belonging to a body that negotiates better terms and conditions (e.g. pay increase, improved conditions) for you
- direct benefits (e.g. sickness benefit)
- support for members if there is a **grievance** (e.g. if a member of a trade union feels they have been treated badly at work) or disciplinary procedure (e.g. when a union member has been disciplined, perhaps for poor timekeeping)
- direct action to support members (e.g. if negotiations over pay break down with employees, union officials may call a strike; this means that union members stop work).

The ability to strike gives unions considerable power: if airline or railway workers go on strike, their companies lose money, profit and their reputation for reliability. Other actions that unions can take include working more slowly (a go-slow) and working to rule – only doing things that fit strictly with the rules set out in a contract of employment.

Trade unions: the impact on the economy

Trade unions may play an important part in determining wages. Where unions are strong they have power to push up wages, increasing costs. In some countries workers' representatives are part of company decision-making. In Germany elected works councils make suggestions about the running of the business. In contrast, unions may call frequent strikes, which can lead to unemployment and disruption.

SUMMARY QUESTIONS

1 Who are the members of trade unions? What benefits can they receive from union membership?
2 With which other bodies do trade unions interact, and for what purposes?
3 What impact might strong trade unions have on the economy?

ACTIVITY

Find out whether trade unions, or similar associations of workers, exist in your country. If so, how many are there and in which industries can they be found? What do they set out to achieve? Compare your findings with those for New Zealand – you can find information on the internet by searching for 'Union Database NZCTU'.

EXAM TIP

You may be asked to discuss the role of trade unions in an economy. Be prepared to give advantages and disadvantages; a one-sided answer will not be sufficient to gain maximum marks.

KEY POINTS

1 Trade unions are set up to protect the interests of their members.
2 Trade unions negotiate with employers and try to secure better working conditions.
3 Trade unions protect the interests of workers within the wider economy. Their leaders meet regularly with government officials and employer representatives.

3.9 Specialisation

LEARNING OUTCOMES

Candidates should be able to:
- describe the benefits and disadvantages of specialisation for the individual.

What is specialisation?

Specialisation involves concentrating on a particular task. Employees specialise in given occupations – for example, teachers, doctors, shop workers. Managers specialise in given activities, such as managing production or managing the accounts of a business.

If people and resources concentrate on things that they can do relatively well, then usually everyone benefits. Specialisation results in an increase in production.

A specialist occupation such as shoemaking enables an individual to produce goods of a very high quality. The shoemaker can concentrate on his work while buying in products and services from other specialists

It benefits individuals to concentrate on what they do best. For example, if an author can earn US$10 an hour from writing a book and it only costs US$5 an hour to have someone paint his house, it will make sense for the author to sit and write while the decorator paints. However, things cannot just be weighed up in money terms – you also need to consider the satisfaction or dissatisfaction you get from a particular activity.

In the modern economy many employees play specialist roles. However, because the economy is changing so rapidly it is important for employees to be flexible by learning new skills. This enables them to adapt to take advantage of new opportunities. Flexibility enables employees to secure higher lifetime earnings.

Division of labour

The principle of specialisation is easily illustrated in relation to the division of labour (specialisation by job task). Figure 3.9.1 shows some of the specialist occupations involved in a factory that makes chocolates.

ACTIVITY

Create a poster to show some specialist workers. With their permission, photograph three specialists in your locality and the type of work they specialise in. How does specialism enable them to earn more than non-specialists? How has specialism enabled them to develop particular skills?

- Dispatch workers
- Administrative staff
- Maintenance workers
- Drivers
- Managers
- Production line workers

Figure 3.9.1 Each of these specialists develops skills from concentrating on one thing

Advantages and disadvantages of division of labour

The table shows some of the advantages and disadvantages of division of labour.

Advantages of division of labour	Disadvantages of division of labour
Increase in skill: by doing something repeatedly the employee becomes more skilled. The skilled employee becomes more productive, producing higher or more valuable output per hour worked.	Dependency: because of specialisation many individuals, groups and processes become dependent on each other. If the person or machine at the previous stage to you is slow, unreliable or inefficient in some other way, your own work will suffer.
Time saving: it takes time to change from one task to another. Specialisation helps to eliminate this.	Unemployment: specialisation in a specific task or job can be harmful if the economy no longer requires that specialism. The individual may find it difficult to find work elsewhere.
Specialisation in 'best lines': division of labour makes it possible for people to concentrate on what they do best. Some people like working with their hands, others enjoy selling things. As employees become more skilled at a set task they often take great pride in what they are able to achieve.	Frustration and boredom: if the work that people have to do is unimaginative and repetitive they may not enjoy work. Accidents are more likely to happen and people will be less motivated to work hard.
Use of supporting technology: specialists can draw on technologies that make their work easier and enhance their skills. Most specialist work is supported by applications such as databases of relevant information, spreadsheet tools for making calculations, applications that enable designers to work on screen and accountancy packages.	Over concentration: by concentrating on specialist skills individuals may not develop other abilities. Their work may require so much focus on particular skills that they may not be able, or have the time, to develop other useful general skills.
Higher earnings: an individual who becomes good at their specialism should be in a stronger position to secure higher earnings.	

KEY POINTS

1. Specialisation of individuals at work is called the division of labour.
2. Division of labour enables individuals to become more skilled and productive.
3. Division of labour increases earnings, but individuals also need to be flexible.

SUMMARY QUESTIONS

1. What are the advantages and disadvantages of the division of labour?
2. What other resources can specialise as well as labour?
3. Give two examples of specialist workers in (a) agriculture (b) manufacturing and (c) service industries.

EXAM TIP

There are a number of advantages and disadvantages to division of labour. In the examination, you might be asked to discuss the topic; remember to consider both sides to gain the best possible mark.

3.10 Motives for spending, saving and borrowing

LEARNING OUTCOMES

Candidates should be able to:
- analyse the different motives for spending, saving and borrowing.

Spending money enables you to enjoy goods and services now; saving enables you to have the money to spend later

DID YOU KNOW?

The rate of interest is an important influence on how much people are willing to save or borrow. A reduction in interest rates makes saving less attractive and borrowing more attractive, which stimulates spending. A rise in interest rates has the reverse effect.

EXAM TIP

There is a variety of factors that can explain why people decide to spend money. You need to be able to discuss these in the examination.

Spending, saving and borrowing defined

- **Spending** is exchanging money for goods. The goods may be for immediate **consumption** (use), or they may be consumer durables. 'Durable' means lasting. **Consumer durables** are items such as radios, bicycles and furniture.
- **Saving** is setting money aside instead of spending it. Savings can be kept in a money box or in a safe place in your house, but it is safer to put money in a bank account or in a savings club.
- Borrowing is when an individual receives money from another individual or financial institution, with the intention of paying it back.

Motives for spending, saving and borrowing

The reason that people behave in a certain way is their motive.

Spending

The main motive for spending money is to buy goods and services that you can consume now: a packet of sweets, a bottle of water, a visit to the cinema. Some spending is on necessities (see Unit 1), such as basic foodstuffs and fuel to cook your food. Other spending is on non-essential goods, such as a new DVD or a computer game.

Spending on consumer durables builds up a stock of wealth that can be enjoyed for a longer period of time (although they lose value each year) – for example, a car, washing machine or television.

When there is a general rise in prices – that is, inflation (see Unit 6) – consumers may put off making expensive purchases and keep consumer durables for longer periods. People spend proportionately more on essentials in a period of inflation as they go up in price, leaving less to spend on other things.

Saving

The main motive for saving is to put money aside in order to make a purchase at a later date. This might be to pay for something relatively expensive or that does not occur regularly – for example, a visit to a relative, a holiday, or school or college fees. Older people might save for their retirement when they are no longer earning.

The **savings ratio** refers to the proportion of income that consumers save. Attitudes to savings vary with culture. For example, people in Asia tend to save more than in the West. In recent years consumers in the US and UK have borrowed a lot to finance spending on consumer goods so that savings ratios are low. In contrast, in rapidly growing economies like India and China many people have been saving more money than spending it.

Savings ratios in selected countries 2005–10

Country	Approximate savings ratios (%)
UK, US	5–10
France, Italy	10
India, China	30

In periods of inflation the savings ratio tends to fall. People may feel that if prices go up, the money saved will only buy less.

The savings ratio may increase during a recession. People save more for the future because they fear that they may lose their jobs.

Borrowing

A major motive for borrowing is to be able to spend more than you receive in income in order to meet your wants and needs. Another motive is to buy an expensive item such as a house or car.

People also borrow money if they anticipate being able to repay it in the future. Borrowing thus becomes a way of raising present income, knowing that the repayment will eat into future income.

When interest rates are low, people will be encouraged to borrow because the cost of future repayment has been lowered.

If prices are expected to rise in the future, people may borrow more now and spend the money, rather than having to pay more at a future date.

DID YOU KNOW?

As income rises, consumers may spend a smaller proportion of each additional unit earned. So a consumer may spend all of the first US$100 earned in a month, but only spend US$50 of an increase from US$900 to US$1,000. The fraction of additional income spent is known as the **propensity to consume**.

ACTIVITY

Find out what has been happening to interest rates in your country over the last year. Plot the base rate charged by the central bank on to a graph. Label the graph to show months in which rises or falls in interest rate are likely to have led to increased saving or decreased saving. Do the same for borrowing.

KEY POINTS

1 Economists use the term 'consumption' to refer to spending on goods that are used up either immediately or over a period of time.

2 Incomes can either be spent (consumption) or saved.

3 Incomes can be supplemented by borrowing, to purchase an expensive item such as a house.

SUMMARY QUESTIONS

1 If consumers spend a smaller proportion of their income as income rises, what will be the impact on:

   a saving
   b borrowing?

2 What is likely to be the effect of rising inflation on spending and borrowing? Explain your answer.

3 What are the main motives for:

   a borrowing
   b spending?

3.11 Income and expenditure patterns

LEARNING OUTCOMES

Candidates should be able to:

- discuss how and why different income groups have different spending patterns.

Patterns of income and expenditure

Studies in different countries have shown that the proportion of income that people spend depends on the size of their income. The table shows the broad findings of these studies.

Size of income	Spending	Saving	Borrowing
High-income household	Not likely to spend all of their income	Will be able to save some of their income	Unlikely to need to borrow
Middle-income household	May spend most of their income	May be able to save a little	Probably borrowing to buy at least some consumer-durable items
Low-income household	Will most probably spend all of their income and this may not cover all their needs	Most low-income households will not be able to save	Many low-income households will have to borrow to meet their needs; however, a problem for low-income households is that they will find it more difficult to borrow – because lenders are less sure about being repaid

Increasing incomes in China have seen rapid rises in consumer spending, particularly among the 20–30 years age group

As people become richer they are likely to spend more. However, they are likely to spend a smaller proportion of additional income than they earn.

Rising consumption is typically associated with rapid industrialisation. For example, Japan's **household consumption** grew by 9.2 per cent a year in the 1970s. South Korea's grew by over 8 per cent a year in the 1980s. Currently China's household consumption is growing at about 12 per cent (for the first decade of the 21st century).

DID YOU KNOW?

Household savings are an important source of funds for business expansion. As households become wealthier they are able to save more. They will deposit their savings in financial institutions such as banks. The banks then lend the money to business and other borrowers.

CASE STUDY Rising consumption in China

One of the major reasons for rising consumption in China is the very fast growth of the economy. Each year during the first decade of the 21st century, China has been able to produce 9–10 per cent more goods than in the previous year. Many young people are benefiting from a rise in income because they have the skills to take up new jobs – for example, in information technology or in the energy industries, as well as in other expanding areas of business. In China currently about 200 million people are entering their twenties and thirties. This group is earning more money in the rapidly growing economy. They are able to spend more, and save more.

Young Chinese people are spending more on their homes and their families. Often they are provided with financial support by their parents. All these factors have led to rapid consumption growth in China.

Questions

1 Why has consumption risen so rapidly in China in recent years?

2 How are young Chinese people able to spend an increasing amount?

3 How are young Chinese people also able to save more?

DID YOU KNOW?

The generation of people up to the age of 29 in China makes up a considerable part of the population (almost 600 million people). This group is likely to spend a higher proportion of income than their parents. There are over 3 million university graduates with relatively high incomes (many continue to live at home). They are more likely to buy brands and modern products.

KEY POINTS

1 The amount a person spends, saves and borrows is influenced by the size of their income.

2 The proportion of income spent, saved or borrowed is influenced by the size of income.

3 Rapid industrialisation gives individuals more money to spend and also more money to save.

SUMMARY QUESTIONS

1 How are richer people able to spend more and save more than those who are poorer?

2 Why are poorer people more likely to borrow than richer people?

3 Why is rising consumption associated with rapid industrialisation of countries?

EXAM TIP

Most people would like to save, but it is not always easy to do so. In the examination you will need to be able to discuss the various factors that can influence decisions to save money rather than spend it.

ACTIVITY

What is happening to consumption and saving in your country? What factors encourage young people to spend more? What factors encourage them to save more? Discuss this in class and see if there is general agreement.

Unit 3 — Practice exam questions

SECTION 1: Multiple-choice questions

Each question has ONE correct answer.

1. What does the phrase *a medium of exchange* mean when describing a function of money?
   a. Price of an item can be measured in terms of money units
   b. Money is a generally accepted means of payment
   c. You can save money because it keeps its value
   d. Borrowers know how much they need to pay back on a loan

2. Which of the following is NOT a function of a commercial or retail bank?
   a. Acting as banker to the government
   b. Keeping money and valuable items safe
   c. Lending money to people and businesses
   d. Paying interest to savers

3. What is the *base rate* as set by a country's central bank?
   a. The smallest amount of money that can be loaned
   b. The shortest amount of time over which loans can be taken
   c. The interest percentage from which all other loan rates are taken
   d. The length of time it takes to get a loan

4. Which of the following is NOT a benefit of share ownership to individual investors?
   a. Public companies can raise capital for expansion
   b. Dividends are paid as a share of profit
   c. Shares may go up in value
   d. Shareholders are protected by limited liability

5. Which of the following is a feature of *division of labour*?
   a. Shorter production times
   b. Specialisation by workers
   c. Lower cost of products
   d. Use of unskilled workers

6. Which of the following workers may receive commission as part of their wage?
   a. A school teacher
   b. A car salesperson
   c. A factory production line worker
   d. A restaurant waiter

7. According to economic theory, why might a lawyer get paid more than a shopkeeper?
   a. A low demand for and a high supply of labour
   b. A high demand for and high supply of labour
   c. A high demand for and a low supply of labour
   d. A low demand for and low supply of labour.

8. What might be a negative *non-wage factor* for a taxi driver?
   a. Low income when not busy
   b. Expense of leasing a taxi vehicle
   c. Need for a driving licence
   d. Working antisocial hours

9. Which of the following is NOT a difference between the spending and saving habits of high-income and low-income families?
   a. High-income earners spend more than low income earners.
   b. High-income earners spend a bigger proportion of their income on essentials
   c. Low-income earners save less than high-income earners
   d. Low-income earners suffer more when prices are rising

10. Which of the following is a benefit to an employee of trade union membership?
    a. Union may strike and halt production
    b. Rising wages leading to rising prices
    c. Ease of negotiation with one union official
    d. Support in the case of a grievance at work

SECTION 2: Structured questions

Country A is a small, highly developed country, whose population lives mainly within its three major cities. Within these urban areas, most people are employed in tertiary occupations, mainly banking, scientific research and high technology. Outside the cities, the countryside is mountainous and the villages are popular ski and walking destinations for tourists, depending on the season. There are also agricultural communities, whose inhabitants are involved in running small family farms.

The Smith family lives in one of the big cities. Mr Smith is employed in commercial banking, specialising in share dealing, and Mrs Smith is an IT consultant. Their daughter Emily is training to be a lawyer, specialising in the banking sector. They live in a luxury apartment in the centre of the city, but also own a country house in the mountains.

The White family lives in one of the mountain villages and owns a small farm. Mr and Mrs White look after the animals and crops on the farm, and their son Hugo helps on the farm during the summer, but works as a ski instructor in the winter season.

1 a Describe ONE function of a commercial bank and ONE function of a central bank. (4)
  b Identify and explain TWO reasons why individuals and companies may buy shares in public companies. (6)
  c Using the information given about the Smith and White families, identify and explain TWO examples of individual specialisation. (4)
  d Discuss the advantages and disadvantages of specialisation to the Smith and White families. (6)

2 The salaries paid to employees in the city banking and technology sectors in Country A are much higher than those paid in other occupations. Farmers such as the White family live on a much lower income than the Smiths and could not afford to move to the city due to the high price of accommodation.
  a Identify and explain TWO reasons why Mr Smith earns a much higher salary in banking than Mr White's income from his farm. (4)
  b Using demand for and supply of labour diagrams, illustrate your answer to 2a in economic terms. (6)
  c Identify and explain TWO non-wage factors that may encourage Hugo White to work part of the year as a ski instructor. (4)
  d Compare the likely changes in earnings over time between Mr White and Mr Smith. (6)

3 Emily Smith and Hugo White are the same age and at the beginning of their working lives. Emily is at a law school, paid for by her parents, and is not earning at present. Hugo earns some income from his work on the family farm and as a ski instructor, but he has saved some money and would like to take a two-year training course to become a teacher.
  a Explain why Emily Smith's parents are willing to pay her law school fees, even though they have had to borrow money from the bank. (4)
  b Explain why the demand for labour is called a *derived demand* and how this may affect Hugo if he qualifies as a teacher and finds a job at one of the country's popular, expensive, fee-paying schools. (6)
  c Using a diagram, compare the supply curves of labour for farm workers and for teachers, and explain why the elasticities are different. (4)
  d Consider the information given and the changes in earnings over time and discuss whether Hugo will benefit, in the long term, from training as a teacher. (6)

4 The Smith family is categorised as 'high income' and the White family as 'low income'. This means that their spending, saving and borrowing habits will be different.
  a Define the three terms *saving*, *spending* and *borrowing*, and explain the link between these uses of money. (4)
  b Explain the likely difference between the two families' *savings ratios*. (4)
  c Explain the likely difference between the two families' patterns of consumption. (4)
  d Using all the information given, compare the effects of rising prices (inflation) on the two families' economic welfare. (8)

Total: 80 marks

SECTION 3: Analysis and critical evaluation

Country B is a large developing nation, with a young, growing population. The government controls a large percentage of the economy, including public transport, health and education provision, as well as the offices that deal with taxation and government statistics. This means that many people are employed in these public sector organisations, which have a reputation for inefficiency and very slow service. Some government employees also receive subsidised housing and public transport.

Trade union membership is encouraged and is widespread in businesses, as it makes negotiations over pay and conditions easier and gives workers the chance to take part in collective bargaining. However, public sector workers have only received pay increases in line with inflation (around 1 per cent) for the last few years. Most employees receive their wages weekly, paid in cash, and only 10 per cent of the population has a bank account.

Economic growth is slow, around 1.5 per cent per year, but privately owned companies are becoming more widespread as public demand for imported consumer goods increases. The government has recently relaxed import controls, which has given the population access to goods from abroad for the first time. Wages in the private companies are increasing at a much faster rate than in the public sector and the gap is widening.

1 a Explain what is meant by a *public sector organisation* and give ONE example from the extract. (2)

  b Why might the government of Country B be concerned about *slow economic growth*? (2)

2 a Give ONE example of a *non-wage* reason why many workers choose public sector employment. (2)

  b Some public sector workers receive *overtime* payments. Explain what this means and give a possible example for a railway worker. (2)

3 Discuss the likely long-term benefits and drawbacks to workers in the public sector in Country B. (5)

4 a Explain what is meant by *wage discrimination*. (2)

  b Some women teachers in Country B are paid less than men. Discuss whether this may be *gender discrimination*. (5)

5 Using the theory of *derived demand*, including a diagram and written explanation, show how falling demand for public transport may affect the number of people employed as bus drivers, and their wages. (5)

6 The government of Country B would like to encourage the population to make more use of banking services. Discuss the best ways to achieve this aim. (7)

Total: 32 marks

4 The private firm

This unit explains how businesses operate in the private sector of the economy (as opposed to the state-owned public sector). The variations in structure and size are considered from small one-person businesses and partnerships to large public companies and multinational firms, are considered, with discussion of why businesses choose one type of structure over another.

The unit goes on to examine the demand for factors of production by businesses. Given that the use of factors of production incurs production costs to a business, the unit examines different types of costs and how these are affected by the output that a business supplies to the market. The unit shows how to calculate revenues and examines the relationship between revenues and costs, to show how a profit is made.

Different types of market structures are compared to show how profits and decisions about price and output are determined by the level of competition in which a business operates. The unit concludes with an overview of reasons for different sizes of firms, and how firms grow and benefit from economies of scale.

LEARNING OUTCOMES

With regard to **business organisation**, candidates should be able to:

- describe the type of business organisation in the public and private sectors
- describe and evaluate the effects of changes in structure of business organisations.

With regard to **costs and revenues of production**, candidates should be able to:

- describe what determines the demand for factors of production
- define different types of costs and perform simple calculations
- analyse situations to show changes in costs as output changes
- define different types of revenues and perform simple calculations.

With regard to **profit**, candidates should be able to:

- describe the principle of profit maximisation
- describe pricing and output policies in perfect competition and monopoly
- discuss the advantages and disadvantages of monopoly.

With regard to the **size of firms**, candidates should be able to:

- describe the reasons for different sizes of firms
- describe and evaluate integration, and economies and diseconomies of scale.

4.1 Sole proprietors and partnerships

LEARNING OUTCOMES

Candidates should be able to:
- describe sole trader and partnership businesses.

Sole proprietors or traders

A street vendor who owns a kiosk from which to sell fruit is a sole proprietor or trader. This business is owned and controlled by one person (though there may be more than one employee). It is the most common type of business and covers activities such as repairing windows, street selling, plumbing and hairdressing. No complicated paperwork is required to set up a sole trader business. Decisions can be made quickly and close contact can be kept with customers and employees. All profits go to the sole trader, who also has the satisfaction of building up his or her own business.

DID YOU KNOW?

Sole traders typically provide much of their own finance, often from their own savings, although they may borrow from a bank or from friends.

A street trader, Rajasthan, India: a sole trader may want to join with a partner to share some of the workload and to bring more finance into a small business

Sole traders may, however, have to work long hours and make special arrangements if they are ill or want a holiday. They do not have the legal protection of **limited liability** (see Unit 3.4): if the business runs up debts, these are the responsibility of the business owner. The debts are **unlimited** and owner may be forced to sell their house and other possessions to pay them off.

Partnerships

A **partnership** is an agreement by two or more partners to run a business together. Partnerships are typically found in professional work – for example, a medical or dental practice, or a group of accountants or lawyers. It may be easier for a partnership to raise the capital needed to start the business and the partners can share skills and the workload. So a group of vets could share knowledge about different diseases and groups of animals, and two or three vets working together might be able to operate a 24-hour service. The business can still function when one of the vets is ill or goes on holiday.

EXAM TIP

In the examination you may be asked to compare a sole trader and a partnership or to discuss why a sole trader may wish to take on partners.

Business partners would be wise to use a solicitor to create a legal document called a **deed of partnership** setting out the terms of the partnership. This will set out how profits will be shared and the different responsibilities and payments to partners. It will set out how much capital each partner would contribute.

Partners may, however, disagree – about how things should be done, the workload and the length of time it may take to reach decisions (all partners need to be consulted). Further disadvantages are that profits will be shared, and that ordinary partnerships have unlimited liability and can rarely borrow or raise large amounts of capital. In some countries the law recognises **limited partnerships** in which one or more of the partners is allowed limited liability in some instances. For example, in some countries large groups of accountants can form a large limited partnership.

> **ACTIVITY**
>
> Interview different local business partners and ask them to explain why they have chosen to work in partnership rather than as sole traders. Ask them about the advantages and disadvantages of operating as a partnership. Share your findings with your group.

> **DID YOU KNOW?**
>
> A sole trader is not necessarily the only person in a business. The sole trader is the *owner*, who may employ others to work for them.

> **CASE STUDY** — Becoming a partnership
>
> Umar inherited a small stall selling fruit in a busy street in Lahore. In the morning he collects the fruit from gardens outside the city and takes them on a cart to his stall. His stall is very popular and people buy his fruit from early morning until late into the evening. He therefore decided to take on a partner, Azhar, to help him run the store, and to collect the fruit in the morning. Azhar and Umar agreed to share the rent on the stall.
>
> ### Questions
>
> 1 Why is it a good idea for Umar to form a partnership?
>
> 2 What details should be set out in a deed of partnership between Umar and Azhar?
>
> 3 What disadvantages could there be as a result of creating the partnership?

> **ACTIVITY**
>
> Working as a group, try to identify sole trader and partnership businesses in your local area. What types of business are the partnerships mainly concerned with? What about the sole traders? Make a list of as many businesses as you can. Compare your list with that of other groups.

> **SUMMARY QUESTIONS**
>
> 1 Give three examples of businesses that would be suitable for setting up as:
>   a   sole traders
>   b   partnerships.
>
> 2 What are the main benefits of setting up a partnership rather than a sole trader business?
>
> 3 In what circumstances would it be preferable for a business to be a sole trader rather than a partnership?

> **KEY POINTS**
>
> 1 A sole trader business is owned by one person. A partnership is owned by two or more people.
>
> 2 In most instances the owners of these small businesses have unlimited liability.
>
> 3 Partnerships are formed to share workloads and to bring in new finance, ideas and skills to a business.

4.2 Private companies

LEARNING OUTCOMES

Candidates should be able to:
- describe private companies.

ACTIVITY

Create a poster that explains why the private company is a good way of setting up and operating a new business. Focus on the benefits to the owners and include examples of private companies in your country or region.

EXAM TIP

Students are often confused between the very important concepts of limited and unlimited liability. Make sure that you know the difference.

Companies

A **company** is a body that has been set up by following established legal guidelines (stating how it should operate) and which is owned by shareholders. The company needs to be registered with the Registrar of Companies in a particular country. In law the company is recognised as separate from its owners.

The shareholders seek to make a return from investing money in a business. The return they receive is called a dividend. The size of the dividend is related to:

- the number of shares they have in the business
- the size of the profit the business makes.

Shareholders of companies choose a board of directors to run the company for them. The main directors of the business are the chief executive, responsible for day-to-day running of the business, and the chair, who runs company board meetings and represents the company, for example when talking to the news media.

A company has limited liability. This means that if the company gets into financial difficulties and has to pay back debtors, the maximum amount that the shareholders will have to pay to meet these debts is the value of their shares in the company.

Private companies tend to be family businesses. Some can be very large: these are some of the well-known confectionery brands of Mars

Private companies

There are two types of companies: private and public. (Public companies are discussed in Unit 4.3.) **Private limited companies** tend to be smaller than public and are often family businesses (i.e. family members may own most or all of the shares in a company, along with friends). However, there are some very large private companies: the American company Mars, maker of the Mars Bar, remains private because the family who owns the business wants to keep control of the main decisions made by the company. Mars operates in over 100 countries. You may have come across some of its products, which include Mars chocolate bars, Uncle Ben's rice, M&M's, Snickers and Milky Way bars.

There must be at least two shareholders, but there is no maximum number. Shares in private companies are not traded on stock exchanges (see Unit 3.4), and usually the shares can only be bought with the permission of the board of directors. You can approach the company and request to buy shares.

Private limited companies usually find it possible to raise more cash (by selling shares) than unlimited liability businesses. This is because shares can be sold to a larger group of investors. The shareholders can also have the protection of limited liability.

To set up a private company it must be registered with the **Registrar of Companies** in your country. To register, the company will have to fill in some important paperwork. If it is already trading it will have to send a copy of its accounts to the Registrar. It will also have to provide details such as:

- the name of the company
- the registered office of the company (and address)
- who the main directors of the company are
- rules about shareholders meetings and the voting rights of shareholders.

If a shareholder wants to sell their shares in a private company they will need permission from the board of directors.

As well as receiving finance to run the business from shareholders, private companies can also borrow money from banks and other lenders. The finance from shareholders is called **equity**, and the finance from banks and lenders is called **loan capital**.

DID YOU KNOW?
A private company can become a public company by making its shares available to the general public rather than just to a small group of invited shareholders. The shares will then be listed and traded through the Stock Exchange.

DID YOU KNOW?
Shareholders in private companies are entitled to read a copy of the yearly financial accounts of the business to see how well their business is doing. Also, if you wanted to buy shares, you could ask to see these accounts.

KEY POINTS
1. A private company is owned by shareholders.
2. Private companies are often family businesses.
3. The shares of a private company can only be traded with the permission of the board of directors.
4. Shareholders in a private company have limited liability.

SUMMARY QUESTIONS
1. What advantages does a shareholder in a private company have that are not available to partners in an ordinary partnership?
2. Who owns a private company? Who controls the decisions made by a private company?
3. A private company runs up large debts and has to sell off its assets. These are not enough to pay off the debts. What is the maximum sum that a shareholder has to contribute to meet these debts?

4.3 Public companies

LEARNING OUTCOMES

Candidates should be able to:
- describe public companies.

What is a public company?

A public company is a company with **shares** traded on one or more national stock exchanges (see Unit 3.4). Large public companies may be listed on several stock exchanges across the world. A quoted company is one with shares appearing in the list of such companies. Dealers buy and sell shares for clients. The clients may be rich individuals or financial institutions such as banks and insurance companies.

The advantage of having shares traded on the stock exchange is that large sums of money can be raised very quickly. One disadvantage is that businesses can be bought and sold by takeover bids that are beyond the control of the original owners. It is also costly to have shares quoted on the stock exchange.

Shares in public companies can be bought by individuals and large financial investors from traders on stock exchanges such as this one

```
Business applies to
stock exchange to be listed
          ↓
Business hires a specialist financial organisation
(e.g. a merchant bank) to help with the
paperwork and the listing process
          ↓
Stock exchange checks accounts of the
company, and checks up on directors
before agreeing the listing
```

Figure 4.3.1 Stages and checks required before a company's shares can be listed on a stock exchange

DID YOU KNOW?

Public companies make a major contribution to the economy. They bring together large sums of financial capital which can be invested to produce goods on a large scale. Large public companies can provide jobs for hundreds of thousands of people in different countries. They can produce many different types of goods and the government benefits from the taxes they pay.

The main benefit of being a public company is that it enables a business to acquire money to invest by attracting finance from people willing to buy shares. Other businesses are pleased to trade with public companies knowing that they have financial backing from shareholders.

Selling new shares can involve risk. Stock exchanges have 'good days', when a lot of people want to buy shares, and 'bad days', when a lot of people want to sell. If the issue of shares coincides with a bad day a company can lose millions of pounds. For example, if a company hopes to sell a million new shares at US$1 each and there are enough buyers it will raise US$1 million. However, on a bad day the company may have to sell its shares for a lower price than it would like.

Shares may be sold by public issue where anyone can apply to buy shares in the company. The shares are advertised in national newspapers and can be purchased on a specific day. Another way of issuing new shares is for the shares in the company to be placed with several leading financial institutions such as insurance companies and pension funds. These institutions agree to buy a certain proportion of the shares on the day they become available.

There are some major disadvantages for public companies:

1. There is a lot of paperwork involved in setting up the business. After that detailed records have to be sent every year to the Registrar of Companies. These include **audited** accounts, meaning that they have been checked by an independent accountant.
2. Public companies can be taken over by others. In 2010 the famous British chocolate manufacturer Cadbury was taken over by the American food company Kraft. Kraft was able to do this by offering a high price for Cadbury shares to the existing shareholders, tempting them to sell and meet the price that Cadbury's shareholders thought their shares were worth.
3. Public companies often concentrate on paying short-term dividends to shareholders rather than building up the business over time. Cadbury's was originally a private company owned by the Cadbury family. They built up the company over many years, putting much of the profit back into improving the business. In recent years, however, directors believed that it was more important to pay dividends to shareholders than invest in the future of the business.

> **ACTIVITY**
>
> Find out the names of three public limited companies that operate in your country. Write a brief report setting out what the company manufactures or the service it provides. Also provide a brief explanation of why these companies need to raise capital through selling shares on Stock Exchanges.

> **EXAM TIP**
>
> Do not confuse the private and the public sectors. A public limited company is in the private sector.

KEY POINTS

1. Shareholders own public companies.
2. Shares in public companies are traded on one or more stock exchanges.
3. Public companies can be taken over by other companies that buy up their shares.
4. Public companies are able to raise large sums of money in equity.

> **DID YOU KNOW?**
>
> Most of the shares in public companies are owned by financial institutions such as pension funds and insurance companies rather than wealthy individuals. For example, in Britain at the end of 2008 only 10 per cent of shares on the stock market were owned by individuals. Why do you think this is?

SUMMARY QUESTIONS

1. Why might a private company decide that it wants to 'go public'?
2. What are the two main methods of issuing new shares?
3. What are the risks to the owners of a public company?

4.4 Multinationals

LEARNING OUTCOMES

Candidates should be able to:
- describe multinationals.

Multinational companies

Multinational companies, as the name suggests, produce and sell products in many countries. They have their headquarters in one country and may focus on a particular region of the world, but many have shareholders worldwide.

DID YOU KNOW?

Some multinationals, such as the Ford Motor Company in the US and the Anglo-Dutch oil company Shell, have grown steadily for more than a hundred years. Others, such as the mobile phone company China Mobile and Ali Baba (a Chinese website business trading goods between businesses), have grown rapidly in recent years.

CASE STUDY | Haier

Haier is the world's fourth largest white goods (for example, refrigerators and washing machines) manufacturer. Since the mid-1980s it has grown rapidly to become a multinational selling 'brown' goods as well — televisions, computers, mobile phones and cameras.

The company was set up in 1984. Between 1984 and 1998 the company expanded in China, developing a strong brand reputation for providing excellent goods and service to customers. From 1998 Haier exported an increasing number of goods to Malaysia, India, Pakistan and Nigeria.

The Chinese multinational Haier is one of the world's leading producers of white goods, manufactured and sold in many countries

Haier then set up its own factories, marketing and research and design centres in other countries: it opened a large factory and research centre in South Carolina in the US from where it sells a range of products to the US market, Canada and Mexico. Haier now has 30 international manufacturing plants worldwide.

Today over 30 per cent of all domestic appliances in China are sold by Haier. One of the reasons for success overseas is that products were adapted to suit local conditions. For example, a Haier fridge can keep food frozen for up to 100 hours after a power cut.

Questions

1. How does Haier fit the definition of being a multinational company?
2. What benefits will Haier receive from operating in different countries?
3. How might consumers in the US benefit from Haier's manufacturing in that country?

EXAM TIP

Make sure that you understand that a multinational does not just sell abroad: it is a company that <u>produces</u> abroad, i.e. it has factories in a number of different countries.

Measuring size of multinationals

The table shows how the size of multinational companies can be measured.

Number of operating countries	The British-Dutch company Unilever has over 300 factories in 90 countries.
Value of all of the shares in the business	By this measure America's giant retailer Wal-Mart, and China's mobile phone company China Mobile, are two of the largest companies.
Number of employees	China's Haier (see opposite) employs 30,000 people across the globe.
Range of products	Tata Industries (India's largest industrial conglomerate) produces a range of products, from steel manufacture to cars and textiles.

Benefits and disadvantages of operating in many countries

Some of the benefits to multinationals from operating in a range of countries include:

- Access to natural resources that may be in limited supply in their own domestic market. For example, giant steel manufacturing companies may be able to gain access to new iron ore deposits.
- A source of labour that may be cheaper than in the home country.
- The opportunity for a global market – in India and China there are over a billion potential customers. Other huge markets include Brazil, Nigeria, Pakistan and Russia.

Disadvantages to multinationals of operating in many countries are that there may be different tastes, requirements and legal standards in different countries. This could make it more costly to produce different models and varieties of products.

Benefits and disadvantages to host countries

Multinationals bring employment, new products and new technologies to host countries. The presence of multinationals can speed up development (see Unit 7). However, multinationals are sometimes criticised for not paying enough for the raw materials, nor to their employees, in poorer countries. They have also been criticised for causing pollution and environmental damage.

SUMMARY QUESTIONS

1. What is a multinational? Give five examples of multinational businesses.
2. Who owns multinational businesses? How do these owners benefit?
3. Give three reasons why a company may become a multinational.

DID YOU KNOW?

Getz Pharma has been one of the fastest-growing companies in Pakistan. It develops a range of molecules for use in pharmaceutical products such as those used to treat cardiovascular diseases, hepatology and infectious diseases. It now markets and sells its products in Asia, the Middle East and Africa.

ACTIVITY

Carry out some research into a multinational that has its home base in your country or operates in your country. Find out how many other countries it operates in. What is the current value of the shares in the company? How many people does it employ? Give examples of the range of its products. Produce a poster or chart to display your findings.

KEY POINTS

1. A multinational is a company that operates in several countries.
2. Some multinationals have grown over a long period. Others, such as internet-based businesses and mobile phone companies, have grown rapidly.
3. Multinationals are able to buy labour and raw materials in more countries and can sell to a much larger market.

4.5 Cooperatives

LEARNING OUTCOMES

Candidates should be able to:
- describe cooperatives.

What is a cooperative?

'Cooperation' means working together in agreement. In a **cooperative** people join together to make decisions, work and share profits. The members are cooperators.

There are many different types of cooperative. Three most commonly found in many economies are:

- farming cooperatives
- production cooperatives
- retailing cooperatives.

Farming cooperatives

Individual farmers want to sell their produce to the market at the best possible price. Onion farmers at Saint André de Majencoules in the Cévennes region of France produce sweet onions which they supply to the market at regular intervals during the year. The onion seedlings are planted in the spring and harvested in August. However, if they were all sold to the market in August they would fetch only a low price.

DID YOU KNOW?

One of the world's best-known cooperatives is the Mondragon Cooperative in the Basque region of Spain. This is an association of cooperatives which employs about 100,000 people. It includes banks, retailers and industrial producers, as well as the University of Mondragon. There are rules in each cooperative about the maximum difference in wages between ground-level workers and managers – for example, sometimes a ratio of 3:1, in other cases a ratio of 9:1.

Onion growers in the Cévennes region of France are organised into cooperatives. Their onions are sold and marketed through the cooperative

The cooperators have therefore set up a large storage unit. The farmers deliver their onions for storing in the unit's cool environment for several months. The cooperative advertises the onions and deals with their customers for the next 12 months – supermarkets, restaurants and other buyers.

The cooperative shares the money from sales between the farmers. The amount they receive is determined by the number of cases of onions of a suitable quality delivered to the warehouse.

EXAM TIP

Cooperatives are a very distinctive type of business organisation; make sure that you can explain how they are different from other types.

Producers' cooperatives

A producers' cooperative (also known as a workers' cooperative) employs all or most of its members. The purpose of this sort of cooperative is to generate benefits for the members, who will:

- share responsibility for the success or failure of the enterprise
- work together
- take decisions together
- share profits (and losses).

Examples of producers' cooperatives include a carpentry cooperative making furniture, or a child-minding cooperative.

Shares in the cooperative are held by the workforce. Most (sometimes all) of the workers own shares. Workers choose a body to represent them by election (e.g. a board). The board then hire managers. Members of the cooperative meet to discuss major decisions.

The main advantage of producers' cooperatives is that the members work together and share the benefits. The disadvantage can be that there are more decision-makers, which can slow down and complicate decision-making.

Retail cooperatives

The first retail cooperative was set up in 1844 in Rochdale, England. Workers were being forced to buy goods from company shops at high prices. The workers therefore put some money into a central fund to buy stocks of goods to sell in their own shop. Often these were simple clothes and food stocks. The profits of the shop were shared according to the amount that the shoppers had spent there.

The owners of a cooperative are the *members*, who usually pay a set minimum subscription. This gives them voting rights to choose, for example, how the cooperative should be run, and what types of goods to stock. Cooperatives usually have strong social principles, which means that many only buy from suppliers who are giving fair prices to growers, say for coffee, tea and other products. Most retail cooperatives believe in the principles of 'fair trade'.

DID YOU KNOW?
The Fairtrade Foundation is a non-profit-making organisation which allows its label to be used on products that meet its internationally agreed standards. Products include a wide range of food and drinks, clothes, flowers and cosmetics.

DID YOU KNOW?
Mitre 10 is a well-known hardware retail cooperative in Australia and New Zealand. The original finders intended to set up 10 stores selling timber, paint and other hardware goods that they would buy collectively. Today there are over 700 cooperative stores, each with an independent owner.

ACTIVITY
Find an example of one or more cooperatives in your area. How is it run? Where does the finance for the cooperative come from? What does the cooperative do? What happens to the money received by the cooperative? Share your findings with your group.

SUMMARY QUESTIONS
1 Why might farmers want to form a cooperative rather than working on their own?

2 What are the main types of cooperative? What are the similarities between these cooperatives?

3 What are the disadvantages of cooperatives to the owners?

KEY POINTS
1 A cooperative is a group of employees, sellers or producers who have banded together to buy, sell and market their products or services.

2 The cooperators often elect a committee to represent them.

3 Cooperators jointly share in the benefits from working together.

4.6 Public corporations

LEARNING OUTCOMES

Candidates should be able to:
- describe public corporations.

DID YOU KNOW?

Government-linked companies (GLCs) are companies in which the government owns some of the shares in the business.

What is a public corporation?

Public corporations are businesses owned by governments. Although the government owns the corporation, the controllers of the corporation are given considerable freedom to make their own decisions. Sometimes they are referred to as stated-owned enterprises (SOEs) or government-owned corporations (GOCs). In India the term public sector undertaking (PSU) is used.

A public corporation is created by passing a law to create the new form of business. The government then appoints a chairperson and a board of managers to lead it.

CASE STUDY: The Saudi Arabian Oil Company

The Saudi Arabian Oil Company is owned by the Saudi government because oil is such an important resource to the Saudi Arabian economy. The Saudi government controls the amount of oil produced, which in turn has an impact on the world oil price.

As in any business, governments usually set yearly targets for particular public corporations. The chairperson and the managers must then decide on the best way to meet these targets. With an oil corporation, the government may set a target for the number of barrels of oil to produce in a country. The managers of the oil company will then decide how much to produce from each oilfield and how to maintain supplies for future years. The managers will also supervise the marketing and selling of the oil. Agreements about how much oil to produce and the price to charge has to be agreed between members of OPEC (Organisation of the Petroleum Exporting Countries).

Questions

1. Why do you think the Saudi Arabian Oil Company is run as a public corporation rather than as a private sector business?
2. What types of decision are made by the Saudi Arabian Oil Company? How are these decisions important to the economy of Saudi Arabia?

EXAM TIP

The process of privatisation has taken place in many countries. You will need to be able to answer a possible question on the advantages and disadvantages of privatisation.

Purposes of public corporations

Public corporations are often created to make sure that important activities that affect the whole nation are carried out well. Indian Railways is a PSU: every day millions of people travel on Indian railways and goods are transported all over India. In most countries there is also a state broadcasting company, such as the British Broadcasting Company (BBC). The purpose of the BBC is to try to present news in a fair way that is not influenced by political or commercial interests.

Sometimes public corporations are set up to preserve jobs. The government is able to support public corporations through money it raises from taxpayers. This enables the government to provide services to locations where it is not economical to provide them, such as water supplies to areas of water shortage. In Libya water supplies are transported over 4,000 kilometres, down a huge water pipe from under the Sahara Desert to major areas of population.

The great man-made river project in Libya was a government project bringing water from under the Sahara Desert along 4,000 kilometres of water pipes to centres of population

Government involvement in a particular industry can also reduce wasteful competition. For example, the government might provide the only electricity or water supply using one set of cables and pipelines. This saves having wasteful duplication of pipelines.

When a business or industry is taken over by the government this is described as **nationalisation**. Selling a public corporation to shareholders is termed **privatisation**.

Figure 4.6.1 Nationalisation and privatisation

Disadvantages of public corporations

Public corporations can become too large and difficult to manage. The lack of competition can lead to higher prices and wasteful use of resources (although, as you read earlier, they can cut wasteful duplication). Subsidising a public corporation through taxes may prevent the revenues from being used more efficiently for other purposes.

ACTIVITY

Saudi Airlines was recently privatised. Carry out some internet research to find out why this happened. What do you expect the benefits of the privatisation to be? Who owned the airline prior to the privatisation? Who owns it now? Produce a report of your findings.

KEY POINTS

1 A public sector business is owned by the government.

2 These businesses have other objectives than just to make a profit.

3 Public sector businesses do not always use resources as efficiently as if they faced greater competition.

SUMMARY QUESTIONS

1 Give examples of three public corporations in different countries.

2 Suggest three reasons why governments set up public corporations.

3 Why are public corporations sometimes privatised?

4.7 Effects of changes on business growth

LEARNING OUTCOMES

Candidates should be able to:
- describe the effects of changes in the structure of businesses
- evaluate the effects of these changes.

Dr Anji Reddy founded Dr Reddy's Laboratories in India in 1984. Today it is one of the world's leading pharmaceutical companies

DID YOU KNOW?

Growing as a business makes it possible to make a brand more widely known, produce and sell goods on a larger scale, and penetrate and sell to a wider range of markets. Typically, larger businesses have lower costs per unit of production than smaller businesses.

Why do businesses grow?

Businesses grow to take advantage of new opportunities. For example, in recent years we have seen an increase in global trade and opportunities to make sales in new countries. If businesses want to take advantage of these opportunities they may have to change their structure. A sole trader or partnership business may be altered to create a company. A private company may change by going public.

CASE STUDY — The growth of Dr Reddy's

Before the 1970s India relied heavily on imported drugs and medicines. However, the government wanted to provide better health care for poorer people and encouraged people to set up their own businesses to achieve this. Dr Anji Reddy set up a small private company selling the basic ingredient of drug compounds to pharmaceutical companies. By the 1980s Dr Reddy wanted to produce the complete products and set up Dr Reddy's Laboratories with US$40,000 of his own capital and a loan of US$120,000.

The new company quickly produced some very successful painkillers. Taking advantage of India's low labour and other production costs, the company grew quickly, and in 1986 became a public company with shares traded on the Bombay Stock Exchange. The company set up its own research foundation to develop new drugs, providing treatments for cancer, diabetes and other medical problems. By the end of the 1990s the company was purchasing US and other international companies to expand across the world. Soon Dr Reddy's shares were listed on the New York Stock Exchange. Today the multinational has subsidiaries in China, Russia, France, Singapore, Brazil, the US, the UK and many other countries. Its shares are owned by investors from many countries.

Questions

1. Why did Dr Anji Reddy set up a private company?
2. How did changing the business to become a public company enable Dr Reddy's company to expand?
3. Is Dr Reddy's a multinational company? Explain your answer.

Dr Reddy could have started off as a sole trader or formed a partnership. However, it made sense to set up a small company and then when the company was successful to become a public company.

As a producer of pharmaceuticals his business needed access to large sums of capital – so forming a company was the right choice. Through expansion the company was able to bring in more finance to build large research laboratories that enabled it to develop new drugs.

As a result of growing to become a large company a number of benefits will arise. These are:

- the ability to raise finance from across the world (Dr Reddy's is listed on several stock exchanges)
- being known across the world
- the ability to engage in extensive research and investment to improve capability
- the power to draw talented people from around the world to work for the company
- adapting new ideas for other countries and markets.

Large international businesses are able to produce large quantities of goods at a low cost per unit. So while the cost of developing a new drug is very high, once it is produced in large production units and sold across the world, the unit cost is very low.

Dangers of going public are that the company may become subject to a hostile takeover bid. This would occur if the majority of shares in a business are bought up by another business. New owners would now have control over the business. Another problem could be that of becoming too large. The company would become more difficult to manage and coordinate.

While some businesses start up as sole traders before forming partnership arrangements and then grow into companies, there are other ways of growing. For example, some businesses will set up immediately as partnerships so that they can enjoy greater access to sources of capital. Other businesses will start out as a private company. The private company structure enables the business to access more capital from shareholders than an individual trader would be able to do on their own.

> **DID YOU KNOW?**
>
> Expanding into an overseas market means meeting different legal standards for production. It often makes sense to work with a local partner organisation, or to take over a local company so as to develop expertise in the new market.

> **ACTIVITY**
>
> Infosys is another example of an Indian company that has grown quickly. Find out more about the growth of Infosys. One way to find this information is to carry out an internet search using the search term 'Infosys growth story'.
>
> Produce a leaflet setting out the key stages in the growth of Infosys and describe the effects of changes in the company's structure.

> **KEY POINTS**
>
> 1. As companies grow they may need to change their structure.
> 2. A private company may change to become a public company to raise more funds and more expertise.
> 3. To get experience of a new international market, partnerships can be formed with businesses in other countries.

> **SUMMARY QUESTIONS**
>
> 1. How are public companies able to raise more finance than private ones?
> 2. What other benefits might there be to becoming a public company?
> 3. Are there any dangers to becoming a public company with shares traded on international stock exchanges?

4.8 The demand for factors of production

LEARNING OUTCOMES

Candidates should be able to:
- describe what determines the demand for factors of production.

Uranium miners in Niger. The demand for miners and their equipment is derived from the demand for the uranium they mine

DID YOU KNOW?

The rewards to the factors of production are:

Land — Rent
Labour — Wages
Capital — Interest
Enterprise — Profit

EXAM TIP

It is very important that you understand what is meant by derived demand. Factors of production are not demanded for their own sake, but for what they can contribute to the production process.

Factors of production

Factors of production are the elements needed by a business to produce goods and services. Examples are land (and the raw materials it contains), labour, capital and enterprise. The **demand** for factors of production is derived in turn from the demand for the products that these factors are used to produce. For example, the demand for agricultural land, labour and machinery is derived from the demand for lentils, maize, rice and other crops which these factors contribute to producing.

CASE STUDY | Uranium production

Many governments and scientists – for example, in India, Pakistan, China, the UK, France and the US – believe that nuclear power is an important source of energy. (In France nuclear energy is the principal source of energy.) To produce nuclear energy you have to process uranium. It can be mined in only a few countries, and the price of uranium has therefore increased from US$10 a pound in 2000 to US$42 in 2010. This has led to an increase in the cost of producing nuclear energy and hence the prices charged for nuclear energy. The demand for uranium is *derived from* the demand for nuclear energy.

This derived demand creates further demands. There is a demand for land, to mine the uranium. Then building the mine involves a huge increase in demand for mining equipment (capital), and working the mine involves a demand for thousands of workers.

Questions

1. Why do you think the demand for nuclear energy has increased in the world in recent years?
2. What has happened to the price of nuclear energy?
3. What has been the resulting effect on the demand for land, labour and capital to mine uranium?

Illustrating the demand for factors of production

Because the demand for factors of production is a **derived demand**, an increase in demand for the end products will lead to an increase in demand for the factors themselves.

Figure 4.8.1 shows that the rise in demand for uranium to produce nuclear energy leads to a rise in the price of uranium from US$10 to US$42. Note that as the demand for uranium increases, more of it is supplied to the market.

Figure 4.8.1 An increase in demand for uranium leads to a rise in the supply and the price of uranium

Figure 4.8.2 shows that as the price of uranium increases this also leads to an increase in demand for miners to mine uranium in countries like Niger. Note the increase in the miners' wages in Niger. In response, more people are willing to make themselves available and to train to be miners of uranium.

Figure 4.8.2 An increase in demand for uranium miners leads to a rise in the supply of miners and an increase in their wages

Combining factors of production

Factors of production are demanded as a combination because they are required to work together. In buying factors of production, buyers will consider the relative prices of factors in order to choose the best combinations.

Important production decisions involve combining factors of production. The chosen combination depends on the relative productivity of these factors compared with their cost.

A labour-intensive industry employs a lot of labour compared with the amount of capital employed.

A capital-intensive industry employs a lot of capital compared with the amount of labour employed.

For example, parts of the textile industry in Bangladesh are labour intensive. This is because labour is not only cheap, but many workers are highly skilled. Increasingly, however, labour is being replaced by machinery that can replace human labour while maintaining efficiency.

The Japanese car industry is highly capital intensive because automated factory machines (capital) are able to produce large outputs at very low unit costs.

DID YOU KNOW?

Uranium is mined in Canada, the US, Brazil, Namibia, South Africa, Niger, Ukraine, Russia, Kazakhstan and Australia. The huge publicly-owned French nuclear power company Areva invested more than US$1 billion in a giant mine in Niger in West Africa in 2010. This will provide the French company with large quantities of uranium to sell to the nuclear industry in South Korea, France and elsewhere.

KEY POINTS

1 The demand for factors of production is derived from the demand for the products they make.

2 Rewards to factors are related to the demand for the products they make.

3 Labour-intensive industries use a high proportion of labour relative to capital and other factors of production.

SUMMARY QUESTIONS

1 What is meant by derived demand? What is the demand for machinery derived from?

2 Why are some industries more capital intensive than others?

3 What do the relative rewards to different factors of production depend on?

4.9 Fixed and variable costs

LEARNING OUTCOMES

Candidates should be able to:
- define fixed and variable costs
- make simple calculations.

Costs

Producing goods costs money. A business enterprise, for example, needs to buy raw materials, pay wages and spend money on marketing the finished product. Economists divide the cost of production into two main types:

- **Fixed costs** do not alter with the quantity of output.
- **Variable costs** increase directly as output increases.

Fixed costs

Fixed costs are costs that have to be paid whether the business is producing nothing or thousands of units. They depend on the type of business, but often include items such as rent and rates, interest on money borrowed and wages, which are not related to how much is produced. Fixed costs can be illustrated as a horizontal straight line: Figure 4.9.1 shows that the costs of a small firm producing footballs are US$200 a week, whether it produces no balls, 5 balls or 25 balls.

Figure 4.9.1 Fixed costs of producing footballs

Variable costs

Variable costs, such as the cost of raw materials, are zero when output is zero and rise directly with output. The table shows the variable costs of the football-manufacturing company.

Output per week	Variable cost (US$)
0	0
5	25
10	40
15	50
20	70

Figure 4.9.2 shows the variable costs of producing different quantities of footballs as a graph.

Figure 4.9.2 The variable cost to a firm producing different quantities of footballs

Average fixed cost

The greater the number of goods produced, the more the fixed costs will be spread over the output. If a bottling plant produces only 100 bottles a week, each bottle produced would involve a very high fixed cost element. In practice, bottling plants produce tens of thousands of bottles a week and the total fixed cost is spread over a large output (resulting in a low average cost per unit).

Figure 4.9.3 shows the **average fixed cost** (AFC) as output increases. As the level of output increases, the fixed cost per unit falls.

Figure 4.9.3 Average fixed cost of increasing output

Average variable cost

Variable costs of production usually include the raw materials and increases in labour to produce more goods, and **average variable costs** (AVC) alter as output increases. For example, a business with a small output will not be able to make good use of variable resources. Two or three workers in a bottling factory would not be enough to handle the machinery efficiently, but a higher number would mean that they could be organised so that each additional worker added to production at an increasing rate. For example, each worker could specialise in one or a small number of tasks.

However, the increase in production cannot keep accelerating (because the equipment and factory floor capacity is limited). Additional labourers would start to get in each other's way and thus work less efficiently, and the average variable cost of producing more would start to rise.

Figure 4.9.4 shows the average variable cost as a curve that falls at first and later starts to rise.

CASE STUDY: Costs at different levels of output

A business has fixed costs of US$1,000 a week. Variable costs at different levels of output are shown in the table.

Output	Average variable cost per unit
100	10 cents
200	8 cents
300	6 cents
400	8 cents
500	10 cents

Questions

1. Illustrate the average variable cost curve on a graph.
2. Explain why it has the shape that it does.
3. Calculate the average fixed cost at each of the levels of output shown in the table.
4. Draw and then explain the shape of the average fixed cost curve.

SUMMARY QUESTIONS

1. Define:
   a. fixed cost
   b. variable cost.
2. Why do average fixed costs fall as output increases, even though the overall fixed cost stays the same?
3. Explain why the average variable cost initially falls and then rises with higher output.

DID YOU KNOW?

Giant manufacturing companies like Coca-Cola have billions of dollars of fixed costs, including advertising and the construction costs of plants and buildings. Spread over many billion units of production, however, the fixed cost element of each can of Coca-Cola produced is only a few cents.

Figure 4.9.4 Average variable cost

KEY POINTS

1. Fixed costs are the same whatever quantity is produced.
2. Variable costs increase as output increases.
3. Average fixed costs fall as they are spread over larger quantities of output.
4. Average variable costs initially fall with more efficient use of factors of production. Once resources are combined less well, they start to rise again.

4.10 Total and average costs

LEARNING OUTCOMES

Candidates should be able to:
- define total and average cost
- perform simple calculations.

By working out the cost of producing items such as footballs, Nike is able to decide on suitable prices to charge to cover costs and make a profit

Total cost

Total cost can be calculated by adding the fixed and variable costs at different levels of output. Figure 4.10.1 shows in graph form the total, fixed and variable costs given in the table below. The shape of the total cost curve makes sense if you think that the more goods produced, the higher the overall cost of producing them.

Output per week	Fixed cost (US$)	Variable cost (US$)	Total cost (US$)
0	200	0	200
5	200	25	225
10	200	40	240
15	200	50	250
20	200	70	270

Average cost

Average cost is the cost of producing a unit of product at a particular output.

To calculate average cost, use the following formula:

$$\text{Average cost} = \frac{\text{Total cost}}{\text{Output}}$$

For example, in the table above, the average cost of producing 10 products would be US$24 (240/10). The average cost of producing 20 products would be US$13.50 (270/20).

The shape of the average cost curve

It is important to know and understand the shape of a typical average cost curve. Figure 4.10.2 shows its characteristic U-shape.

It has this shape because:

1. Average fixed cost is falling as output levels increase. This effect pulls the curve down at a slower and slower rate. So if fixed costs are US$1,000, producing two units rather than one will lower the curve from US$1,000 to produce 1 unit, to US$500 to produce 2 units. However, at much higher levels of output – for example, producing 1,000 units rather than 999, you will only be reducing the average fixed cost from US$1.11 to US$1.00 – that is, by just a few cents.

2. Average variable cost falls initially as the firm is able to combine its factors of production more efficiently. However, there comes a point at which inefficiencies creep into the production plant (see Unit 4.9).

Figure 4.10.1 Fixed and total cost

Figure 4.10.2 The shape of the average cost curve

The lowest point on the average cost curve shows the point at which the business is combining its resources most efficiently. We call this lowest point the **optimum output** level.

CASE STUDY: Calculating average cost

A firm has calculated that its total costs (fixed + variable costs) at different levels of daily output are as follows:

Output per day	Total cost (US$)	Average cost (US$)
0	10.00	
1	15.00	
2	18.00	
3	20.00	
4	21.00	
5	23.00	
6	26.00	
7	30.00	
8	35.00	
9	41.00	

Questions

1 Copy the table. Using the data given, calculate the average cost of production for a firm at different output levels, and complete the final column for each level.

2 At what point does average cost start to rise?

3 Explain why average cost starts to rise at this point.

ACTIVITY

Working in groups of three or four, prepare a presentation for the rest of the class. Choose one of the following topics: an explanation of fixed costs and how they are illustrated; variable costs (explained and how they are illustrated); total costs; average costs; average fixed and average variable costs.

DID YOU KNOW?

Businesses need to be able to calculate the cost of producing individual units. If a company like Nike can establish the cost of producing a soccer ball or pair of trainers, it will be able to price its products to ensure that it makes a profit.

KEY POINTS

1 Total cost measures all the costs at given levels of output.

2 Average cost is calculated by dividing the total cost by the units produced.

3 Average cost shows the cost of producing a typical unit at a particular level of output.

SUMMARY QUESTIONS

1 How would you calculate the average cost of producing a given level of output?

2 Why does the average cost curve have a U-shape?

3 Compare the shape of the total cost curve with that of the average cost curve.

4.11 Output and costs

LEARNING OUTCOMES

Candidates should be able to:
- analyse situations to show how total and average costs vary with output.

Variable costs of manufacturing paint include the raw materials that are mixed into the paint, and the tins. Fixed costs include costs such as interest on money borrowed by the manufacturer and the lighting and heating of the factory

ACTIVITY

Working in groups of three or four, identify five products that your families buy regularly. Set out a list of the likely fixed costs and variable costs of producing these products. Explain how the costs of producing one of these items would vary with output.

Costs and output

We are now in a position to examine the relationship between the various types of costs and output levels.

Total and average cost

CASE STUDY — Manufacturing paint

A paint manufacturer has calculated that fixed costs for the business are US$1,000 per week. These are made up of the costs of advertising, transporting paint to the store, lighting and heating, as well as the rent and rates of running the business. The variable costs of manufacturing the paint consist of the materials that go into the paint, and the labour required to manufacture it – the more that is produced, the greater the number of people employed (so their wages vary with the quantity produced).

The fixed and variable costs are set out in the following table.

Number of tins produced	Total fixed cost (US$)	Total variable cost (US$)	Total cost (US$)	Average cost (US$)
0	1,000	0		
100	1,000	1,000		
200	1,000	1,800		
300	1,000	2,300		
400	1,000	3,200		

Questions

1. Copy the table and complete the columns for total cost and average cost.
2. What is the optimum output? Explain your answer.
3. Explain the changes in the average cost curve as output increases.

Fixed, variable and total cost

CASE STUDY — Canning tomatoes

The total costs for a canning plant that specialises in canning tomatoes are:

- The fixed costs – interest paid on a loan, rent and rates, and the cost of energy to run the plant.

- The variable costs – the tomatoes, the cans and the labels.

Output (units)	Total fixed cost (US$)	Total variable cost (US$)	Total cost (US$)
0			
100		1,200	
200			3,800
300		2,400	
400	2,000		4,700
500			5,400

Questions

1 Some of the figures are missing from the table. Copy the table and fill in the missing numbers.

2 Now calculate the average fixed cost, the average variable cost and the average total cost at each of the levels of output shown in the table.

DID YOU KNOW?

A tax paid per unit sold or produced is a variable cost – for example, an output tax charged on the number of a particular good produced, such as US$1 per pair of trainers. A lump sum tax, such as a vehicle tax or rates on property and land, is a fixed cost.

DID YOU KNOW?

It is not always easy to decide which costs are fixed and which are variable. For example, wages for full-time workers are a fixed cost for a business, whereas when a firm pays piece rates these would count as variable costs.

The following table summarises some key terms and their meanings.

Total fixed cost	The sum of all of the different types of fixed costs at different outputs
Total variable cost	The sum of all of the variable costs at different outputs
Total cost	The sum of total fixed cost and total variable cost at different outputs
Average fixed cost	The total fixed cost divided by the level of output
Average variable cost	The total variable cost divided by the level of output
Average total cost	The total cost divided by the level of output

KEY POINTS

1 Business costs consist of fixed and variable costs.

2 Total cost is calculated by adding together all the costs at each level of output.

3 Total cost rises with output.

4 Average cost is the total cost divided by the level of output or sales.

SUMMARY QUESTIONS

1 How would you calculate average fixed costs of production?

2 What is the relationship between total costs and the level of production?

3 How does average cost change as a result of changes in the level of output of a manufactured good?

4.12 Total and average revenue

Revenue

Revenue is the sum of money that a business receives from making sales. Obviously sales revenue increases with the quantity of goods sold. Mars earns revenues from its sales of chocolate bars to supermarkets and other shops. Tata Tea earns revenue from its sales of different types of tea. Shell earns revenue from selling oil and petrol.

To calculate the total revenue from selling tea, multiply the number of packets sold by the price per packet. The average revenue is the price charged for each packet

Total revenue

To calculate **total revenue** (in order to calculate the value of sales made by a business), multiply the quantity of goods sold by the price they are sold for:

Total revenue = Quantity of goods sold × Price

TR = Q × P

Average revenue

The **average revenue** is the price received for selling a given quantity of goods. It is helpful for a business to know its average revenue because this can be compared with the average cost of making and/or selling that item.

The best way of illustrating this is to show the market price – that is, where demand and supply meet. Take the example of footballs produced by a major sports good producer. The market price (where demand cuts supply) is US$10. At this price the business is prepared to supply 1,000 footballs a week to sports shops. Sports shops are happy to buy 1,000 footballs a week.

So what is the total revenue?

1,000 (Q) × US$10 (P) = US$10,000

LEARNING OUTCOMES

Candidates should be able to:
- define total and average revenue and perform simple calculations.

EXAM TIP

It is very important to understand the differences between the various types of cost and revenue. There are usually several questions on these in the multiple-choice paper.

DID YOU KNOW?

At low levels of output total revenue will always be below total cost. This is because total revenue starts at zero, whereas total cost nearly always has a fixed cost element. Businesses therefore make a loss if they only produce a small output. As output increases and the product is sold, total revenue should start to catch up with, and then overtake, total cost.

On Figure 4.12.1 this is illustrated by the shaded area OPAQ.

So what is the average revenue?

The average revenue is simply the price: US$10.

This is because every ball will be sold to shops for US$10 each.

Total and average revenue

The total revenue is the sum of all of the revenues received by a supplier. The table shows the weekly average and total revenue of a company that supplies footballs to shops in a particular country for a price of US$10 each.

Sales	Average revenue (= price) (US$)	Total revenue (total value of all sales) (US$)
100	10	1,000
200	10	2,000
300	10	3,000
400	10	4,000
500	10	5,000
600	10	6,000
700	10	7,000
800	10	8,000
900	10	9,000

Figure 4.12.1 The market price (average revenue) for a supplier of footballs

Figure 4.12.2 shows this data in graph form. Notice the straight line starting at zero and then rising by US$10 for each sale made.

Figure 4.12.2 Total revenue rises in proportion to the number of sales made

ACTIVITY

Working as a group, propose an idea for a business that sells a product or service. Decide on a price that you would charge for your chosen product or service. Calculate how many units of the product or service you could sell each week. Then calculate what your weekly total revenue would be.

KEY POINTS

1. Revenues are receipts from sales.
2. Total revenue is calculated from adding the value of all sales made.
3. Average revenue is the total revenue divided by the quantity sold.

SUMMARY QUESTIONS

1. How would you calculate the average revenue from the sales of a product?
2. What is the relationship between average revenue and price?
3. How does total revenue alter with the volume of sales made?

4.13 Profit maximisation

LEARNING OUTCOMES

Candidates should be able to:
- describe the principle of profit maximisation as a goal.

Shareholders in businesses like Tata Tea expect to receive a large dividend – their share of the profit of the company

Figure 4.13.1 The profit maximising point: the greatest difference between total revenue (TR) and total cost (TC)

Making a profit

The main aim of a business is to make a **profit**. There may be wider goals, such as building a reputation for quality or helping to build a stronger community, but most businesses will place an emphasis on profit. Many businesses set targets, one of which will be to meet, or exceed, given levels of profit. The directors who control the business will be responsible for seeing that these targets are met – they may have large salaries to reflect the responsibility that they carry for achieving this.

One group that is very interested in the profits is the shareholders. We saw in Units 4.2 and 4.3 that companies are owned by shareholders. They risk their money when they buy shares but, as their name suggests, they receive dividends, their share of the profits. Good profits, and so good dividends, are important for convincing the shareholders that the company is strong and that they should continue to invest their money in it.

To *maximise* is to make something as large as possible, and a business will want to maximise its profits. Analysis of costs and revenues helps us to find out how much businesses should produce, and what prices they should charge, in order to maximise their profits. The **profit maximising point** of a business is the point at which there is the greatest difference between total revenues (TR) and total cost (TC). Figure 4.13.1 shows this as a graph.

CASE STUDY | An example of profit maximising

The table gives the figures for a business producing men's suits. You can see that the greatest difference between the total revenue and total cost occurs in the fourth row, when there are sales of 300 units at a price of US$15. In other words, the best profit that the company can make is to produce 300 units and charge US$15 per item. The **profit maximising output** is therefore 300 sales.

Sales (number of units)	Price per unit (US$)	Total revenue (US$)	Total cost (US$)	Total profit (US$)
0	30	0	1,000	−1,000
100	25	2,500	2,000	500
200	20	4,000	2,800	1,200
300	15	4,500	3,200	1,300
400	10	4,000	3,700	300
500	5	2,500	4,300	−1,800

At very low outputs the business would make a loss because it has fixed costs of £1,000 to cover. A lower price would mean a greater number of sales, but at prices below US$20 the business would find total revenues falling, because sales are rising less proportionately than the fall in price (demand is relatively more inelastic). Another problem for the business is that as it produces more to sell initially, its costs rise only slowly, but above 200 units of output costs rise at an increasing rate, as resources are combined less efficiently.

Questions

1 Why would the firm prefer to sell 300 units than 200 units?

2 Why would the firm prefer to sell 300 units than 400 units?

3 How does:
   a total cost change with higher levels of output?
   b total revenue change with higher levels of output?
   c total profit change with higher levels of output?

4 What is the profit maximising point?

EXAM TIP

Profit maximisation is a very important concept in relation to a private firm. You need to be able to discuss why this is the case.

Other goals

Businesses may have other goals than profit maximisation – for example, they may seek to maximise sales in order to reduce the sales of their competitors. Businesses may also want to draw attention away from their high profits. The government and other regulatory bodies might ask questions about how they are able to make such large profits.

Other goals include building a good reputation – for example, through having a good name for quality and safety. In 2010 Toyota received adverse publicity in the world's press because of a fault in its car braking system. The chairman of Toyota made a statement saying that Toyota's priorities should be: (1) safety, (2) quality and (3) selling large numbers of cars – in that order.

ACTIVITY

Study the national newspapers in your country to find stories about businesses making higher than average profits. In what industries do these firms operate? How do you think they are able to make such large profits?

KEY POINTS

1 Profit maximisation is achieved when the difference between total cost and total revenue is greatest.

2 Studying total costs and total revenues helps a business to identify the output at which it will maximise profit.

3 Businesses may have other goals than profit maximisation.

SUMMARY QUESTIONS

1 How can shareholders share in business profits?

2 What is profit maximisation?

3 How can a business maximise its profits?

4.14 Price and output in perfect competition

LEARNING OUTCOMES

Candidates should be able to:

- describe pricing and output policies in perfect competition.

Some grades of grain, such as this in Nebraska, are almost identical. The produce therefore creates a competitive market for grain – particularly if there are many producers

Price competition

Businesses compete with each other to make sales. The greater the competition, the closer the prices charged by rivals. Take the example of three petrol stations that are located close together. They display their prices on signs that are clearly visible so that motorists can choose which petrol station to buy from. The motorists know that the petrol in the pumps is almost identical. If one petrol station charges more than its rivals it will lose sales. In this situation the prices charged are likely to be identical. Even a 1 cent difference in fuel prices per litre will lead to motorists choosing the cheaper petrol.

Competition can also be intense when there are lots of producers of identical agricultural products – for example, the same grade of grain.

Perfect competition

As a way of analysing how businesses compete with each other, economists have developed a theory of **perfect competition**. Perfect competition does not exist in a pure form because there are always differences between sellers – for example, the cashier in one petrol station may be friendlier and more helpful than the cashier in a rival station.

The idea of perfect competition that economists have modelled is based on the following assumptions:

- There would be lots of firms competing with each other.
- Each firm would produce an identical product.
- Each firm would know exactly what the others were producing and the prices they were charging.
- There would be no barriers to new firms entering the market, and no barriers to exit, so that firms could enter or leave the industry easily.
- Each firm would only produce a very small percentage of the overall production in the industry, because consumers could immediately switch to a cheaper supplier.
- There would be lots of buyers, each of whom would know the prices charged by different sellers.

Given these conditions, economists believe that:

- Businesses would all charge the same price.
- This price would be the minimum they could charge without going out of business.
- The price would be equivalent to the lowest average cost of producing goods.
- At the market price the average cost of production would be the same as the average revenue received for selling.
- No firm would risk charging more than the market price, because they would make no sales if they did so.

DID YOU KNOW?

Within markets that have near perfect competition there are lots of buyers and sellers of an almost identical product, such as varieties of rice or corn. However, in these cases some suppliers will still have advantages over competitors – for example, close proximity to customers.

Price takers

Under perfect competition a business would be a **price taker**: it would take its price from the market. The alternative would be a **price maker** – that is, a business that chooses at what price to sell its products. You will read about this in Unit 4.15.

Illustrating average cost and average revenue in perfect competition

Figure 4.14.1 shows the price a firm would receive under perfect competition and how many products it would supply to the market.

The diagram indicates the following points:

1. The business would produce OQ of output. This is the point at which the average revenue (AR) line is equal to the average cost curve.
2. The AR line is a horizontal straight line. It is at the market price, which the firm takes from the market.
3. The market price is OP.
4. Total revenue is exactly equal to total cost. The area OQAP (total revenue) = the area OQAP (total cost).

Figure 4.14.1 A price-taking firm under perfect competition

DID YOU KNOW?

The theory of perfect competition is based on economists' idea that something they call normal profit should be included as a fixed cost for a business. As a fixed cost it is part of the average cost curve. The normal profit is the reward that a business person would need to keep their business running (rather than close down).

EXAM TIP

Economists understand that perfect competition may not exist in practice, but they still regard it as a very important concept. You will need to demonstrate that you know why this is.

KEY POINTS

1. The idea of perfect competition helps economists to understand what an absolutely competitive market would be like.
2. In perfect competition suppliers would be price takers.
3. Businesses would produce at the point where:
   output × average revenue = output × average cost.

SUMMARY QUESTIONS

1. Why have economists created a model of perfect competition?
2. How are prices determined under perfect competition?
3. Why would a business not raise its prices if it was operating in a perfectly competitive market?

ACTIVITY

Identify markets in which the market largely determines the price at which a producer can sell its product. Compare the prices charged by different producers in this market. How similar are they? Compare your findings with those of classmates.

4.15 Pricing and output policies in monopoly

LEARNING OUTCOMES

Candidates should be able to:
- describe pricing and output policies in monopoly.

Branding products helps to differentiate them and give the producers some elements of monopoly powers. This in turn enables them to charge higher prices

DID YOU KNOW?

In some countries – for example, the UK – the government defines a monopoly as existing in law if it has 25 per cent or more of the market. This is because when it has a substantial share of the market it has power to influence price and other aspects of competition.

What is a monopoly?

Monopoly is the opposite of perfect competition. In a pure monopoly there is only one firm in an industry, so there is no competition. There are very few pure monopolies in the real world, but there are local examples in, say, the only shop or petrol station in a remote area. There are businesses that are so large that they can benefit from the same advantages as monopolies – for example, Microsoft, which provides the operating system for most computers. Microsoft is able to use its virtual monopoly position to create exclusive deals with computer manufacturers.

In some countries government-owned public corporations have monopoly powers. For example, state-owned oil companies sometimes manage all of the oil reserves in a particular country. This Unit looks at how the lack of competition enables companies to benefit from monopoly-like powers.

Price makers

One of the main features of a monopoly is that it acts as a price maker. A price maker chooses what price to charge rather than having to charge a price that is identical or very similar to the prices charged by rivals. Microsoft, mentioned above, is able to choose the price it charges to computer manufacturers. Of course it would not want to make this price unaffordable to computer manufacturers.

The demand curve under monopoly

A downward-sloping demand curve occurs when more of a product is demanded at lower than at higher prices. Monopolists are faced with a downward-sloping demand curve for their products. The monopolist will want to set prices at the profit-maximising output. Figure 4.15.1 shows the demand curve for the output of a monopolist. It also shows the average cost of producing goods.

The monopolist will choose a price where the difference between cost and revenue is maximised.

Figure 4.15.1 The demand curve for the output of a monopolist

In Figure 4.15.1 you can see that the monopolist is charging a price (P) that is higher than the average cost (C) of making that output of goods. Sales revenue for the monopolist is OPAQ (price × quantity produced). Total cost for the monopolist is OCBQ (average cost × quantity produced). The monopolist is therefore making profit over and above normal profit.

NB The monopolist's demand curve is the same as the industry demand curve because he is the only supplier. He can choose price or output, but not both.

The features of a monopoly

The key features of a monopoly are:

- There is only one firm in the industry and it controls the market.
- It is very difficult for new firms to enter the industry.
- The monopolist is the price maker – that is, the setter of prices.
- Monopolists make profits over and above normal profit.

Examples of virtual monopolies include Microsoft Internet Explorer®, for accessing the internet, and Google for carrying out an internet search (although in China, Baidu is the leading search engine).

How do monopolies occur?

As we have seen, when businesses have monopolies, or have monopoly powers, it is difficult for rivals to enter the same industry. The monopoly may have occurred for various reasons:

- The government may give a business the legal right to be the only one in the industry. This may be the case with energy companies, railway companies, suppliers of water and other important public services.
- Through first mover advantage: a business may be the first to enter an industry, be very efficient and quickly develop a monopoly. It may build up a reputation and position that are difficult for others to match. Microsoft and Google are examples.
- Through economies of scale: the business is able to produce a very high output at low average cost. Smaller firms are unable to compete.
- Through marketing and branding: Nike and Coca-Cola spend billions of pounds on advertising and promotion; high costs of advertising deter other firms from setting up in competition. Nike and Coca-Cola do not have a complete monopoly, but have monopoly-like powers in most markets in which they operate.
- Some businesses are also 'natural monopolies'. A natural monopoly occurs when resources are located in a limited geographical area and are easily exploited in that area. For example, 'rare earth' elements that are used in battery powered cars are only available in some locations. Currently they are most plentiful and easy to extract in China. This gives Chinese producers a natural monopoly in 'rare earth' production.

ACTIVITY

Identify some of the products that you consume where the business appears to have monopoly powers. Are the prices of these products relatively high compared with other products that you buy, where there appears to be more competition between producers and sellers?

KEY POINTS

1. A pure monopoly exists when there is only one firm in the industry.
2. Firms have monopoly powers when they control a large percentage of a particular market. In the UK this is more than 25 per cent of market share.
3. Monopolists are price makers.
4. Monopolists maximise profits when there is the greatest difference between their total costs and total revenues.

SUMMARY QUESTIONS

1. What is the difference between *monopoly* and *monopoly powers*?
2. How can businesses develop monopoly powers?
3. What are the key features of monopoly?

4.16 Different sizes of firms

LEARNING OUTCOMES

Candidates should be able to:
- describe the main reasons for different sizes of firms.

Shell began as a sole-trader business, before becoming a partnership trading in seashells and liquid fuel. Today the company is a huge multinational

DID YOU KNOW?

Forbes is a widely read American business magazine. It publishes a list of the world's largest companies.

DID YOU KNOW?

The definition of a small business varies, but usually refers to a business employing fewer than 50 people. A **micro-business** employs fewer than 5 people.

Measuring the size of a firm

There are different ways of measuring the size of a firm:

- The **number of employees**: a firm may be large but employ relatively few employees (because they use a lot of capital). Many automobile factories use robots for work once done by hand.
- The **value of sales** made by the business is a good way of measuring the size of retail businesses such as supermarkets.
- The value of the financial **capital employed**: for example, the Forbes List of the top 100 companies measures size by the value of all the shares in the business (the **market capitalisation**).
- The size of the **market share** of a business: the percentage of all the sales made by a company. Market share can be a useful indicator of the extent of a business's monopoly powers.

Why do large businesses exist?

There are various reasons why large businesses exist:

- To meet demand: large companies (e.g. Procter and Gamble in the US) supply household goods such as washing powder, toothpaste and soap worldwide. Bao Steel (China) produces steel worldwide for construction projects, particularly in the rapidly growing Chinese economy.
- When there are considerable economies of producing on a large scale (see Unit 4.18): Coca-Cola distributes cola-based drinks and bottled water on a huge scale worldwide. It is able to operate from large factories with very low average unit costs.
- When the supply of goods depends on employing large sums of capital: nuclear energy can only be developed economically on a large scale. This also applies to motor vehicle manufacture, aircraft and ship building, and major construction projects such as skyscrapers and bridges.

The table shows some multinational companies that dominate global trade.

Examples of large multinationals	Country of origin
China Mobile (mobile phones)	China
Wal-Mart (retailing)	US
Unilever (household goods)	UK/Netherlands
Tata (conglomerate)	India
Lukoil (oil)	Russia
Air France (airline)	France
Emaar Properties (construction)	Saudi Arabia

DID YOU KNOW?

Shell began as a small shop in East London owned by Marcus Samuel, who imported seashells from the Orient. His sons set up a partnership importing paraffin from China and Japan. By the early 20th century they had formed a company producing and trading in oil. The market for seashells was limited, but for oil it became global.

ACTIVITY

Choose 10 large multinational businesses. For each one find out the number of employees, the value of sales made and the marketing capitalisation in a recent year. (You should find this information in the company report.) Rank the companies in order using these different classifications. How does the order vary according to how you classify size?

Why do small firms exist?

Most businesses are small, and even large multinationals that dominate global trade are only a small proportion of the businesses in any one country. There are several reasons for the existence of small firms, many of which are important for their country's economy:

- Some are new businesses that have just set up, hoping to play an increasingly important role as they grow.
- They may supply a local market, e.g. a local corner shop, restaurant or hairdresser.
- They provide essential components and supplies for larger businesses.
- There may be only a limited demand for their product. An example might be suppliers of specialist medical supplies for patients with rare diseases.
- Their owners may prefer to run a small enterprise.
- Personal services requiring attention to detail, such as hairdressing, are often suitable for small firms.

EXAM TIP

Small firms still play a very important role in economies all over the world. You will need to be able to discuss why such small firms still continue to exist.

SUMMARY QUESTIONS

1 Explain whether the following types of industrial production are more suitable for large-scale or small-scale businesses:

    television broadcasting   baking bread   coffee shops
    computer manufacture   wind energy turbines
    selling fruit   postal services

Give reasons for your answers.

2 Explain two good ways of identifying the size of a particular company. Choose a local company and explain which of these methods you think is better, and why.

3 Why are small businesses so important to the economy?

KEY POINTS

1 There are several ways of measuring the size of businesses.

2 Classifying large and small businesses by market share indicates how much competition a business faces.

3 Some businesses are large through demand for their products.

4 Small businesses can take advantage of limited demand.

4.17 Different forms of integration

LEARNING OUTCOMES

Candidates should be able to:
- describe and evaluate integration.

Vertical integration in tea manufacture involves businesses joining together at different stages of production – for example, a tea processor taking over tea estates that grow tea

DID YOU KNOW?

In order to expand, many firms will try to merge with or take over others. If a business wishes to take over another business it will set out to purchase more than 50 per cent of the shares. As soon as it has a 50 per cent share plus one share, it is in control. It can then make all the decisions as it cannot be outvoted by other shareholders.

Integration

To integrate means to join together. In business **integration** may be in the form of a **takeover** or a **merger**.

A merger occurs when two businesses combine to form a single company. It is similar to a takeover except that the existing shareholders of both businesses retain a share in the new business.

A takeover occurs when one business gains control of, or acquires, part of another business. A business may be prepared to sell off one of its divisions which it no longer wishes to keep.

Mergers and takeovers take place because:

- there is too much supply in the market, relative to demand. A firm may take over part of a rival in order to control supply to the market
- to get access to new markets, perhaps in other countries
- to acquire new technologies from other businesses
- to acquire dynamic products.

CASE STUDY | Tata Tea takes over Tetley

Tata Tea is part of India's giant conglomerate Tata, which has a range of divisions, each focusing on a specific area, such as steel, motor vehicles or tea. Each of these divisions operates as a separate company with its own board of directors. In 2005 Tata Tea took over the larger British tea company, Tetley. There were many advantages to be gained from doing this, one of which was the internationally respected brand names belonging to Tetley, the company's expertise in producing flavoured and herbal teas, and its access to international markets in Europe and North America. Tata has a strong base in growing tea and owns a range of tea estates. It has access to a huge market in India, with over 1 billion potential customers. Tata has now been able to build a strong brand image of providing quality tea across the world, with increased sales and profits in most countries.

Questions

1 Why do you think that Tata wanted to take over Tetley?

2 Why do you think the takeover has been successful?

3 What type of integration was involved in the takeover?

4 What are the benefits of this type of integration?

Types of integration

The table sets out different ways in which businesses can merge, or integrate.

Horizontal integration	Firms join together at the same stage of production. They can learn from best practice in each company and concentrate on processing activities in the most efficient plants. The increased size of the business provides economies of scale.
Vertical integration	It may be *forward* – that is, taking over a firm at a later stage of production (for example, a business with tea estates taking over a company that processes tea) – or *backward* – that is, taking over a firm at an earlier stage of production (for example, a firm that advertises and markets tea taking over one that processes it). The advantage of this sort of integration is that the firm gains control over its supply chain.
Lateral integration	Occurs when there is a merger of firms that use the same distribution channels. For example, a company selling tea may join with a firm selling coffee, so that the goods can be distributed together to supermarket chains.
Conglomerate integration	For example Tata Industries, which is able to spread interests and risks over many industries. Profits from one established business can be used to develop a new business area. So, for example, Tata Steel and Tata Tea profits could be channelled into the growing Tata IT company. A large conglomerate also builds up a high profile, enabling it to raise finance more easily.
International integration	Global companies like Tata buy up other companies worldwide. In China, for example, Tata Tea has invested in Chinese tea companies producing green tea. A **joint venture** is a good way of entering a new international market. In this case a new company is set up, owned by Tata and a Chinese company.

DID YOU KNOW?

A conglomerate business is made up of a range of companies or divisions producing products that are not necessarily related. The conglomerate looks for opportunities for growth and profits in a range of unrelated fields.

EXAM TIP

You need to be able to discuss both the advantages and disadvantages of a firm merging with, or being taken over by, another.

ACTIVITY

Study the newspapers to find examples of takeovers and mergers. What type of integration is involved? What are the advantages of the integration? Compare your findings with those of others in your group.

KEY POINTS

1 Businesses can grow through takeovers, acquisitions and mergers.
2 Integration involves the joining together of businesses.
3 Integration gives access to new markets, technologies and large-scale production.

SUMMARY QUESTIONS

1 Why might two steel manufacturers at the same stage of production join together?
2 What is lateral integration? What would be the benefits?
3 What is the advantage of conglomerate integration?

4.18 Economies and diseconomies of scale

LEARNING OUTCOMES

Candidates should be able to:
- describe and evaluate economies and diseconomies of scale.

Shenzhen, China: the concentration of many leading-edge electronics factories provides external economies of scale to all firms in the industry, including a pool of highly skilled workers

Figure 4.18.1 Economies of scale

Economies of scale

Economies of scale are the advantages of producing on a scale large enough for a business to be able to cut the cost of individual units of production. Economies of scale enable a business to reduce its average cost curve. Figure 4.18.1 illustrates the average cost curve for a growing business in three successive time periods. In period 2 it can produce a larger output at a lower average cost than in period 1. In period 3 it can produce a large output at a lower average cost than in period 2.

Businesses can benefit from two main types of economies of scale:

- **Internal economies**: the advantages that a firm gains from its own growth.
- **External economies**: the advantages gained from the growth and improvement of a firm's industry and locality.

Internal economies of scale

Technical advantages

Large firms can benefit from better techniques of production. Automated plant and equipment (e.g. in a confectionery manufacturing company) may be so expensive to install that only large companies can afford it. Automated production lines enable very high production at low unit cost and can be run 24 hours a day, 7 days a week.

Financial advantages

Large firms usually find it easier and cheaper to borrow money. A huge multinational like Tata Tea was able raise extra capital for the takeover of Tetley by issuing new shares to existing shareholders. Tata can borrow money at a low rate of interest because the bank is confident that the loan will be repaid.

Managerial advantages

Large companies are able to attract the best managers worldwide because of the high salaries they can pay.

Commercial advantages

Large firms are able to buy and sell in bulk. They obtain discount for bulk purchases. The cost of creating a global advertising campaign can be spread over billions of people who will watch the television advert across the globe.

Risk-spreading advantages

Large firms can spread their risks in various ways:

- Product diversification – producing and selling lots of different products.

- Market diversification – producing and selling in many different countries and regions.
- Supplier diversification – using several different suppliers in case one is unable to supply on time.
- Production diversification – having several different production plants.

Internal diseconomies of scale

If an organisation is too large, managers may not be able to manage it effectively. There may be technical problems with complicated equipment. If a firm is producing more than it can sell, the proportion of advertising costs may increase. If the business produces too many products for too many markets and a number of them fail, the losses may have a damaging effect on the development of the company's other products.

External economies of scale

External economies arise from the growth of the industry rather than a particular firm. All firms benefit from external economies of scale, such as:

- improved communications and transport links, such as a new railway line that cuts distribution costs
- improved educational facilities, such as a new college or university training people in the skills needed by local businesses
- the development of suppliers, supplying components to all the firms in an industry
- improved housing and social amenities that encourage workers to move to an area
- the development of banking and insurance services in an area.

External diseconomies of scale

There can be problems arising from the growth of an industry. Labour and other costs can increase as more competitors hire more labour and buy more land and machinery. There may also be congestion and pollution from the business activities.

> **DID YOU KNOW?**
>
> Over a quarter of a million people now live in the Chinese city of Shenzhen. The city has grown rapidly (since 2000) to become a centre for high-technology industries – particularly multinational electronic companies like China Mobile, Apple and Nokia. There is a large, young and highly skilled labour force, and a university specialising in science, engineering and technology.

> **EXAM TIP**
>
> You need to be able to demonstrate that you understand there are both advantages and disadvantages of a firm growing in size.

> **KEY POINTS**
>
> 1. Internal economies of scale enable larger businesses to produce with lower unit costs.
> 2. Economies arise from better technology, management and marketing, as well as diversification.
> 3. External economies result from the growth of an industry or improved services in a region reducing costs for a range of businesses.

> **SUMMARY QUESTIONS**
>
> 1. Explain the difference between an internal and an external economy of scale.
> 2. What benefits can a firm gain from being larger than its rivals?
> 3. How can external economies help more than one firm?

4.19 Advantages and disadvantages of monopoly

LEARNING OUTCOMES

Candidates should be able to:
- discuss the advantages and disadvantages of monopoly.

Large pharmaceutical companies spend substantial sums of money each year on the research and development of new products. This may help to justify their monopoly position

The advantages of monopoly

We saw in Unit 4.15 that pure monopoly exists where there is just one business in a market. Virtual monopoly means that large firms have powers as if they were in fact monopolies. This can be seen with some internet companies, such as Google, the world's leading search engine, and Amazon, the leading online bookseller. Facebook is the world's leading social networking site. The obvious advantage to these businesses is the ability to build very strong brands, with high sales and high profits. Their shareholders receive good dividends. Consumers also benefit from a fast, accurate and reliable service, though they may not have much choice.

Figure 4.19.1 shows how, through economies of scale, a large business with monopoly-like powers can produce at lower cost than smaller rivals. Provided that the monopolist does not take too much profit, some of the benefits of low-cost production are passed on to consumers. The monopolist has an incentive to produce high-quality products and services to maintain the monopoly position.

Figure 4.19.1 Large businesses using monopoly powers are able to produce at lower cost than smaller rivals

Public sector monopolies also benefit from economies of scale. For example, in Cuba the government runs all the hospitals and is able to run one of the best hospital services in the world. It is able to ensure that high-quality resources are provided in the hospitals and that medical supplies are bought in bulk.

The disadvantages of monopoly

There are a number of criticisms of monopoly:
- Monopolies can be inefficient because of a lack of competition.
- Monopolists might restrict the quantity of goods they supply to the market in order to keep prices high.

DID YOU KNOW?

A private sector monopolist is a large company owned by shareholders that is in a monopoly position, such as Microsoft or Coca-Cola. A public-sector monopolist is a government-owned business. Examples are a government-owned railway or broadcasting service such as the BBC.

- Monopolies might produce poor-quality products because there is no opportunity for a rival to produce a better-quality product.
- Monopolies may not invest in developing new products because they can sell existing ones.

CASE STUDY | The pharmaceutical industry

An advantage of monopoly is that profits can be ploughed into research. This is particularly important in the pharmaceutical industry, which is dominated by very large multinational companies. It usually takes several years to identify new medicines and drugs. The new formulations are produced after painstaking laboratory trials. They are then extensively tested in clinical trials before being launched onto the market. Only large monopoly-type companies can afford to engage in this type of research.

However, pharmaceutical companies are sometimes criticised for not making life-saving drugs and medicines available at affordable prices in poor countries. The pharmaceutical companies often will not permit important drugs from being produced in bulk for these countries. The pharmaceutical companies say they have spent billions on developing these drugs and therefore are entitled to charge high prices.

A criticism of large pharmaceutical companies is that they often spend more on advertising than they do on research activity.

Questions

1. How can monopoly in the pharmaceutical industry help in the fight against disease and illness?
2. How can the existence of monopoly prevent poorer patients from getting the treatment they need?

ACTIVITY

Identify a business in your locality that has a local monopoly. How does the owner of the business benefit from the monopoly position? What are the advantages to consumers of products produced by the monopoly? What are the disadvantages to consumers?

KEY POINTS

1. Monopoly enables a business to dominate a market.
2. Monopoly typically enables a dominant producer to produce at a low unit cost.
3. Monopolies can provide high-quality service to consumers.

DID YOU KNOW?

A monopolist sets its own price. It will charge a price above the average cost in order to make a profit. Monopolies make profits in excess of those that would be made in a competitive industry.

EXAM TIP

You will often be asked to discuss, which usually implies that there are two sides to an argument. If, for example, you were asked to discuss the role of monopolies in an economy, you would need to consider both their advantages and their disadvantages to gain a good mark.

SUMMARY QUESTIONS

1. Give an example of a situation in which it may be beneficial to have a monopoly producer.
2. In bioscience – the development of new seeds and crops – there are just a few large companies introducing most of the new products. What are the benefits and drawbacks of having just a few companies in bioscience?
3. Why are monopolists unlikely to produce at the lowest point of the average cost curve?

Unit 4 — Practice exam questions

SECTION 1: Multiple-choice questions

Each question has ONE correct answer.

1 Which of the following is NOT included in a deed of partnership?
   a The responsibilities to be carried out by each partner
   b Each partner's investment in the company
   c How profit may be shared between the partners
   d How much each partner must earn in revenue

2 Which of the following may be a benefit to a multinational corporation of moving production away from its home country?
   a A wider market to sell products to
   b Lower production costs
   c Better communication within the business
   d Lower marketing costs

3 A sole trader sells doughnuts from a market stall for US$1 each. The stall costs US$20 to rent and each doughnut costs US$0.30 to make. If she makes and sells 100 doughnuts, what will the AVERAGE TOTAL COST be?
   a US$0.50
   b US$0.30
   c US$0.20
   d US$1.00

4 Which of the following is a benefit of limited liability to shareholders?
   a Only a fixed amount may be invested by each individual
   b Dividends are paid on each share owned
   c Personal assets do not have to be sold to pay company debts
   d Shares may be bought and sold on the stock exchange

5 An external economy of scale may be:
   a Low costs due to bulk buying
   b Lower interest on bank loans
   c Training courses at local colleges
   d Product diversification

6 This week, a flower-selling company sells 50 plants for US$5 each and 100 plants for US$2 each. What is the company's AVERAGE REVENUE for the week?
   a US$2.00
   b US$5.00
   c US$3.50
   d US$3.00

7 According to economic theory, how might a firm maximise profits?
   a Sell as much of the product as possible, at a range of prices
   b Sell where there is the biggest difference between costs and revenue
   c Sell at the lowest possible price to increase demand
   d Sell at a price just below that of the competition

8 Which of the following is most likely to be a capital-intensive business?
   a A car factory
   b A hotel
   c A school
   d A restaurant

9 Which of the following is NOT true in the economic model of perfect competition?
   a Companies produce identical products
   b Companies charge different prices to different consumers
   c There are many buyers and sellers of the product
   d Companies make normal profit in the long term

10 Which of the following is a disadvantage of monopoly power to consumers?
   a Advertising expenditure is high
   b Economies of scale are unlikely
   c There are barriers to entry into the industry
   d Prices may be higher

SECTION 2: Structured questions

Penelope is a sole trader who has recently set up a small pizza takeaway shop in a popular tourist town. At present she runs the shop on her own, but the hours are long and she has not taken a break for the last 18 months. The business is seasonal to some extent, but the town attracts visitors all year round, so she does not want to close the shop for a holiday period, as she feels she may lose business to one of her many competitors. Penelope is considering going into partnership with a friend who has recently lost her job as a chef and is willing to put money into the pizza business. Penelope would like to expand and open another takeaway shop or a restaurant. Penelope has spoken to a business adviser, who has suggested that she also considers the option of forming a private limited company.

Her business costs and revenues are as follows:

Rent of shop	US$250 per week
Penelope's wage	US$150 per week
Business rates	US$140 per week
Electricity bills	US$30 per week
Marketing leaflets	US$10 per week
Pizza ingredients (average)	US$2.50 per pizza
Pizza boxes	US$0.30 each
Selling price of pizzas	US$7.50 (average)

1. a Define *fixed costs* and give two examples from Penelope's business. (4)
   b Define *variable costs* and give two examples from Penelope's business. (4)
   c Identify and explain TWO advantages to Penelope of operating her business as a sole trader. (6)
   d As a sole trader, Penelope has unlimited liability. Explain what this means and how it may affect Penelope's future plans for her business. (6)

2. a Calculate total fixed costs for Penelope's business for one week. (4)
   b Calculate Penelope's total variable costs if she produces 50 pizzas. (4)
   c Calculate Penelope's profit or loss if she produces and sells (i) 120 pizzas and (ii) 175 pizzas in a week. (6)
   d Calculate and comment on Penelope's average fixed costs for the output levels. (6)

3. Penelope is trying to decide whether to expand her business by forming a partnership with her friend, or to start a private limited company. She needs to consider the advantages and disadvantages of both options.
   a Explain ONE advantage and ONE disadvantage to Penelope of expanding her business by taking on a partner. (4)
   b Explain ONE advantage and ONE disadvantage to Penelope of expanding her business by starting a private limited company. (4)
   c Penelope needs to measure the size of her business in order to give information to prospective investors. Identify and explain TWO possible ways she could do this and decide which would be the best. Justify your decision. (6)
   d Referring to the information in the case and your answers to 3a and 3b, discuss the best way for Penelope to expand her business. Justify your decision. (6)

4. Penelope's major competitor in town is the branch of a major multinational pizza takeaway and delivery company. This company sells pizzas at an average price of US$6.50, due to economies of scale in the production and marketing costs achieved by the large company.
   a Explain what is meant by *economies of scale* and *multinational company*. (4)
   b Identify and explain TWO likely examples of economies of scale in this type of business. (4)
   c If Penelope reduces the price to US$6.50 in order to compete with the multinational company, explain what may be the implications for her sales, profits and future plans. (5)
   d Evaluate the view that 'local businesses like Penelope's are likely to remain small'. (7)

Total: 80 marks

SECTION 3: Analysis and critical evaluation

Country B is a medium-sized developed nation, whose economic and business environment is dominated by tertiary businesses, many in banking and insurance. The public sector in the country is also very important, as tax rates are high and welfare benefits very generous. The government provides a wide range of health and education services and promotes high public awareness of healthy eating and environmental issues. Taxation on products such as cigarettes is high, leading to high prices, but this has not reduced demand to any great extent.

- The population is fairly static, only growing at approximately 0.2 per cent a year; there is a net emigration to other countries of young professional workers seeking high-paying jobs elsewhere.
- The unemployment rate is low and there are unfilled job vacancies for low-skilled workers in the public sector.
- Consumers are increasingly demanding healthy food products and there is an increasing interest in energy-saving products, such as light bulbs.
- The government of Country B has recently decided to subsidise IT training for older workers, via a public sector training agency.
- Energy is becoming a major issue as the country is reliant on an unreliable neighbouring nation. The government is considering a plan to build a nuclear power station, with the potential capacity to supply the entire country's needs.

1 a Explain what is meant by *public sector* and give an example from the text. *(2)*

  b Explain why 'net migration' may lead to a 'static population'. *(2)*

2 a Suggest ONE example in the text of a change in consumer demand. *(2)*

  b Illustrate your example for (i) with a supply and demand diagram, clearly labelled with change in price and quantity. *(2)*

3 Discuss whether the government provision of essential services will always lead to the best-quality service for the population of Country B. *(5)*

4 a Explain, using a diagram, why high taxes should lead to a decrease in quantity demanded for a product or service. *(2)*

  b Discuss the possible reasons why high taxation may not have led to a decrease in the consumption of alcohol and cigarettes. *(5)*

5 Using the example of government provision of training and education in Country B, explain why this is an example of intervention to correct market failure. *(5)*

6 Using information from the text and the concept of social costs and benefits, discuss the development plans for the nuclear power station in Country B. *(7)*

Total: 32 marks

5 The role of government in an economy

Unit 5 examines the part played by a government in the economy. Government roles vary in countries across the world, but all play a major part in that they create a framework against which economic decisions can be made by individual consumers and by individual producers.

Governments have a fundamental responsibility to try to make sure that the economy runs smoothly. In a smoothly running economy there is steady yearly growth in production of useful goods and services. The economy then generates high levels of employment and rising wage levels. At the same time it is essential that the government ensures that general prices of goods and services only rise slowly and that there is not too much inequality of incomes. Governments also play a direct role in the economy as producers of goods and employers of labour, particularly in the provision of public goods.

This unit identifies and explores major government economic policies, and how taxation and subsidy are used in their management. It also looks at the necessity of regulations and the creation of a framework of rules within which a country's economic activity takes place.

> **LEARNING OUTCOMES**
>
> With regard to **the role of government**, candidates should be able to:
>
> - describe the role of government as a producer and employer.
>
> With regard to **government policy**, candidates should be able to:
>
> - describe the policies of full employment, price stability, economic growth, redistribution of income and balance of payments stability
> - discuss possible conflicts between government aims
> - describe types of taxation and their impact.
>
> With regard to **government influence on private producers**, candidates should be able to:
>
> - discuss the influence of government on private producers through regulation, subsidies and taxation.

5.1 The government as a producer and employer

LEARNING OUTCOMES

Candidates should be able to:
- describe the role of government as a producer of goods and services
- describe the role of government as an employer.

Singapore, one of the largest ports in the world. The government plays a significant role in supporting the country's major industries: these include financial services and pharmaceutical and biotechnology businesses

The government as a producer of goods and services

In some countries – Cuba and North Korea, for example – the government plays a major part in owning and running many large industries or important businesses in an industry. In some other countries, such as Singapore, the government owns major holdings of shares in large businesses considered to be of national importance.

CASE STUDY — Cuba

In Cuba between 75 and 90 per cent of people work in government industries – for example, the biotechnology and pharmaceutical industries. Since the 1980s the Cuban government has invested heavily in biotechnology: Cuba's Centre for Genetic Engineering and Biotechnology is the leading research institution in the country and has developed vaccines against hepatitis B, various strains of influenza and the only effective treatment in the world for diabetic foot ulcers. Cuba has set up research poles – that is, centres for pharmaceutical and biotech research – in each of its 12 provinces. Pharmaceuticals bring in nearly US$400 million to the economy each year. Tourism is also an increasingly important industry managed by the government. The sugar and tobacco industries are also important. The government discourages private businesses because it wants to make sure that all Cubans earn similar incomes.

The government is able to ensure that funds are allocated to priority areas like biotechnology, enabling Cuba to be a leading country in pharmaceutical research and production. However, a weakness of government ownership is that there is no scope for enterprising individuals to develop enterprises or to make profits for themselves.

Questions

1. What reasons can you think of for the government taking control of production in some of the industries mentioned in this case study?
2. What benefits and drawbacks to Cuban citizens might result from such a high level of government control?
3. See if you can find out other countries where the government makes lots of economic decisions. Why do you think that the government makes so many of the decisions in the countries you have identified?

EXAM TIP

Make sure that you are able to discuss the various reasons for government intervention. You can use examples from your own economy.

Governments typically take responsibility for production for a number of reasons:

- **To produce essential goods and services.** Some products are regarded as essential – for example, health and education. In Sweden employees pay about 50 per cent of their income in tax to pay for education, health care, care of the elderly and other social service industries provided by local and national government.
- **To supply merit goods. Merit goods** are produced on the basis of individual or society needs rather than ability to pay. Again, these would include health and education services to which everyone is entitled; some governments provide these for all citizens.
- **To supply public goods.** These are goods that the private sector would be reluctant to provide because it is difficult, and often impossible, to get people to pay for them. Examples are road repairs and traffic lights – goods from which everyone benefits but not everyone would be prepared to pay for.
- **To control natural monopolies.** Some industries are **natural monopolies** – such as the supply of water and electricity coming from a huge dam. If this was owned by a private company, it might charge high prices. Government ownership of natural resources can make sure that everyone gets them at a fair price.

The government as an employer

The government is a major employer in all countries. Some people work directly for the government as civil servants – for example, as tax collectors, accountants, passport checkers – or they carry out office work on behalf of the government – for example, producing reports that evaluate recent research. Another group of government employees includes workers in public services such as education and health care. A third group works for state-controlled businesses – for example in Cuba for state-run pharmaceutical companies (see case study), or in Sweden for the national post office service.

Employees in the public sector may have more secure employment because the government can raise the funds through taxes to pay them. Public-sector employees often receive state pensions when they retire. Money earned by government employees will mainly be spent in the national economy.

ACTIVITY

Identify one industry where there is a natural monopoly in your country. Is this industry publicly owned? What benefits are there to citizens from public ownership? Write notes on your findings to compare with others in your group.

EXAM TIP

You may be asked to discuss government intervention in an economy. You will need to consider both the possible advantages and disadvantages of such intervention. A one-sided answer will limit the number of marks you could be awarded.

SUMMARY QUESTIONS

1. Give three examples of public sector production in a country that you are familiar with. In each case explain why production is carried out by the public sector.
2. Why should natural monopolies be owned by the government? Illustrate your answer with examples.
3. What benefits are there to public sector employment?

KEY POINTS

1. In some countries a large percentage of goods is produced by the public sector.
2. The public sector can step in to produce merit goods and public goods that the private sector may not produce.

5.2 Government policy: full employment

LEARNING OUTCOMES

Candidates should be able to:

- describe the aims of the government's policy of full employment.

Villagers in Bihar, India working on a flood protection scheme. The scheme provides work in areas of unemployment while improving the agricultural infrastructure

EXAM TIP

You may be asked to explain what is meant by full employment. You will need to be able to define the term very clearly to gain maximum marks.

Full employment

It might seem that full employment means that everyone has a job. However, at any time people are moving jobs, so there will be an element of temporary unemployment. If everyone was in employment, wages would start to rise and employers would have to compete to attract new employees. Economists therefore define full employment as a situation where most people are in work, but there are enough people out of work to prevent wages from starting to rise at an increasing rate. Employers seeking to recruit new workers can attract them without this leading to a surge in wages in the economy.

The **rate of unemployment** in an economy can be measured as follows:

$$\text{Unemployment rate} = \frac{\text{Number of unemployed}}{\text{Labour force}} \times 100$$

Every month government statistical offices calculate unemployment rate figures. In most countries unemployment rates are higher among younger workers, people with the lowest educational qualifications, minority groups and people in rural areas.

Why the government seeks to achieve full employment

Unemployment wastes resources that could be used to make goods. High levels of unemployment are costly to the government: tax revenues fall and spending on the unemployed increases. Rising levels of unemployment and falling incomes for poorer people can lead to social unrest and rising crime figures.

Labour is the most important resource in the economy. When people are in employment that they enjoy, they feel happier, are able to feed themselves and their families and do not have to rely on the government for handouts. Most people regard full employment as a desirable state.

DID YOU KNOW?

Structural unemployment involves major changes in the industrial structure of a country – some industries decline and others grow. Cyclical unemployment occurs when there is a general decline in demand across the economy.

ACTIVITY

How close to full employment is the economy in which you live? Find out the latest statistics for the unemployment rate. Look at recent newspapers for stories about national, or regional and local, employment. What actions (if any) is the government taking to bring about full employment? Set out your findings in a newspaper report called *Employment Supplement*. This should include facts and figures that would interest employers and general readers of a national newspaper.

Dealing with unemployment

Governments need to identify cures – that is, policies to deal with the different causes of unemployment. These are shown in the table below.

Cause	Possible cures
Temporary	Publicise job vacancies
Seasonal	Not necessarily a problem if employees can find a second job in addition to their seasonal work
Technological	Provide educational and training opportunities focusing on new technical skills required for new jobs
Frictional	Training in job areas where there are shortages of supply; providing more information through government and private labour recruitment agencies about job opportunities – to reduce the period of 'search unemployment'
Structural	Encourage people and businesses to move into growth areas of the economy – regions and occupations
Cyclical, demand-deficient	Government increase in its own spending in times of recession; lower business taxes to reduce costs and encourage employment of more labour

The more serious the type of unemployment, the more it will cost the government to provide a cure. The job creation scheme in Bihar, India (see photo opposite) shows how unemployed people can be given a purpose and earn an income while carrying out work of national importance, in this case a scheme to protect valuable agricultural land from flooding. A similar scheme in Trinidad in the West Indies ensures that roads and verges are kept clean.

Governments need to identify the cause of unemployment (see Unit 6.5) in order to deal with it effectively. If it is a result of job seekers not having enough information about job opportunities, the government can create job centres and job noticeboards, maybe online. If it results from too few workers with the right skills, the government can subsidise or run job creation schemes.

EXAM TIP

There may be a question on unemployment and how to deal with it. You should be able to discuss the various actions that could be taken by a government to reduce the rate of unemployment in a country.

KEY POINTS

1. Full employment occurs when almost everyone who wants a job has one.
2. Economists feel that a small amount of unemployment may be helpful to the economy.
3. The government can use a range of policies to try to create full employment, depending on the type of unemployment.

SUMMARY QUESTIONS

1. How would you define:
   a full employment
   b the unemployment rate?
2. Outline three major problems of not being at the point of full employment.
3. Describe three policy measures that the government can employ to deal with long-term unemployment.

DID YOU KNOW?

The government's main aims in seeking to secure full employment are to:
- maximise the use of resources in the economy
- minimise human suffering, poverty and potential social unrest arising from people being out of work.

5.3 Government policy: price stability

LEARNING OUTCOMES

Candidates should be able to:
- describe the aims of the government policy of price stability.

Rising prices over time are a worry to the government – particularly when there is a general rise in prices, referred to as inflation

Price stability

When prices are stable it is easier for households, businesses and governments to make economic decisions. For example, if savers invest US$100 for a year expecting an interest rate of 5 per cent, they can expect to receive US$105 at the end of the year. If prices remain stable, US$105 at the end of the year should buy more than US$100 at the start of the year.

Inflation can be a major cause of concern for economists. It occurs when there is a general rise in the price of goods and services in the whole economy. Of course, not every price will rise, but average prices will. In many countries, average prices are measured by the government using the **Consumer Price Index** (**CPI**). (This is explained in Unit 6.1.)

Small increases in general prices are not a bad thing. Slowly rising prices encourage producers to supply more goods to the market. However, problems arise if prices start to rise more quickly – for example, above 2 per cent per year – and when the changes in prices are unpredictable. It is in situations like this that prices become unstable.

The unpredictable nature of inflation makes life very difficult for government and business planning. Most businesses sell goods on credit. They supply now, expecting to be paid a given sum at a future date. However, inflation may reduce the value of the sum that is eventually paid. This makes businesses reluctant to supply goods on credit. In a similar way, each year governments set out a **national budget** showing the taxes to be raised for government spending. Inflation will reduce the value of some of the taxes received. A further problem caused by inflation is that when prices of domestic products rise they become less competitive when compared with imports.

The main reason that governments want price stability is to enable accurate planning. Price stability enables businesses to carry out their business with more certainty.

DID YOU KNOW?

General increases in prices within an economy are worrying, particularly if changes are sudden and unpredictable. Economists agree that small and predictable rises can be a good thing because they encourage firms to produce more. For example, in 2010 the UK government target for inflation was 2 per cent. Rises above this would be unsettling for the economy.

EXAM TIP

You need to understand why the government tries to create price stability, such as the types of policies it would use to deal with excessive inflation.

ACTIVITY

What is the current level of inflation in your country? Is it rising or falling? Can prices be described as stable or are they changing in an unpredictable way? Create a short report to present to the class, setting out the implications of price changes in your country. The report should show the impact of price changes for consumers, businesses and the government.

Government policy to create price stability

A **prices and incomes policy** is a set of measures by which the government sets prices and wages to create stability. There are a number of policies that can be implemented:

1. **Direct control** of prices. The government can set prices for goods and impose limits on wage increases for public sector employees. The problems with doing this are that:
   - the price system no longer operates as an efficient system for signalling the preferences of consumers
   - there may be conflict between the government and businesses that want to raise prices, and trade unions that want increases in wages.

2. The government could reduce its own spending and raise taxes in a period of inflation. This would work in the following way:
   - Reduced government spending lowers the demand for goods in the economy, leading to falls in prices.
   - Increased taxes mean that taxpayer incomes fall. They have less to spend, leading to a fall in demand, and a fall in prices.

3. Controlling the **quantity of money** available for spending in the economy. In Unit 1 we saw how the central bank controls the supply of money in the economy, and the interest rate. By printing less money, and raising the cost of borrowing money (raising the interest rate), it is possible to discourage people from borrowing and spending.

The central bank can also impose restrictions on other banks, requiring them to reduce their lending. This then reduces the quantity of money available for spending, which can also reduce price inflation.

EXAM TIP

You need to be able to show that you understand that there may be conflicts between different government objectives. For example, policies to reduce the rate of unemployment in a country could lead to a rise in the rate of inflation.

DID YOU KNOW?

Government management of how much it spends and how much it raises from taxes on people and business is called **fiscal policy**.

KEY POINTS

1. Quickly rising and unpredictable changes in prices unsettle an economy.
2. In periods of inflation, government and business find it more difficult to calculate how much they will receive at future dates from creditors.
3. Inflation makes an economy's goods less competitive.
4. Governments can create price stability through implementing a range of policies.

SUMMARY QUESTIONS

1. What is inflation and how can it make prices unstable?
2. What direct actions can the government take to control prices?
3. How can the government reduce demand in the economy in order to manage prices?

5.4 Government policy: economic growth

LEARNING OUTCOMES

Candidates should be able to:
- describe the aims of the government policy of economic growth.

The hydroelectric power scheme at Three Gorges Dam, China, is an example of government investment to support economic growth

ACTIVITY

Find out from newspapers and the internet the most recent figures for economic growth in the following countries: India, China, Brazil, Russia, the US, Pakistan, Japan, the UK and your own country. Set out these figures in the form of a table.

Economic growth

An essential part of government policy is to grow an economy. Over time an economy needs to be able to provide better living standards, so that people have more goods to consume, more leisure time and better environmental and other living conditions. This is most likely to take place if there is a growth in **Gross Domestic Product** (**GDP**). GDP measures the total value of goods produced in the economy in a given period – usually one year (or a quarter – that is, a three-month period). It is important for a country's economy that the **GDP per head** of population is increasing. It is calculated by dividing the country's GDP by the number of people. More information about GDP can be found in Unit 6.7.

China has one of the fastest-growing economies in recent times. A report by China's National Bureau of Statistics in February 2009 showed how GDP has risen in recent years, as well as the production of major goods. The table shows this growth.

Year	Growth (%)
2004	10.1
2005	10.4
2006	11.6
2007	13.0
2008	9.0

The next table shows the percentage increases of raw materials in finished goods in 2008.

Goods	Percentage increase
Cloth	5.1
Sugar	14.0
TV sets	6.5
Fridges	8.2
Hydroelectric power	20.6
Aluminium	17.0

The government and economic growth

Governments place a very high priority on **economic growth**. Tables are often drawn up ranking countries by GDP per head, and by how fast their economy is growing. Rising GDP per head means that:

- incomes within a country are rising
- the standard of living of people within a country is rising

- the government is able to raise more in taxes and to use this money to meet its objectives, such as providing public goods for citizens.

Government investment in major projects that improve an economy helps to support growth, such as the Three Gorges Dam project in China which supplies huge quantities of electricity.

Sustainable economic growth

Sustainable economic growth occurs when the growth is maintained over a period of time. An important aspect of sustained growth is that there is investment for future generations. Investment can be in roads, ports, railway lines and other parts of the economic infrastructure to make the economy more productive. It can also be social and welfare investment – for example, in schools, hospitals and clinics, providing a healthier and more educated population. Both of these types of investment improve the productive capacity of the economy over time.

The trade cycle

The nature of economic growth is that it does not take place in a steady way. The UK economy experiences periods in which the rate of growth is rising, followed by periods in which the rate of growth falls. In some periods there is even negative growth. The cycle of growth and recession is termed the **trade cycle**.

Most advanced economies have experienced periods of growth and recession in recent years, including an international recession in 2008–9. In a period of recession, spending in the economy falls, as does the output of goods. This leads to reductions in employment. Figure 5.4.3 shows the UK recession, which started in the second quarter of 2008 and ended in the first quarter of 2010.

Government policy is to try to prevent recession, or at least minimise the effects, and to stimulate growth. Growth can be encouraged by:

- making it easier for business to conduct business – for example, by lowering taxes
- providing incentives for businesses to set up in growing industries – for example, wind power energy
- employing people in productive activities in the public sector
- encouraging investment by both the private and public sectors.

EXAM TIP

You may be asked to discuss economic growth, and you will need to be able to contrast its potential advantages and disadvantages.

Figure 5.4.3 The UK recession 2008–9. The vertical axis shows changes in GDP (output) compared with the previous quarter

DID YOU KNOW?

The reverse of a recession is a period of economic growth known as a recovery. Recovery can then lead to a boom, as experienced in India and China in 2010.

KEY POINTS

1. Economic growth is measured by changes in GDP over time.
2. Improving growth increases production, living standards and government revenues.
3. Sustainable growth involves maintaining growth over time.

SUMMARY QUESTIONS

1. Why does the government place importance on economic growth?
2. How does investment help to sustain economic growth?
3. How can the government encourage economic growth?

5.5 Government policy: redistribution of income

LEARNING OUTCOMES

Candidates should be able to:
- describe the aims of the government policy of redistribution of income.

Public distribution system shops in India provide the poor with basic food supplies at subsidised prices

DID YOU KNOW?

The southern Indian state of Kerala has the widest network of public distribution shops of all Indian states. Subsidies from the state government account for 50 per cent of all spending on cereals by the poor.

Inequality and poverty

In all economies there are people with fewer goods and services than others (in **relative poverty**), with some not receiving enough to meet even basic needs (in **absolute poverty**). This **inequality** between rich and poor can mean, for some, high levels of infant mortality, malnutrition, starvation, ill health and low life expectancy. A key government policy in all countries is to redistribute income more equally through society.

However, a study published in the US in 2007 by the economist Emmanuel Saez showed that inequality in the US had achieved an all-time high. The top 0.01 per cent of income earners in the country were taking home 6 per cent of US wages, and the top 10 per cent of wage earners received almost half of all wages. The remaining half of wages was earned by the bottom 90 per cent of wage earners.

ACTIVITY

Find figures that show inequality between high and low wage earners in your country. How do these figures compare with those in the US?

CASE STUDY | Redistribution in India

About a quarter of the population of India is estimated to live in poverty and the Indian government has created a range of measures to redistribute income to the poorest groups. This includes the provision of food subsidies and public goods to rural areas. In the 1950s the Indian government created a public distribution system (PDS) and set up supply depots to provide everyone with basic foods. This system was changed in 1997 to target the poor, so that from that time they were able buy basic foods at half their actual cost. Since 2000 the poorest 15 per cent receive even cheaper food. They are entitled to a maximum of 35 kilograms of wheat and rice at very low prices (about 2 rupees per kg) per month.

The second government redistribution scheme is in the provision of public goods. From the 1970s a Minimum Needs Plan was introduced to provide clean water, schools, health facilities, electricity and roads to rural areas. By 2010 most villages had a primary school and access to electricity and piped water. Over half of Indian villages can now be approached by a paved road. However, there is still a substantial lack of publicly funded health facilities, and in a number of states publicly provided goods are of poor quality (e.g. irregular electricity supply, water supplies that dry up). As a general rule, the greater the GDP of a particular state, the better and more extensive the public goods provision.

Questions

1 In what ways do the two schemes described above illustrate redistribution of income?

2 Who are the principal beneficiaries of these schemes and who will pay for the schemes?

3 Can you identify similar redistribution schemes in your own country? Explain how they work.

What is poverty?

Poverty is usually assessed by a person's income: someone is considered poor if their income falls below the minimum level necessary to meet basic needs. This minimum level is called the **poverty line**, which countries identify in different ways. Information about income is collected by surveying a sample of the population. The World Bank identifies US$1.25 as the poverty line. In 2005 about 1.4 billion people in the developing world (1 in 4) were living on less than this per day. This number is falling, but not as quickly as economists and governments across the world would like.

Redistributing income

Governments can redistribute income through government spending, through subsidies and through taxation (see Unit 7.2).

- **Government spending**. The government can use the money that it receives from taxes and other revenues to spend on goods and services that benefit the poor more than the rich. Examples include roads to remote rural communities, and public education and health systems.
- **Subsidies**. This is where the government pays a sum of money to a consumer or a producer. For example, in India poorest members of the community receive a ration card enabling them to buy food at below cost price from public distribution shops. Alternatively the government could pay a subsidy to a producer so that they can supply it to the market at a lower price – for example, subsidies to rice and wheat farmers.
- **Taxation**. The government can tax the rich and redistribute this income – for example, through spending on public goods.

EXAM TIP

There may be a question about how a government could redistribute income. You would need to be able to discuss the different policies that could be used.

DID YOU KNOW?

Another country committed to reducing poverty is Pakistan, from 26 per cent of the population in 1990 to 13 per cent by 2015. There are many initiatives, such as a food support programme for poor families – the initiative includes the provision of cheap roti (bread), free medicines and educational support for deserving students.

KEY POINTS

1 Redistribution of income involves transferring income or benefits from the rich to the poor.

2 Redistribution can be achieved through taxation, subsidies and spending by the government on public goods.

SUMMARY QUESTIONS

1 Explain two ways in which the government can redistribute income from the rich to the poor.

2 Define *poverty*.

3 What are *public goods*? How can the provision of public goods help to reduce inequalities?

5.6 Government policy: balance of payments stability

LEARNING OUTCOMES

Candidates should be able to:
- describe the aims of the government policy of balance of payments stability.

ACTIVITY

Create a poster setting out the major exports and imports of a well-known country – for example, the US, Japan or South Africa. Use pie charts to illustrate the major types of exports and imports.

DID YOU KNOW?

An *export* is a good or service sold to another country in return for payments. An *import* is a good or service bought from another country. Pakistan exports textiles, rice, wheat and sporting goods to developed countries such as Australia, the US and the UK. It imports petroleum from countries like Saudi Arabia, industrial machinery from Japan and China, and trucks and automobiles from Japan and the US.

The balance of payments

The **balance of payments** is a financial statement that sets out the monetary transactions between a country and the rest of the world in a particular period of time. The most important part of this is the **current account balance** which compares a country's **exports** with its **imports**. Other parts of the balance of payments include capital flows, such as investments in shares in foreign companies, and the running down or building up of foreign currency reserves.

China is the country with the largest balance of payments surplus. Manufactured goods like textiles provide an important component of this surplus

When the value of exports is greater than the value of imports there is a current account surplus, as shown in the table of figures for China in the first half of 2009:

	Credit (thousand US$)	Debit (thousand US$)	Balance (thousand US$)
Trade in goods	521,262,315	402,285,697	118,976,618
Trade in services	54,928,329	71,585,222	−16,656,894
Trade in goods and services	576,190,644	473,870,920	102,319,724

The account shows that China has exported US$118,976,618,000 more of goods than it has imported. In the same period it imported more services than it exported. Overall it exported a lot more than it imported.

This is good for a growing economy. China is supplying large parts of the world with textiles (T-shirts, shirts, suits, dresses, and so on) and manufactured products such as refrigerators and televisions. Exporting these products enables China to earn foreign currency to buy essential raw materials that it needs to develop the country – for example, copper from parts of Africa, oil from Saudi Arabia, and iron and steel from Australia.

Problems of having a deficit balance

If some countries have a surplus in their current accounts, others will run deficits. For example, the World Economic Outlook database (October 2008) showed that the countries with the largest current account deficits were the US (US$731,214 billion), Spain (US$145,141 billion) and the UK (US$105,224 billion).

Having a deficit is not necessarily bad, provided a country is able to attract inflows of capital from countries with a surplus, and a country has a large economy. The problem is more serious if an economy is quite small, such as those of Lithuania and Estonia, which had substantial deficits in 2010.

Creating a balance

In the short term it does not matter if a country has a surplus or deficit on the balance of payments, provided it is not too large. In the longer term the government will seek to make sure that the account balances. In other words, if you have a few years of deficits (because your exports are not competitive enough) you would want to turn this into surpluses in succeeding years, to pay off the deficits.

Deficits may mean that a country is not competitive in the international market. Not enough foreigners want to buy exports from that country. The currency of the country may lose value in international exchange because nobody wants to hold that currency in case it loses further value. Governments need to take action, therefore, to make sure that their economy remains competitive. This might involve:

- providing subsidies to industries, particularly industries that may do well in the future
- protecting the domestic market against foreign imports – for example, by taxing imported products
- encouraging consumers to buy domestically produced products.

You will often read reports in the newspaper about the competitiveness of your country. These reports refer to the ability of your country to sell exports, and the ability of home producers to sell goods in the home market, rather than consumers buying foreign imports.

ACTIVITY

Carry out an internet search for 'List of countries by current account balance'. This will give you a list of countries according to whether they have a surplus (top of the list) or a deficit (bottom of the list). Where does your country fit into this list?

EXAM TIP

You will need to be able to discuss the policies that a government could take to overcome the problem of a balance of payments surplus or deficit.

KEY POINTS

1. The current account of the balance of payments compares export and import values.
2. It is important for a country's industries to be internationally competitive.
3. Governments take action to make sure that in the longer term deficits are covered by surpluses.

SUMMARY QUESTIONS

1. Which country has the largest balance of payments surplus and which the biggest deficit?
2. What are the main components of the current account of the balance of payments?
3. Why does the government try to make sure that deficits are matched by surpluses in the longer term?

5.7 Conflicts between government aims

Conflicting aims

Governments managing their economies often face conflicting policy aims – for example:

- Spending more money to stimulate growth can lead to rising prices, resulting from increased demand. If, however, spending is reduced to cut back the demand that is causing inflation, this will lead to a fall in growth.
- If the government tries to create full employment, labour becomes increasingly scarce. Employers have to compete more strongly to attract labour. They raise wages, which in turn leads to rising wage inflation.
- If the government tries to redistribute income, this may involve taxing richer people at higher rates. Richer workers may feel that they are unfairly penalised for working hard and may decide to migrate: this is the 'brain drain'. This in turn might slow down economic growth.

Trade-offs

The government has to balance its various policy aims. For example, it may have to **trade off**, or accept, a little more unemployment for a little less inflation. Economists may need to fine-tune the economy, creating the best possible balance between policy objectives. **NAIRU** is an example of this. This is the Non-Accelerating Inflation Rate of Unemployment and involves allowing just enough unemployment in the economy to prevent inflation rising above a given target figure. Prices are allowed to increase gradually and some unemployment is tolerated. NAIRU involves living with manageable inflation and acceptable unemployment.

A suitable mix

The government should be trying to achieve:

- a state of almost full employment
- inflation held at a manageable rate – for example, about 2 per cent
- year-by-year sustainable growth of the economy
- the reduction in inequality over time
- international payments balanced so that deficits in some years are balanced by surpluses in others.

Economies need to be quite strong to achieve this. They will probably have a strong resource base that makes them competitive in the world, and a government able to manage the economy carefully.

LEARNING OUTCOMES

Candidates should be able to:
- discuss the possible conflicts between government aims.

Oil and gas fields provide Norway with a healthy balance of payments position. The surplus is invested in a sovereign wealth fund for the future

EXAM TIP

You need to be able to discuss the possible conflicts between different government aims. The more you recognise these, the higher your mark is likely to be.

EXAM TIP

Students sometimes think that examples should always come from the UK. This is not the case. You will be rewarded for the inclusion of appropriate examples from your own country.

Successful economies

Many economies experiencing high rates of GDP growth and those that are rich in resources often have quite high levels of inequality. Not so in Norway!

CASE STUDY | Norway

Norway's natural resources include petroleum, hydro-power, fish, forests and minerals. The oil and gas industry accounts for over 30 per cent of exports and Norway runs a surplus in most years on its balance of payments. The government controls the petroleum sector through large-scale enterprises, owning the majority of shares. Because oil and gas reserves will eventually run out, the government saves almost all state revenue from this sector in a sovereign wealth fund (a reserve owned by the government for the nation). From 2004 to 2007 the economy grew at between 2.5 and 6.2 per cent, but moved into recession in 2008–9. The country was one of the first in Europe to move out of recession in late 2009. The government used some of the sovereign wealth fund to increase spending to get the economy growing again. Norway uses the 'Nordic economic and social model': taxes are high, to pay for a large welfare state, spending on schools, hospitals and care for the elderly. There is almost full employment, and there is a strong emphasis on redistribution to create gender and other forms of equality. In 2009 and 2010 inflation averaged about 2 per cent.

Questions

1 Describe the Norwegian economy in terms of:
   a the level of employment
   b the rate of growth
   c redistribution of income
   d inflation.
2 What is the importance of the oil industry, and of the sovereign wealth fund, to Norway's prosperity?
3 See if you can find out (for example, in the World Factbook) the most recent annual figure for GDP annual growth, the inflation rate and the balance of payments on current account for Norway.

SUMMARY QUESTIONS

1 Explain how the policy objectives of full employment and low inflation may clash.
2 Do high growth rates always lead to the increased redistribution of income?
3 What is NAIRU and why is it desirable?

EXAM TIP

You will need to demonstrate that you understand that it would be very difficult, if not impossible, to achieve success in all of these policy objectives at the same time. There will, therefore, be an opportunity cost of taking one set of decisions rather than another.

DID YOU KNOW?

The Nordic model is used by Norway, Sweden, Denmark and Finland, made up of a mixed market economy with a generous welfare state. This model may be difficult to finance in periods of recession: the economy of Finland suffered badly in the crisis of 2008–9, leading to rapidly growing unemployment and rising government debt.

KEY POINTS

1 There is often a clash between policy aims (e.g. full employment and low inflation).
2 The government needs to trade off and balance its five main economic policy objectives.

5.8 Types of taxation

LEARNING OUTCOMES

Candidates should be able to:
- describe types of taxes and their impact.

Progressive taxes are ones that redistribute income from the rich to the poor

EXAM TIP

You need to be able to discuss in the examination the various reasons why governments impose taxes.

Reasons for taxing

A tax is a payment made by individuals or businesses to the government. The government imposes taxes for various reasons:

- **To raise revenue**. The earliest taxes were raised by governments to pay for the expenses of the rulers of a country and to finance wars. Today, taxes are levied to raise money to cover a range of government expenditures – for example, on building schools, hospitals and roads, paying for defence and a police force.
- **To discourage certain activities** – for example, those that some see as antisocial in terms of the damage to health and pollution that they cause, such as smoking or driving. So cigarettes, cars and fuel may be heavily taxed.
- **To discourage the import of goods**. Import taxes are referred to as **tariffs**. They can be levied as a percentage of the value of imports (an *ad valorem* **tax**) or a set tax on each item imported (a **specific tax**).
- **To redistribute income from the rich to the poor**.

Direct and indirect taxes

Economists make a distinction between:

- **direct taxes**, for which the burden falls on the person paying it – for example, when you pay income tax it is taken directly from your wages and paid to the government
- **indirect taxes**, which are imposed by government on goods and services, but are eventually paid by consumers rather than by the businesses that collect the tax for the government in the first instance.

DID YOU KNOW?

The payer of a direct tax has no choice about whether they pay the tax. In contrast, consumers can choose to buy a good with a tax on it or not. Because of this element of choice, some people believe that the government should rely more on indirect than direct taxes.

Progressive, regressive and proportional taxes

If income is going to be redistributed then the rich need to pay more in tax than the poor.

Progressive tax takes a greater proportion of income from a wealthy person than from a poor person. So someone earning

US$5,000 a year might pay 5 per cent of this in tax, a person earning US$10,000 would pay 15 per cent and a person earning US$20,000 would pay 30 per cent.

A **regressive tax** is one where the poor pay a higher percentage of their income in tax than the rich. This happens when the government imposes a tax at a set rate. For example, a person may pay US$20 for a licence to fish in a river, and US$100 a year to tax their car, or pay some other set rate tax. You can see that US$20 would be a higher percentage for a poor person to pay than a wealthy person.

Progressive taxes redistribute income in favour of the poor. Regressive taxes redistribute income in favour of the rich.

Proportional tax refers to a situation in which tax rises in proportion to the income of the taxpayer.

Figure 5.8.1 shows the relationship between income and the percentage of tax taken.

Figure 5.8.1 The relationship between income and the percentage of tax taken

Common taxes

Taxes that are common to most countries include the following:

- **A tax on incomes**. This is often a progressive tax. Higher-income earners pay a larger percentage of income in tax. It is a direct tax.
- **A tax on purchasing**. An example of this is value added tax. Producers and sellers of goods pay the tax to the government as a percentage of the value they add in the production of an item. The shop then makes the customer pay the tax. The tax is thus indirect. If the government taxes goods that are bought by the rich more than those bought by the poor, the purchase tax system would be progressive.
- **A tax on company profits**. This is a direct tax. The government can make it progressive by increasing the rate as profits increase.
- **Taxes on imports**. These are indirect, as they are passed on to consumers.
- **Taxes on specific products** – for example, cigarettes, alcohol, petrol, etc. These are indirect. They may be regressive if they hit the poor harder than the rich.

EXAM TIP

Questions in the examination on different types of taxation often require you to include appropriate examples of particular taxes.

SUMMARY QUESTIONS

1 Identify three types of indirect tax. Who pays indirect taxes? Who collects them?
2 Why might progressive taxes be fairer than regressive taxes?
3 What is the difference between an *ad valorem* (percentage) tax and a specific tax? Give an example of an *ad valorem* tax.

KEY POINTS

1 Direct taxes are paid directly to the government. Indirect taxes are paid through an intermediary rather than the person on whom the burden of the tax falls.
2 Progressive taxes are designed to place a greater burden on the rich than on the poor.

5.9 Government influence on private producers: regulation

LEARNING OUTCOMES

Candidates should be able to:

- discuss the government's influence of private producers through regulation.

Environmental regulations are very important. For example, there are rules about what type of waste can enter water systems. Firms can be fined for failing to comply with these regulations

DID YOU KNOW?

Some economists are in favour of more regulation to limit the externalities (social costs of business activity) and other market failures. Others believe that there is too much regulation, limiting the ability of the free market to supply goods that meet customer needs. These economists think that too much regulation raises costs and leads to inefficiency.

Regulation

Regulations are rules. They can be rules imposed by a government, backed up by penalties. In the world of business, the aim of regulations is to influence the behaviour of firms and individuals in the private sector. For example, government regulations cover who can set up a bank, how much the bank is allowed to lend and even the amount of interest the bank is allowed to charge for loans. The table shows some of the areas covered by regulations.

Area covered by regulation	Examples
Methods of production	Management of waste and pollution, rules protecting the health and safety of production workers (e.g. wearing of safety protection equipment)
Setting up a new business	Paperwork to be filled in to register the business, rules protecting shareholders, filing of tax returns
Rules about prices	Prices that can be charged for supplying certain products (e.g. agricultural products, minimum wage rules)
Product standards	Quality of food products, labelling of contents of a product
Disclosure of information	Information that companies must produce in reports to shareholders, information about how certain products can be used
Providing goods on credit	Information that must be given about the cost of the credit to the borrower, rules setting out the possibility of the borrower pulling out of a credit agreement
Providers of certain products and services	Who can supply certain products, such as repairs to gas pipes, building construction
Supply of harmful products	Health warnings on cigarettes

Regulations can be in the form of laws governing the actions of private firms and individuals. They can also be created by granting licences and permits to firms that meet certain conditions. Inspection by qualified inspectors can then make sure that the businesses are complying with the regulations. Failure to do so can mean fines or loss of the licence.

The benefits of regulation

Governments use regulation to improve efficiency. Regulations are also used to redistribute income.

Governments regulate firms and industry where there are monopoly powers. Monopolists may restrict output or artificially raise prices. There are many regulations covering anti-competitive practices by firms, such as a group of suppliers jointly fixing prices. Governments also use regulations to limit the effect of externalities, such as where pollution is created in production – for example, regulations covering carbon emissions by vehicles – and production processes.

Some industries involve a high level of regulation, e.g. the banking sector, the oil industry, and pharmaceuticals. These industries need to be carefully controlled in the public interest.

Regulation makes it possible to strike a balance between private firms seeking to make a profit and the interests of the people who use their services and the wider public.

The disadvantages of regulations

Regulations usually raise business costs and can involve a lot of time. To comply with regulations a business must:

- learn the regulations that relate to it
- fill in all the paperwork relating to the regulations
- create systems and methods that fit with the regulations.

Some business people complain that they are over-regulated. They mean that they have to spend so much time and money complying with the regulations that they cannot concentrate on running their business.

Countries with a greater number and complexity of regulations lose competitiveness because of the cost of complying with the regulations. However, these countries also gain a competitive advantage because their standards – for example, product standards – may be higher than those of competitors.

> **EXAM TIP**
>
> You may be asked to discuss regulations. Try to refer to both their advantages and disadvantages and give a balanced perspective on their importance.

> **ACTIVITY**
>
> Study the World Bank's Doing Business database (**www.doingbusiness.org**). The World Bank collects data from most countries, setting out the costs of regulation in certain areas, such as setting up a business and getting credit. Where does your country rank in terms of the number of regulations that it has? How does this compare with a neighbouring country?

> **DID YOU KNOW?**
>
> Some economists believe that governments regulate too much. They believe that every regulation imposes a cost of compliance and that these costs are greater than the benefits they create.

> **KEY POINTS**
>
> 1. Regulations are rules imposed by government backed up by penalties.
> 2. Regulations are designed to modify the behaviour of businesses and individuals in ways that benefit society.
> 3. Regulations can impose costs and time burdens on private businesses.

> **SUMMARY QUESTIONS**
>
> 1. Identify three different business activities that are regulated by governments. In each case give an example of a regulation.
> 2. Who benefits from government regulation? Illustrate your answer by focusing on a specific regulation.
> 3. What are some of the disadvantages of high levels of regulation?

5.10 Government influence on private producers: subsidy

LEARNING OUTCOMES

Candidates should be able to:

- discuss the government's influence on private producers through subsidies.

The government has given smallholders in Malawi subsidies in the form of vouchers to buy seeds and fertiliser, and they have been able to raise production of agricultural products

Subsidies

Most subsidies are sums of money provided by the government to a producer or supplier for a specific purpose. They may be provided for several reasons:

- **To encourage the production of goods of national importance**. For example, the government may provide subsidies to farmers to produce essential food supplies. The subsidy guarantees an income to the farmer.
- **To encourage the development of new products and industries**. In the short term these products and industries may be uncompetitive, resulting in losses being made by private producers. For example, in many countries the government provides subsidies to encourage the development of new forms of energy, such as wind and solar power.
- **To provide support for industries that are in decline and that are major employers of labour**. If the industry did not receive a subsidy it might not make a profit. Closing the industry could have negative externalities, such as unemployment, which would result in the government having to make unemployment payments to those out of work. The subsidy is thus both socially desirable and economically sound from the government's point of view.
- **To protect domestic industries against foreign competition**. The subsidy has the same effect as lowering the cost to the supplier.

DID YOU KNOW?

In recent years governments in many countries have given subsidies to householders to introduce energy-efficient products in their houses (e.g. part payments to install loft insulation, solar panels and energy-efficient light bulbs).

EXAM TIP

You need to be able to discuss the potential usefulness of subsidies. This means that you need to be aware of both potential advantages and disadvantages.

In addition to the subsidies listed above there are some additional subsidies to consumers to enable them to make purchases. For example, Unit 5.5 gave the example of food subsidies given to poor households in India to purchase essential food supplies.

Illustrating the effect of subsidising a supplier

When a supplier receives a subsidy it will be encouraged to produce more for the market. This leads to a shift to the right of the supply curve. When the supply curve shifts to the right this leads to an increased supply at lower prices. Figure 5.10.1 shows that a subsidy of 10 cents per unit supplied has led to an increase in supply from S to S1. The quantity supplied has increased from Q to Q1.

Of course, a subsidy does not always lead to an increase in supply. For example, in a loss-making industry the more likely effect will be to stop supply from falling rather than leading to its increase.

Figure 5.10.1 Increase in supply resulting from a 10 cent subsidy

CASE STUDY: Subsidies to smallholder farmers in Malawi

In 2005 Malawi had a severe famine, following a lack of rain, and 40 per cent of the population needed food aid. In contrast, by 2007 Malawi had become a net maize exporter. Increased rains have helped, but perhaps more important has been the provision of government subsidies for seeds and fertiliser.

Eighty per cent of all Malawians are smallholder farmers. The farmers were given vouchers by the government enabling them to buy fertiliser and seeds at one-third of the market cost. The farmers have to make a contribution to the cost of the fertiliser and seed rather than being given it. The results have been excellent, with the yield per hectare increasing from an average of about 1.2 tonnes per hectare to 2.2 tonnes per hectare. The government has also started to distribute vouchers for pesticides.

Questions

1 Explain how the subsidies will have affected production of crops.
2 Why might it be better to give farmers vouchers rather than cash subsidies?
3 Draw a diagram to show the impact of the subsidy on the supply curve and market quantity of crops produce on the smallholdings.

ACTIVITY

Carry out research using a national newspaper to find examples of subsidies provided in your country. Who receives the subsidies, and why?

KEY POINTS

1 Subsidies are incentives provided by the government to individuals and households in order to carry out desired activities.
2 Subsidies are granted to support declining industries, to produce essential products and to protect domestic industries.
3 The effect of a subsidy is to push the supply curve to the right.

SUMMARY QUESTIONS

1 What would be the effect of subsiding producers in a declining industry?
2 What would be the effect of subsidising producers in a new and growing industry?
3 Why are subsidies sometimes given to consumers?

5.11 Government influence on private producers: taxes

LEARNING OUTCOMES

Candidates should be able to:

- discuss the government's influence on private producers through taxes.

Figure 5.11.1 Taxes on fuel in many countries are high. The incidence of the tax falls mainly on motorists

PETROL
Duty 90¢
Product 50¢
VAT 30¢
Retailer delivery 10¢

DID YOU KNOW?

Corporation tax is a tax on company profits. The higher the tax, the less profit available to return to shareholders and to reinvest in the business.

Taxes

Taxes act in the opposite way to subsidies. The government can use them to discourage certain activities as well as to raise revenue. However, if it sets a tax rate too high it can discourage some desirable business activity. For example, in February 2010 Unilever, one of the world's largest producers of household goods, threatened to move its manufacturing operations away from Britain because of high tax rates. The chief executive said: 'We ... have choices where we put research laboratories ... manufacturing facilities and ... where we put senior management.' At that time Unilever employed 174,000 workers around the world, with 9,000 of these in the UK. Corporation taxes in Britain then were 28 per cent compared with 15 per cent in Germany and 12.5 per cent in Ireland.

The incidence of sales taxes and price elasticity of demand

The price elasticity of demand for a product determines how much revenue the government is able to collect from **indirect sales taxes**. When a sales tax is increased, the supply curve of a good shifts to the left. The sales tax acts as a cost to a business. The supply curve shifts upwards by the amount of the tax.

Figure 5.11.2 compares an increase in a sales tax by the same amount for a good with an elastic demand curve, and for one with an inelastic demand curve.

Figure 5.11.2a (product with elastic demand) shows that the increase in the sales tax leads to a relatively large fall in the quantity demanded (Q to Q1), compared with the impact of the sales tax shown in Figure 5.11.2b (product with inelastic demand).

Figure 5.11.2 The incidence of a sales tax with (a) elastic demand (b) inelastic demand

The diagrams also show how much of the tax will be paid by the seller and how much by the customer. **Incidence of tax** refers to who pays the major part of the tax. In Figure 5.11.2a the incidence of the tax falls mainly on the seller. This is because the total amount of tax that will have to be paid is P1ACD. Out of this the consumer pays PP1AB – that is, the increase in price from P to P1 multiplied by the quantity now traded in the market 0Q1. The seller has to pay the rest of the tax DPBC.

If demand is elastic, sellers will of course be able to raise their prices only a little.

In contrast, in Figure 5.11.2b, with inelastic demand the size of the rectangle DPBC (the incidence of the tax to the seller) is much smaller than PP1AB (the incidence of the tax to the buyer). If demand is inelastic, sellers are of course much better placed to shift the incidence of the tax to the buyer.

Where knowledge of elasticity is useful

Knowledge of elasticity and the impact on indirect taxes helps the government to set tax rates for VAT and other sales taxes. It also helps governments to decide how much import taxes they can charge to discourage imports.

The government should also consider elasticity in tax levels for licences – for example, car licences – waste and pollution charges, and local business taxes.

Imposing taxes that are too high can lead to:

- falling sales and falling incomes – and hence rising unemployment as workers are laid off and businesses close
- an incentive for businesses and individuals to avoid paying taxes, leading to an 'undercover' economy involving tax evasion.

Effective taxes

Effective taxes should focus on producing desirable goods and services and discourage businesses from carrying out undesirable activities. They should not discourage effort and initiative. They should also provide suitable revenues for the government. Effectively designed tax systems should create a good relationship between government and private producers. They should be simple to operate and understand, and not need excessive form-filling by taxpayers.

SUMMARY QUESTIONS

1 Give three reasons why the government taxes private producers.

2 When the government imposes a sales tax on a good with an inelastic demand, who does the bulk of the incidence of the tax fall upon? Explain why.

3 What are the dangers of making taxes on private producers too high?

EXAM TIP

Make sure that you understand incidence of tax. This indicates precisely who is paying particular parts of a tax.

EXAM TIP

Price elasticity of demand is a very important concept in economics. Its role in relation to indirect taxation is a good example of how it can be usefully applied.

DID YOU KNOW?

Goods with inelastic demand, which many governments tax at quite a high rate, include cigarettes and petrol. The incidence of these taxes then falls largely on consumers.

KEY POINTS

1 Taxes should be designed to support government objectives without discouraging effort and initiative.

2 Taxes are seen as a cost to business.

3 The incidence of sales taxes depends on the price elasticity of demand for the product being sold.

Unit 5 — Practice exam questions

SECTION 1: Multiple-choice questions

Each question has ONE correct answer.

1. Why might a government take responsibility for production in an economy?
   a. To make a profit
   b. To widen consumer choice
   c. To supply merit goods
   d. To supply demerit goods

2. Which of the following is a public sector employee?
   a. A bank cashier
   b. A taxi driver
   c. A private school teacher
   d. A tax collector

3. What may be a disadvantage of a high rate of economic growth for a government?
   a. Increasing rate of employment
   b. Increasing tax revenues
   c. Increasing risk of inflation
   d. Increasing wages

4. Which of the following is NOT a method governments may use to decrease unemployment?
   a. Increase unemployment benefit
   b. Reduce the rate of interest
   c. Introduce worker training schemes
   d. Reduce corporation tax

5. Which of the following policies might be used to control inflation?
   a. Increase government spending
   b. Increase interest rates
   c. Increase the money supply
   d. Decrease direct taxation

6. Which of the following is NOT an example of fiscal policy?
   a. Provision of merit goods
   b. Taxation on polluting businesses
   c. Lowering interest rates
   d. Progressive income tax

7. What might be a government method of income redistribution?
   a. Environmental taxation
   b. Control of the supply of money
   c. Regressive sales tax
   d. Progressive direct taxation

8. Which of the following would indicate a balance of payments deficit on a current account?
   a. Revenue from taxation greater than government spending
   b. Value of imports greater than value of exports
   c. Government spending greater than revenue from taxation
   d. Value of exports greater than value of imports

9. Which of the following is NOT an example of a government regulation on business?
   a. Display of health warnings on cigarettes
   b. Payment of minimum wage
   c. Display of information on food labels
   d. Payment of income tax

10. A government may seek to limit monopoly power of a big company because:
    a. They benefit from economies of scale
    b. They use up many resources
    c. They may exploit consumers
    d. They pay higher wages to workers

SECTION 2: Structured questions

Country A is a medium-sized nation, whose economy has been growing at an average rate of 5 per cent per year for the last five years. The population is growing at around 3 per cent per year and unemployment is low, and falling. Out of a total workforce of 12 million citizens, only 600,000 people are currently recorded as unemployed and seeking work. Incomes and prices are rising and the consumers of Country B are increasingly demanding imported products. The government of Country B has the following economic objectives for the next few years:

- Inflation to be low, at a maximum of 3 per cent per year
- Economic growth steady at 4 per cent
- Maintain a balance of payments current account surplus
- Redistribute income in order to help the poorest families

1 a Explain why the government of Country B may have set the objective of low inflation. *(4)*

b Explain, with the use of a diagram, why inflation in Country A may increase due to higher wages. *(6)*

c Suggest ONE policy the government of Country A may implement to control inflation. *(4)*

d Discuss whether measures to control inflation may have other negative consequences for the economy of Country A. *(6)*

2 a Using information in the text, calculate the unemployment rate for Country A. *(4)*

b Why might rising GDP lead to falling unemployment in Country A? *(4)*

c With the help of a diagram, explain why falling unemployment may lead to increasing inflation in Country A. *(6)*

d Discuss the extent to which 'full employment' may be a major objective for the government of Country A. *(6)*

3 a The government of Country A would like to redistribute income to help those on lower incomes. Explain why a government may have this objective. *(4)*

b Explain how a *progressive* tax system may help to redistribute income. Give an example. *(6)*

c The government of Country A subsidises the production of basic foodstuffs, such as milk and bread. Using a diagram, show how this may affect production levels and prices. *(4)*

d Discuss the ADVANTAGES and DISADVANTAGES of taxing higher-income earners at a higher rate to help pay for benefits for unemployed people in Country A. *(6)*

4 a Explain what is meant by a *balance of payments current account surplus*. *(3)*

b Explain why rising incomes may lead to higher demand for imported goods. *(3)*

c Suggest TWO ways in which the government of Country A may protect domestic firms from foreign competition. *(6)*

d Considering the case study information and economic objectives of Country A, discuss the extent to which these aims may conflict with each other in the short term. *(8)*

Total: 80 marks

SECTION 3: Analysis and critical evaluation

Cool Pops is a private sector soft drinks producer and distributor in Country A. The company's traditional products are low-priced, flavoured fizzy drinks, such as lemonade and cola. Profits have been steady in past years, although a large percentage goes to the government in corporation tax. Cool Pops has relied on being the government-licensed monopoly seller of soft drinks in Country A, but is now facing major competition from imported brands, especially light versions of fizzy drinks and fruit juice-based products. The managing director of Cool Pops would like support from the government to help develop a range of new drinks and prevent the company from going out of business, with the loss of thousands of jobs. He has put a proposal to the government for financial support as follows:

- Cool Pops will continue to produce the traditional products and sell them at low prices, in order to satisfy demand from low-income consumers.
- Cool Pops will open a new factory in a rural area, where a substantial number of the population are unemployed.
- Cool Pops will develop a new range of healthier soft drinks, which will enable the company to compete with imported brands.
- Cool Pops will look for new markets outside Country A, specifically within two neighbouring countries, whose populations have similar tastes.

1 a Explain what is meant by a *monopoly seller*. (2)
  b Explain why a monopoly seller may be able to charge high prices to consumers. (2)

2 a Suggest ONE way in which imported products may threaten the Cool Pops market share. (2)
  b Illustrate your example for 2a with a supply and demand diagram showing the changes in price and quantity. (2)

3 Discuss how the high percentage of corporation tax payable may have affected Cool Pops' ability to develop new products. (5)

4 a Explain, using a diagram, why falling demand for Cool Pops' products may lead to job losses. (2)
  b Discuss the possible reasons why the government of Country A may decide to support the Cool Pops company. (5)

5 Explain why government support for Cool Pops may be seen as protectionist in this case. (5)

6 Using information from the text, discuss to what extent government support may guarantee the survival of Cool Pops in the long term. (7)

Total: 32 marks

6 Economic indicators

Unit 6 explains how economic indicators provide good measures of major changes taking place in economies, showing how quickly an economy is growing and indicating possible problems, such as rising prices and unemployment.

The unit explains how indicators such as the Retail Price Index are used to decide policies, such as setting the rate of interest, and points out that businesses and trade unions use these as a basis for setting wage increases. Reference is made to charts that show how governments use indicators, such as numbers employed, as a basis for devising policies that will attempt to create jobs.

The material in Unit 6 also shows how some indicators, such as Gross Domestic Product and the Human Development Index, move in the same direction as the economy, while others, such as unemployment, move in the opposite direction to the economy.

LEARNING OUTCOMES

With regard to **prices**, candidates should be able to:
- describe how the Retail Price Index is calculated
- discuss causes and consequences of inflation.

With regard to **employment**, candidates should be able to:
- describe changing patterns and levels of employment
- discuss causes and consequences of unemployment.

With regard to **output**, candidates should be able to:
- define Gross Domestic Product (GDP)
- describe simple measures and indicators of comparative living standards, such as GDP per head, and the Human Development Index (HDI).

6.1 The Retail Price Index

LEARNING OUTCOMES

With regard to **prices**, candidates should be able to:

- describe how the Retail Price Index is calculated.

Average prices are measured by governments using the **Retail Price Index (RPI)** or the **Consumer Price Index (CPI)**. This index measures changes in average prices over a year. Measurements are made by recording prices of goods and services that most people will be expected to buy, or put in an imaginary shopping basket. Government statisticians decide what goods to include in this basket. This list should be updated to take account of changing spending patterns.

Most governments measure prices in similar ways. This unit uses the example of Kenya. The examples show some of the difficulties involved in accurately measuring average price changes.

A basket of goods

The imaginary shopping basket for a typical family in Kenya contains, for example, milk, bottled water, sugar, tea, meat, cooking fuel, school books and mobile phone charges. The contents included in the basket are fixed in the short term, but the prices of individual goods change.

Shopping in a supermarket in Kenya. The Consumer Price Index (CPI) measures general increases in the prices of a basket of goods. Changes in food prices are particularly important in Kenya as this is the largest item of household expenditure (and how these prices change over time)

DID YOU KNOW?

Food prices (especially for rice, maize, flour and coffee) have a prominent weighting in the price index in Kenya. When they rise, this will have a major impact on inflation as measured by the price index.

Figure 6.1.1 A helpful way of thinking about the price index is to imagine the contents of a shopping basket bought by a typical household

A price index uses a single number to indicate changes in prices of a number of different goods. This is calculated by comparing the price of buying the basket of goods with a starting period, called the **base year**. The base year is given a figure of 100. So if the average price of goods in the basket today is 10 per cent higher than the base year, the price index will be 110. Changes in average prices (the cost of the basket of goods) can be measured on a monthly, quarterly or annual basis.

Inflation

Inflation is a persistent or sustained rise in the general level of prices over a period of time. So not every price will rise, but average prices will. The effect of this rise on ordinary people will vary, depending on what they buy.

Price inflation in Kenya is measured by the Kenya National Bureau of Statistics (KNBS). One of its responsibilities is to decide on the 221 goods and services to be included in the price index, or 'basket'. The selection is made after carrying out a survey of spending patterns – that is, what most people in Kenya are buying. From time to time the items in the basket will change: in 2010 the basket was 'widened' to include internet charges, computers and primary and secondary school transport fees.

Statistics covering the prices of all items in the CPI are gathered each month in 10 areas of the capital, Nairobi, and 15 other price collection zones across Kenya selected for their high expenditure levels.

Weighting

The weighting is a figure given to a category of goods according to the percentage of a typical household's income that is spent on it. Statisticians have found that typical families in Kenya spend 40 per cent of their income on food, so this is given a weighting of 40 per cent in the price index.

> **EXAM TIP**
>
> The examination may require you to define inflation, so make sure you are able to give a full and accurate definition.

> **DID YOU KNOW?**
>
> The 'average annual' rate of inflation is computed as a percentage change of a twelve-month average of the CPI. The 'year-on-year' inflation rate is calculated as a percentage change of the CPI between the current month (e.g. April 2011) and the same month a year ago (e.g. April 2010).

CASE STUDY | Rising inflation in Kenya

In 2008, inflation rose sharply in Kenya, largely as a result of rising food prices. The overall annual average inflation was 26.2 per cent, compared to 9.8 per cent in 2007. The main causes of this were:

- an increase in average food prices of 37.5 per cent
- an increase in average oil prices of 18 per cent.

Questions

1 What effect do you think that a rate of inflation of 26.2 per cent is likely to have on people in Kenya?

2 Why do you think that changes in food prices are so important to people living in Kenya?

3 Are some Kenyans likely to have been more affected than others by the high inflation figure? Explain how.

4 Suggest a way of measuring inflation in Kenya.

> **DID YOU KNOW?**
>
> From time to time, weighting of items in the basket needs to be adjusted. For example, more frequent use of mobile phones in Kenya between 1993–4 and 2005–6 meant that the weight attached to spending on mobile phone use was increased from 5.75 to 12.7 per cent.

Calculating average price changes

Calculating average price changes will give the rate of inflation. The calculation involves two sets of data:

- The price data (collected each month).
- The weights (representing patterns of spending, updated each year).

With this data it is possible to construct a weighted price index. A consumer spending survey has been carried out that shows the percentage spend of typical households in an imaginary country. The table on the left shows how the percentage spend forms the basis of the weighting given to the categories.

Category	Percentage spend	Weight
Food	40	4
Clothing	20	2
Transport	10	1
Other household goods	30	3
Total	100	10

The weighting for food is twice that for clothing because typical households spend twice as much on food as on clothes

The next stage is to identify price changes in each of these product categories. Let us suppose that surveys carried out in supermarkets, shops and other retail outlets across the country show the following changes since the base year:

- Food prices have increased by 20 per cent.
- Clothing has increased by 10 per cent.
- Transport has fallen by 10 per cent.
- Other household goods have increased by 30 per cent.

To find out the **average change in price** we need to take account of each of these price changes in terms of how much consumers spend on that item (the weight). For example, the increase in food prices of 20 per cent will have a major impact on average prices because 40 per cent of household income is spent on food. In contrast, even though transport prices have fallen by 10 per cent, this will have a smaller impact on average prices because consumers only spend a tenth of their income on transport.

To create a **weighted price index** we need to multiply the weight for each item by the price index for that item. This is shown in the table below.

Product category	Weight price index	Weighted price index
Food	4 × 120	= 480
Clothing	2 × 110	= 220
Transport	1 × 90	= 90
Other goods	3 × 130	= 390
Total		1180

Finally, divide the weighted price index by the total number of weights:

$$\frac{1180}{10} = 118$$

This shows that prices have risen on average by 18 per cent (i.e. from the base year figure of 100 to 118 in the new year).

> **EXAM TIP**
>
> Make sure you understand this difference: the price index shows how much the price of that item has risen by compared with a base year of 100; the weighted price index shows the price index times the weight attached to the product category.

Problems involved in using a price index

The price index is designed to show general increases in prices and how they affect consumers. There can be some problems, however, with its use as an indicator:

- The index does not necessarily show how price changes affect typical consumers. For example, in Kenya the weighting attached to food in the index was reduced from 50 per cent to 40 per cent. However, food purchases for a poor person in Kenya may make up 80 per cent or more of their spending.
- The index makes comparisons with a base year. However, if prices were low at the base year, the comparison may exaggerate the price rise. If prices were high at the base year, the index comparison may suggest that subsequent price changes have been low (especially if the base year is at the top or bottom of the trade cycle fluctuation).
- Some items, for example fuel and food, are subject to quite a lot of variation.

For indicators to provide useful information, it is essential that the statistics gathered are accurate.

> **DID YOU KNOW?**
> In Kenya separate indexes are calculated for low-income households and medium- to high-income households in recognition of the way that they purchase different baskets of goods each week.

> **ACTIVITY**
> Working in a group, find out the monthly inflation rate of your country, or a large country in your part of the world. You should find this information published each month by your national statistical office. With your teacher's help, try to find the rate on the internet or in a national newspaper. Plot the current rate on a large chart and display this in your classroom to monitor ongoing changes. Then try to find the inflation rate of another country and compare it with your own.

> **KEY POINTS**
> 1. Inflation is a persistent or sustained rise in the general level of prices over a period of time.
> 2. A price index can be used to measure price increases by reducing prices to a single number starting at 100 in a base year.
> 3. The price index measures changes in an average basket of goods bought by a typical consumer or family.
> 4. Weighting items in the basket makes it possible to take account of the relative importance of spending on different items when measuring average price changes.

> **SUMMARY QUESTIONS**
> 1. What items are likely to be included in a basket of goods bought by a typical consumer in your country? Which categories of items should be given the greatest weights?
> 2. What two sets of data are required to calculate a CPI?
> 3. Why is it necessary periodically to alter the list of items included in a country's 'shopping basket' of items included in the CPI?

6.2 Causes of inflation

LEARNING OUTCOMES

With regard to **prices**, candidates should be able to:

• discuss causes of inflation.

Causes of inflation

A cause is a factor that has an effect on something else. For example, a cause of inflation might be that people increase the amount of money they spend. The effect might be an increase in prices.

Inflation is usually the result of a number of causes. It may occur when a number of prices rise at the same time, say for oil, food and housing or rented accommodation.

In examining inflation, economists distinguish between **cost-push** and **demand-pull** factors. These are explained below.

Cost-push factors

Cost-push refers to the costs that a business has to meet, such as wages and raw materials. As costs rise, the business will often pass these on to consumers by increasing the prices for the product they are selling.

Food costs

In the previous Unit we saw that 40 per cent of the weighting in Kenya's Consumer Price Index (CPI) is allocated to food. In the years 2000–10 the food supply in Kenya has been badly affected by droughts in the north of the country.

At the same time, the price of basic foodstuffs, including the price of cereal crops on global markets, has been increasing. There is increased competition for cereal crops as a result of the growth of huge economies like China and India, and also as a result of cereals being used as alternative **biofuels**. Whatever the cause, high food prices lead to higher costs for other businesses.

Raw material costs

Despite the world recession in 2008 and 2009, the costs of raw materials such as steel, copper, oil and gas have risen. These raw materials are at the centre of modern economies, so as their prices rise, there is an effect on many other prices.

Wage costs

Wage costs are another major cause of cost-push inflation. If food and fuel prices rise for workers in Kenya, they will press their employers for higher wages. If, however, the wage increase is not matched by higher labour productivity, in other words, if the workers do not produce more goods to sell, production costs will rise.

Land costs

Land prices in many countries have risen as land is used more intensively. For example, the Ethiopian government has granted

Rising oil and energy costs are a major cause of cost-push inflation that affects many businesses across an economy

EXAM TIP

In the examination, you need to show that you understand that inflation can be the result of more than one cause.

long-term leases to overseas companies to use land for large-scale agricultural production of grain and other crops. Land is also increasingly being used for housing as the world population increases. This leads to land price inflation.

Exchange rate costs

Changes in the exchange rate between currencies can have a major impact on business costs. For example, if the Kenyan Shilling (KES) loses value against the South African Rand (ZAR), people will have to pay more for imported goods, oil and food from South Africa.

Demand-pull inflation

Demand-pull inflation occurs when rising demand pushes up the price of goods. This happens when people have more to spend. This is most likely when an economy is near to full employment. Businesses compete for resources and this will lead to a rise in prices.

CASE STUDY | Monetary inflation

Monetary inflation provides a good explanation of demand-pull inflation. It illustrates clearly the impact of economic indicators on the economy.

The idea of monetary inflation is not new. One of the best explanations was provided by the American economist Milton Friedman in the book he wrote with Anna Schwartz, *A Monetary History of the United States, 1867–1960,* published in 1971.

Friedman and Schwartz argued that if governments increase the quantity of money, there is more to spend on new goods. If, however, there are not enough goods being produced for the people who want to buy them, manufacturers will be able to put up prices. The authors concluded that price levels are linked to the quantity of money available. In their words, 'inflation is always and everywhere a monetary phenomenon.'

This work was published in 1971 and became a model of good practice in using detailed statistical analysis over a long period (in this case in the US) to make the link between prices and the quantity of money.

Questions

1 What connection did Friedman and Schwartz identify between the quantity of money and the level of prices?

2 What statistics did the authors study and use to make their claim?

3 How can monetary inflation also be described as demand-pull inflation?

4 With what economic indicators was Milton Friedman primarily concerned?

KEY POINTS

1 Causes of inflation can be split into cost-push and demand-pull factors.

2 Rising costs include agricultural prices, raw material costs, labour costs and weakening exchange rates.

3 Demand-pull occurs when demand increases and is usually associated with monetary inflation.

SUMMARY QUESTIONS

1 Define cost-push inflation, explaining one type of cost-push inflation.

2 How is an increase in the quantity of money in the economy likely to affect price levels?

3 When the exchange value of a country's currency falls, how is this likely to impact on import prices?

6.3 Consequences of inflation

LEARNING OUTCOMES

With regard to **prices**, candidates should be able to:

- discuss consequences of inflation.

Inflation is a sustained rise in the general level of prices. Mild inflation of one or two per cent is not particularly harmful because it encourages producers to supply more to the market. When inflation rises more quickly it can disrupt economic decision-making because it becomes difficult for businesses, governments and even ordinary people to make plans. Inflation results in a loss of value of units of currency. The reverse of inflation is **deflation**, when prices start to fall. Deflation (negative inflation) discourages businesses, who may restrict supply to markets.

There are many historical examples of rapid inflation. When prices rise rapidly governments are often tempted to print more money. Where the quantity of money increases, people lose confidence in it and businesses push up prices because they see money as being less valuable. The government is forced to print more money, but it becomes worthless. In the first decade of the 21st century, the government of Zimbabwe printed so much money that citizens started exchanging goods and services rather than use money to make payments.

The table below shows how inflation affects people in different circumstances.

Maize grain is a major staple food in many countries. An increase in the price of maize and other food staples can have a major impact on the livelihoods of the poorer members of society

Income level	Effect of inflation
Low income	They can afford fewer goods, including basic necessities. People resort to buying the lowest-priced products available.
Fixed income	There is a fall in real income (what can be afforded with money coming in). Because money loses value, people on fixed incomes save less and spend more.
High income	There is less income to spend on some luxury items. People may, therefore, switch to cheaper alternatives and cut back on some extravagant purchases. They may save less and spend more.

Who loses out in a period of inflation?

The poor

Poor people are the first to suffer in times of inflation. For example, in Kenya, an important part of people's diet is maize grain. In recent years there have been several droughts, reducing the supply, and so raising the price of maize. Drought has hit Kenya every two or three years and this has forced the country to buy expensive imports to meet its people's needs. This has pushed up inflation.

DID YOU KNOW?

Deflation can be as harmful as rapidly rising prices. When prices are falling business income from sales falls. Businesses become reluctant to invest and they reduce the numbers of employees.

People on fixed incomes

People on fixed incomes are those whose incomes remain the same, or nearly the same, during periods of inflation. They may be poorly paid workers who are not in a trade union, or pensioners. Workers who are unskilled and so have less bargaining power, such as office cleaners and car park attendants, also suffer in times of inflation. Skilled workers in well-paid jobs may be able to bargain with their employers to receive wage increases. This is often the case for people who work for the government: civil servants, teachers, the police and armed forces.

Savers

Many people like to save some money each month for future needs. Their savings may be deposited in a bank or kept in a safe place. However, during a period of inflation savings lose their value. When the money comes to be spent it is not worth as much as when it was first saved. Similarly, money saved in a pension scheme can lose value by the time the saver becomes old enough to draw on it.

Businesses

A lot of business activity involves supplying goods on credit, perhaps to other businesses. Payment may be required one month, three months or six months later. When money starts to lose value quickly, businesses become reluctant to supply on credit. Therefore, inflation is very harmful to business activity.

In contrast, people who borrow money in a period of inflation are likely to gain. When they come to pay back the sum they have borrowed, the value of their repayment will have fallen.

Mild inflation

As mentioned above, a small level of inflation is not necessarily a bad thing. Gently rising prices encourage businesses to supply more to the market and help to increase profits. In fact Milton Friedman argued that the government should increase the quantity of money. However, this should be done in a planned way that anticipates growth in production in the economy.

Deflation

Deflation refers to a general fall in the level of prices. Typically, this will occur when there is a general fall in demand for goods – for example, if people are spending less through uncertainties over rising unemployment. This is likely to be harmful to the economy as businesses will start to lay off workers and reduce levels of production.

ACTIVITY

Argentina and Turkey have both experienced rapid inflation. Carry out some internet research to find out when these periods of inflation occurred and how the governments in the two countries managed to stabilise prices. Try to find out what caused the inflation in these countries.

EXAM TIP

Make it clear in the examination that you understand that inflation can have varying effects on different groups of people in an economy.

KEY POINTS

1. In a period of inflation the economy becomes less stable. Groups such as the poor and those on fixed incomes suffer most.
2. Rapidly rising prices can quickly destroy business confidence and the willingness of business people to supply goods on credit.
3. A mild level of inflation can have a positive effect on business confidence.

SUMMARY QUESTIONS

1. Which two of the following groups would suffer least in a period of high inflation? Savers, pensioners, poor households, employees whose skills are in great demand, borrowers, or the government? Explain your answers.
2. Explain why a period of very mild inflation may not be harmful for an economy.
3. Explain why high inflation can be damaging for long-term business planning.

6.4 Patterns and levels of employment

LEARNING OUTCOMES

With regard to employment, candidates should be able to:

- describe changing patterns and levels of employment.

Employment

Employment is the work that people do in an economy. Over time, patterns of employment change: some industries go into decline and jobs disappear while new types of industries and jobs develop.

Government statistics provide indicators showing what jobs people do and how many are employed. These are important for governments. (Ideally everyone who wants a job should be able to find work that meets their own needs, as well as the needs of the economy as a whole.)

Skilled full-time workers producing modern products are best placed to earn high wages and to help an economy to grow

CASE STUDY: Labour force indicators in the UK

The table below presents a picture of employment in the UK from May to July 2009.

	All aged 16 and over (thousands)	Total in employment (thousands)	Employment rate (%)
Men	24,109	15,461	64.1
Women	25,340	13,430	53.0

Source: Labour Force Survey

The table is extracted from data in the Labour Force Survey. It shows that out of a possible 50 million people in the UK over 16, about 29 million are in work. The employment rate among men is higher than among women.

The survey also shows the breakdown of employment by age structure. For example, almost 11 million jobs are held by people in the age category 35–49. Over 80 per cent of people in this age category are employed, compared with only 25 per cent for the age category 16–17.

There are over 18 million people in full-time jobs, 6.5 million doing part-time jobs and almost 4 million people who are self-employed (i.e. working for themselves, perhaps running a small enterprise).

There are 23 million people working in the private sector, while just over 6 million people work in the public sector.

Questions

1. What reasons would you put forward to explain why only 29 million people aged over 16 are working in the UK? What will the others be doing?
2. What is meant by the employment rate? Why do you think that the employment rate is higher among men than among women?

DID YOU KNOW?

Core workers are at the heart of an organisation. They have full-time well paid jobs. Their work is supported by a more flexible labour force of part-time and temporary contract workers. Terms of employment, such as wage rates and job security, are less good for contract workers.

3 What is the difference between the public and private sectors? Who pays employees in these two sectors?

4 Why is the self-employed sector of the economy likely to be important for the future development of the UK economy?

The table (right) shows the different status of employees in a workforce.

Participation rates

The number of people available to work in an economy depends on:

- the number within the working age range
- the number within that age range who are prepared to participate in work. This is the **participation** rate.

$$\text{participation rate} = \frac{\text{number who are prepared to work}}{\text{number within working age range}}$$

Participation rates vary from country to country, depending on various factors:

- Social attitudes: in some countries it is acceptable for women to go out to work. In others they may be expected to stay at home and focus on looking after their children and the home.
- Number going to school and university.
- Age at which people stop work and **retire**.
- Facilities available to enable groups to work. In some countries, shops, offices and industrial premises are adapted to enable people with disabilities to participate in work.

The industrial structure

Another way of examining patterns of employment is to look at the industrial structure of the economy.

The table below gives some statistics from the UK, from June 2009: jobs are divided into 14 categories (A–O), using a classification known as the Standard Industrial Classification.

Job	Category	Number
All jobs	(A–O)	30,997
Agriculture, forestry and fishing	A–B	488
Mining, energy and water supply	C–E	191
Manufacturing	D	2,885
Construction	F	2,170
Distribution, hotels and restaurants	G–H	6,816
Transport and communications	I	1,854
Finance and business services	J–K	6,409
Education, health and public administration	L–N	8,193
Other services	O	1,991
Total services	G–O	25,263

Type of employee	
Full time (core workers)	Very important to the economy. They may work for the same employer for a number of years and develop increased knowledge and skills, enabling them to produce high-quality products for the economy.
Part time	Able to combine work with other commitments, such as bringing up a family.
Self-employed	Work for themselves. The businesses they set up may take on others and grow to become major employers in the future.
Employed workers	Work for someone else (e.g. large businesses or the government).
Private sector workers	Work for businesses. Most employees in developed economies, such as the US, UK or Germany, work for large companies, some of which employ thousands of workers.
Public sector workers	Employed by the government, for example, in the Civil Service. In India the biggest employer is the government-run Indian Railways.
Skilled employees	Have developed skills through training and practice. Typically, they are relatively well paid compared with **unskilled** workers.

> **DID YOU KNOW?**
>
> In many countries, tourism is a major provider of employment that swells the size of the tertiary industry. Hotel work, excursions and trips are all 'services'.

By studying the chart opposite, you should be able to see that most jobs in the UK are in service occupations.

The industrial structure is split into three main areas:

- Extractive (primary industry)
- Manufacturing and construction (secondary industry)
- Services (tertiary industry)

These areas are outlined below.

Extractive industries

Extractive industries use natural resources. Examples include farming, mining and drilling for sources of oil. Farmers grow and harvest crops and farm livestock, miners take out, or extract, fuel and minerals from the ground. Extractive industries sometimes produce raw materials like iron ore (for making steel) and oil (for making petrol, plastics, fibres, and so on). Some primary products can be sold direct to consumers, for example fish and oranges sold by a grower at the farm gate.

Manufacturing and construction industries

Manufacturing and construction industries use raw materials and parts from other industries to make and assemble new products, such as chocolate, furniture, cars and oil rigs. House, factory and bridge building are examples of construction industries. **Semi-manufactured** refers to goods that are partly made and will need further processing by manufacturing industries.

Service industries

Service industries are particularly important in the modern world. **Services** give something of value to people, but are not physical goods. Examples of services are being served in a restaurant, or having a bank look after your money for you. Society has gone through three waves of development. In modern third wave societies services dominate employment in advanced economies.

In the **first stage**, countries are dominated by agriculture and farming. This is still the case for many developing countries, such as such as Côte D'Ivoire and Ghana in West Africa, where over 90 per cent of the population live in rural areas.

In the **second stage**, countries are dominated by manufacturing, when industries such as coal, steel, car manufacture and engineering become important.

In the **third stage**, services become the most important sector of the economy, with many people working in insurance, banking, leisure entertainment, tourism and hotels. This can lead to countries being highly developed in some areas, while still having districts where people live in considerable poverty.

In modern, third-wave societies, computers and robotised machinery have replaced many manufacturing jobs.

> **ACTIVITY**
>
> Societies have developed in three stages, sometimes also called 'waves'. Group the following activities under the headings of primary, secondary and tertiary industry.
>
> Building, Cinema attendant, Electrician, Sign writing, Cloth making, Coal mining, Laundry, Fire fighting, Book publishing, Civil service, Selling lottery tickets, Banking, Oil drilling, Food manufacture, Key cutting, Public transport, Fishing, Retailing, Food selling

150

CASE STUDY: Employment by major industry sector in the US

The US is frequently given as an example of a third-wave society. The following data is drawn from information provided by the US Bureau of Labour Statistics. It shows percentages of people employed in the three sectors. The table includes a prediction for the future.

	1996 (%)	2006 (%)	2016 (%)
Primary industry	2.4	1.8	1.6
Secondary industry	16.9	14.5	12.7
Tertiary industry	81.7	83.7	85.7

Source: US Bureau of Labour Statistics

Questions

1 Describe the key trends that are taking place in the data.

2 Why do you think that the figures for primary and secondary industries show a decrease?

3 Do you think that the patterns of change from 1996 to 2016 are likely to continue?

ACTIVITY

Find statistics for your own economy to find out how the working population (i.e. people who are of working age) is distributed between primary, secondary and tertiary occupations. You will need to examine statistics from the government department responsible for collecting employment statistics. Obtain some information from the past five years so that you can see the trends in the three sectors.

The data shown for the US is very different from **Newly Industrialised Countries** (NICs). Brazil is a NIC and roughly 20 per cent of the working population there is still engaged in agriculture and other primary industries, and a further 15 per cent in manufacturing, with the remainder working in services. In Ghana in West Africa, over half the working population still works in primary industries, including cocoa growing and other forms of small-scale agriculture. About 25 per cent of Ghana's population is engaged in services.

In all countries, the percentage of people employed in tertiary industries tends to be higher in urban than in rural areas.

KEY POINTS

1 The structure of employment refers to the employment rate, proportions of men and women working, differences between public and private sector employment and other structural differences.

2 The structure of employment in an economy changes over time.

3 As economies develop, the main change is an increasing proportion of jobs in the service sector.

SUMMARY QUESTIONS

1 Explain the difference between the primary, secondary and tertiary sectors of an economy. Give examples of industries that would fit into each sector.

2 What is meant by the 'participation rate'? What are the key factors influencing rates of participation?

3 Between 1990 and 2005 the employee percentage working in manufacturing fell in these countries: Australia, Barbados, China, Colombia, Finland, France, Iceland, Ireland, Japan, Poland, Republic of Korea and the UK. Give four reasons why you think this may have occurred.

6.5 Causes of unemployment

LEARNING OUTCOMES

With regard to **employment**, candidates should be able to:

- discuss causes of unemployment.

Machines taking jobs away from humans is an example of technological unemployment

What is unemployment?

As we have seen, employment usually refers to the use and payment of labour. Unemployment typically occurs when people who want to work are not able to find jobs.

Measuring unemployment

The International Labour Organization (ILO), an agency of the United Nations, defines unemployed people as those who are:

- without a job, but who want a job and have actively sought work in the last four weeks and are available to start work in the next two weeks
- out of work, have found a job and are waiting to start it in the next two weeks.

There are two major statistics to look at when examining unemployment:

1. The total number of unemployed people in an economy. Is this rising or falling over time?
2. The unemployment rate. This rate measures the percentage of the working population who are unemployed. Note that the 'working population' consists of those with jobs as well as those who are unemployed. Is this rate rising or falling over time?

What causes unemployment?

Unemployment and inflation are two of the most serious economic problems. It is not surprising that governments pay so much attention to indicators that measure unemployment.

Unemployment is caused by a range of factors, some of which are more harmful than others in that they affect more people and have a longer-term impact on the economy. Figure 6.5.1 shows the range of unemployment types: the factors that cause them are explained in the next paragraphs.

Less serious (shorter term, affecting fewer people) → **More serious** (longer term, affecting more people)

Temporary | Seasonal | Technological | Frictional | Structural | Cyclical

Figure 6.5.1 Types of unemployment

ACTIVITY

Identify the current rate of unemployment in your country. How does this compare with figures for your region and for the world? Study news reports to get the figures for your country. Do newspaper reports suggest any of the causes for unemployment? As a group, collect monthly statistics for unemployment in your country and display these on a poster in your classroom.

Temporary unemployment

Temporary unemployment is short term, occurring usually while people are leaving one job to go to another, or perhaps when they are leaving school or university before going on to work.

Seasonal unemployment

Seasonal unemployment occurs in countries where there are distinct seasons and harvest times. For part of the year there will be plenty of jobs, such as harvesting sugar cane or picking fruit and vegetables. In the rainy season or winter, fewer jobs will be available.

Technological unemployment

New technology frequently replaces older methods that might have required more labour. For example, the use of tractors and giant harvesting equipment on modern farms has reduced the demand for agricultural labour. Automatic bottling, canning and packaging equipment has reduced the need for factory labour. However, new technology also helps to create new jobs by leading to economic growth. Computer technology has taken away the need for many factory workers, but it has created new opportunities for office workers and people setting up small businesses from home.

Frictional unemployment

Frictional unemployment occurs when the market system does not work as smoothly as it should – as its name suggests, there are *frictions* in it. This sort of unemployment occurs when there is a mismatch between the demand for, and supply of, labour. This might occur when employers are trying to recruit highly skilled construction workers but too few workers have been trained with the skills required.

Another cause of frictional unemployment might be **search** unemployment. This occurs when workers who have lost their previous jobs are searching for new ones, but are unable to find them because there is too little information about availability.

Structural unemployment

Structural unemployment arises when there are longer-term changes in the economy, affecting specific industries, regions and occupations. In the previous Unit we saw that one of the main structural changes in economies has been the move away from primary and secondary industry to services. This has led to rural and urban poverty in areas where agriculture and manufacturing industry are in decline.

Cyclical unemployment

On a larger scale, a major cause of unemployment across the globe is cyclical unemployment, also called **demand-deficient** unemployment. This is unemployment resulting from a substantial fall in demand that affects the economy as a whole.

Dealing with unemployment

Because there are many causes of unemployment, governments need to identify cures, that is, policies to deal with them. These are shown in Figure 6.5.1. The more serious the type of unemployment, the more it will cost the government to provide a cure.

DID YOU KNOW?

In Mauritius the sugar cane harvest depends on weather conditions. Once the hurricane season starts (usually in December) there are fewer available jobs in this industry.

KEY POINTS

1. 'Unemployment' refers to people seeking work who are unable to find a job.
2. Some of the causes of unemployment are more serious and long term than others.
3. Structural and cyclical unemployment are the most deep-seated causes of long-term unemployment.

SUMMARY QUESTIONS

1. What type of unemployment is caused by:
   a. the decline of an industry
   b. the end of the agricultural harvest?
2. What is the difference between the level of unemployment and the rate of unemployment?
3. Why is structural unemployment likely to have long-term consequences?

6.6 Consequences of unemployment

LEARNING OUTCOMES

With regard to employment, candidates should be able to:
- discuss consequences of unemployment.

Unemployed people queuing for work in the US. Recent studies in the US link unemployment with increased levels of stress, crime and people losing a sense of self-worth

DID YOU KNOW?

The International Labour Organization classifies some workers as 'vulnerable'. They are poorly paid and often work for employers who do not apply employment laws. They are particularly at risk in periods of economic recession or when they try to press for their employment rights.

EXAM TIP

Make sure that you are prepared to answer a question that involves a discussion of the various consequences of unemployment.

Who suffers from unemployment?

High or rising levels of unemployment creates consequences for:
- people who are unemployed
- the communities in which they live
- businesses
- the government
- the economy.

People who are unemployed

The United Nations Convention on Human Rights lists the right to work as an essential human right.

> Everyone has the right to work, to free choice of employment, to just and favourable conditions of work and to protection against unemployment.

As well as providing income for a wage earner and their family, work brings a sense of self-worth from playing a role in society, and a sense of satisfaction and achievement, particularly when the work is enjoyable and challenging.

Unemployment means that people losing their job have all the privileges and benefits of being part of the workforce taken away. In some countries, it is possible to claim unemployment pay based on contributions made during the time at work. However, in many countries this right does not exist.

Large numbers of people losing work through **cyclical unemployment** can lead to widespread poverty and hardship (unemployed people are more likely to suffer from stress and illness and have lower life expectancy). Cyclical unemployment was a particular feature of the 1920s and 1930s and, more recently, occurred in the global recession of 2007–9.

CASE STUDY | The impact of unemployment on individuals in the US

Studies in the US show some of the harmful effects of unemployment. The most obvious effect is the inability to pay bills and meet financial commitments, such as mortgage payments on a house. In the US, health insurance is often tied to having a job, so without a job medical bills can build up rapidly. Unemployment insurance in the US is unlikely to pay more than half of what a worker would have earned in wages.

Without a job, individuals lose contact with fellow workers and lack a sense of purpose for many hours a day. A further damaging effect is a lack of self-esteem. Studies show that unemployment leads to rising crime, suicide and bad health.

Questions

1 What impact is unemployment likely to have on a person's savings?

2 What are the consequences of being unemployed for someone who becomes ill in the US?

3 Why might unemployment lower a person's self-esteem?

4 How are the problems of being unemployed in the US likely to be similar for unemployed people in your own country?

The communities in which they live

Areas of high unemployment often have poorer facilities, for example, there are fewer shops and recreational facilities. There is an increased likelihood of social problems, such as higher crime rates and drug abuse. Businesses often play a major part in supporting community activities. For example, the huge US car manufacturer General Motors plays a prominent part in supporting local orchestras, sponsoring sports teams and providing educational scholarships for needy students in the areas in which it operates.

Businesses

Increased unemployment has an effect on business known as a **ripple** or **multiplier** effect. This means that as unemployment increases people have less income to spend and so businesses make less money from sales. Some businesses close down, others reduce the size of their labour force. In 2009, General Motors closed down many of its car plants in the US because of falling demand for cars during a major recession. The ripple effect was that other factories supplying General Motors with engine systems and other components had in turn to lay off workers or shut down completely.

The government

When unemployment is rising, ideally the government should increase its own spending. It can set up job-creation projects, perhaps to reduce youth and long-term unemployment. Unfortunately, however, government revenues fall in periods of recession. More unemployed people mean that fewer people are paying taxes and more are claiming benefits. As businesses start to close down or make reduced profits, they pay less in corporation tax (profits tax) to the government. Tax revenue then falls, spending rises and there is a greater likelihood of a budget deficit.

The economy

All the above problems are likely to damage an economy. Rising unemployment has a downward effect on the trade cycle. This in turn creates cyclical unemployment. When major businesses start to lay off workers there is a much wider ripple effect on the economy. Initially, the local economy is affected, but this quickly spreads to the regional economy, where component suppliers lose steady orders, and then further to the national and even the international economy.

ACTIVITY

Carry out some personal research using older relatives and friends to find out what impact unemployment has had in your area, either today or in the past. Find out what impact this had on local people and the local community. Write a report to present to the class.

KEY POINTS

1 High and rising unemployment has a negative effect on many groups within the economy (e.g. the unemployed and the communities in which they live).

2 The government loses revenue in times of rising unemployment, making it more difficult for it to combat the effects of unemployment.

3 Rising unemployment on a large scale has a negative effect on the trade cycle.

SUMMARY QUESTIONS

1 Who else suffers from unemployment in addition to the unemployed?

2 Describe two ways in which governments can lose revenue when unemployment is rising.

3 What effect does rising unemployment have on the wider economy?

6.7 Gross Domestic Product

LEARNING OUTCOMES

With regard to **output**, candidates should be able to:

- define Gross Domestic Product (GDP).

Street vendors, Nigeria. All countries have an element of unreported income from these types of businesses, whether market traders in Rome or street traders in Mumbai or Lagos. If they do not provide detailed statistics of their sales to the tax authorities, this can lead to extensive under-reporting of the country's GDP

DID YOU KNOW?

An International Monetary Fund paper titled *Comprehensive Measures of GDP and the Unrecorded Economy* has defined hidden economic activities as 'legal production deliberately concealed from the public authorities to avoid payment of taxes'.

What is GDP?

Gross Domestic Product (GDP) is a measure of the total value of goods produced in an economy in a particular period, such as a year or quarterly. It is the most common measure of national income and indicates how an economy is growing. Rises in GDP indicate that the value of goods being produced is increasing.

Comparisons of GDP can be made over time. The following statistics, based on the *World Factbook*, compare GDP in Nigeria in 2008 and 2009 and make comparisons with 10 and 20 years earlier.

	1989	1999	2008	2009
GDP (US$ billions)	78	125	320	330

Measuring GDP

There are several ways of measuring GDP. The important thing is to use a method that yields accurate results.

The output method

This involves adding up the output produced by the various industries in the economy. In Nigeria:

- Agricultural output makes up about 40 per cent of GDP.
- The service sector makes up about 30 per cent of GDP.
- The oil industry is responsible for over 20 per cent of GDP.
- Manufacturing is responsible for over 5 per cent of GDP.

It is important not to double-count outputs. For example, oil output will be used for manufacturing.

To avoid double-counting, statisticians only count the value added by each industry (and not inputs that have already been counted once).

The expenditure method

Add together the final spending on outputs produced by a country. There are four types of spending:

- Consumer spending (by households on goods and services).
- Investment spending (by businesses on premises, machinery and equipment).
- Government spending (on goods, services and investment).
- Net exports (the difference between exports and imports).

Nigeria's GDP is the output of the Nigerian economy, including exports to other countries. Spending by Nigerians on imports is deducted from GDP because the spending leaves Nigeria, to be spent on the output of foreign countries.

The income method

This involves adding together the incomes earned for producing all the goods that year. Only incomes earned for producing outputs are included. Therefore, 'transfer payments', such as pensions and unemployment benefit, are not included because no work was produced to earn those incomes.

GDP per head

The figure for GDP per head of population is probably more informative than the total value of GDP, but it does not take account of the way income is spread out or distributed between the different income groups in the population.

Nigeria has Africa's highest population, with about 150 million people. The GDP is 330,000 million (US$ equivalent). This gives an income per head of about US$2,200.

To calculate GDP per head we simply divide GDP by the population of the country.

$$\frac{US\$330,000 \text{ million}}{150 \text{ million}} = US\$2,200$$

Real GDP

When calculating GDP, it is important to take account of the effect of inflation – this usually means taking it out. Rising inflation can distort increases in GDP. Economists, therefore, make a distinction between **nominal** GDP and **real** GDP.

- Nominal GDP figures are ones that have not been adjusted for inflation.
- Real GDP figures are ones that have been adjusted for inflation.

This involves calculating the value of the GDP produced in a particular year in terms of the prices of a base year.

For example, if the nominal GDP and inflation both double between 2005 and 2010 real GDP will stay the same. For example, if 2005 was given an index of 100 as the base year:

Nominal GDP = US$10,000 in 2005 and US$20,000 in 2010.

The price index would be 200 in 2010 (prices doubled).
US$20,000/2 = US$10,000. Therefore, real income stays the same.

Problems in measuring GDP

It is not easy to measure GDP. One difficulty is that some economic activity is simply not recorded. For example, Italy and Nigeria both have a substantial 'underground' or 'unrecorded' economy. For instance, there are many roadside businesses selling farm products, where tax is not declared. In Nigeria, there is also a substantial local film production and distribution industry (Nollywood) where films are sold through hidden channels. It is estimated that this unrecorded economy in Nigeria could account for up to 40 per cent of all trades made, leading to a substantial under-reporting of Nigeria's GDP.

ACTIVITY

Using national newspapers or by carrying out an internet search using 'GDP' and the name of your country, find answers to the following:

- The most recent GDP figure for your country.
- The figure for GDP per head.
- The growth rate for GDP in your country over the last year.
- The inflation rate in your country.

What would be the effect of the inflation rate on real GDP in your country?

KEY POINTS

1. GDP is a measure of the value of output produced in an economy in a period of time, used to measure economic growth.
2. GDP can be calculated by adding together the outputs of the various industries, total expenditures in the economy or incomes earned.
3. Real GDP is a measure that takes inflation into account.
4. GDP per head calculates GDP per person in the economy.

SUMMARY QUESTIONS

1. Define GDP, GDP per head and real GDP.
2. Why might comparisons of the GDP of two countries provide an inaccurate picture of the relative size of output in those countries?
3. Why is GDP such an important indicator for economists?

6.8 Comparing living standards

LEARNING OUTCOMES

With regard to **output**, candidates should be able to:

- describe simple measures and indicators of comparative living standards, such as GDP per head and the Human Development Index (HDI).

Standard of living

A person's standard of living refers to the level of material comfort that they are able to enjoy in terms of the goods and services which they can buy or use.

Making comparisons using GDP

In the previous Unit we saw that Gross Domestic Product (GDP) measures the total value of goods produced in an economy in a given period of time. Until the 1970s, GDP was widely regarded to be a good measure of living standards.

The argument was that if an economy produced more goods, people in that country would become better off. GDP and GDP per head were regarded as good ways of measuring the economic growth of a country.

It might be claimed, therefore, that the economic indicator GDP would be a good way of:

- measuring the growth of economies over time
- making comparisons between levels of production, income and spending between countries.

Barbados ranks as 'very high' in the Human Development Index because of high income per head, long life expectancy and high rates of enrolment in schools coupled with high literacy rates

CASE STUDY | Comparing countries

The World Development Indicators database produced by the World Bank set out the following ranking of the world's top 10 economies in terms of GDP in 2008.

Ranking	Economy	US$ millions
1	US	14,204,322
2	Japan	4,909,272
3	China	4,326,187
4	Germany	3,652,824
5	France	2,853,062
6	UK	2,645,593
7	Italy	2,293,008
8	Brazil	1,612,539
9	Russian Federation	1,607,816
10	Spain	1,604,174

> **Questions**
>
> 1 Why is the US top of the world GDP indicators table?
>
> 2 What would a country need to do to move up the GDP indicators table?
>
> 3 Why might the GDP indicators table not give a clear picture of how well off individual people are in the countries listed?
>
> 4 Is measuring GDP a good way of measuring economic growth and comparing standards of living in different countries? Give reasons for your answer.

Criticisms of using GDP as an economic indicator

Since the 1970s there has been a lot of criticism of linking GDP with standards of living. These criticisms are explained below and overleaf.

1. It does not take into account inequality in society. For example, the Brazilian economy grew rapidly in the first decade of the 21st century compared with other smaller countries. However, Brazil has amongst the highest income inequality in the world. The richest 10 per cent of Brazilians receive 50 per cent of GDP, while the poorest 10 per cent receive less than 1 per cent. Most countries around the world have not been very successful in reducing inequality in recent years. For example, in Britain between 1997 and 2007, the percentage of national income going to the richest 20 per cent of households rose from 40.9 per cent in 1997 to 42.6 per cent in 2007. During the same period the share taken by the poorest 20 per cent of families fell from 7.7 per cent to 7.2 per cent. So although GDP per head in a country might rise over time, prosperity does not necessarily make much difference to the living standards of poorer people.

2. GDP simply measures the value of goods produced. GDP calculations do not take into account the harmful effects of growth, such as pollution and waste. A country that produces more food does not necessarily produce healthy food. Cigarettes are counted as 'goods' even though they create lung cancer and other illnesses.

3. GDP calculations are not very good at making comparisons between countries. This is because GDP is usually calculated within a country using the currency of that country. For example, GDP in South Africa is measured using the South African Rand (ZAR), but the value of the Rand may change over time against other currencies. For example, on the 29 October 2008 the exchange rate between the South African Rand and the US dollar was 10 rands to one dollar. At the time, the GDP of South Africa was worth about 25 billion US dollars. However, the value of the rand was falling against the dollar. This means that the value of South Africa's GDP as measured in dollars may change quite dramatically on a day-to-day basis.

> **ACTIVITY**
>
> Find out the most recent published figure for GDP in your country. Compare this with the GDP of another country with a similar-sized population.
>
> What factors might explain the difference in your country from that of the country you have chosen to compare it with?

4   Standard of living is not the same thing as quality of life. People may have more goods but they are not necessarily better off or happier. In recent years, economists have suggested that a person's quality of life depends on a range of factors, including being healthy, being free from stress and worry or living in a pleasant climate – all factors that are not measured by simple GDP calculations.

Human Development Index

The Human Development Index (HDI) is a broader method of measuring quality of life. The well-known economists Mahbub ul Haq and Amartya Sen led a team of economists that developed this for the United Nations Development Programme.

The HDI contains three elements:

1   Standard of living, as measured by GDP per head.
2   Life expectancy at birth.
3   Education as measured by:

   a adult literacy (given a **weighting** of two-thirds)

   b primary, secondary and tertiary enrolment in education (given a weighting of one-third).

Achievement in each of these three areas is measured by how far a country has gone in attaining the following goals:

- Real GDP per head of US$40,000. Real GDP is the value of goods produced in a given period when we have taken out the effect of price rises caused by inflation.
- Life expectancy of 85 years.
- Adult literacy and enrolments of 100 per cent.

These goals have not yet been fully attained by any country, so the actual indicators are expressed as decimal shares of the ideal. Therefore, 0.5 represents halfway towards the goal. The HDI score for any country is measured between 0 and 1. The highest score is 1.

Using Human Development Indices, countries are ranked into four categories: very high, high, medium and low. Here are some of the countries in the very high, medium and low categories, with their ranking in brackets and the HDI score as a decimal.

Primary and secondary school enrolment and adult literacy are given important consideration in Human Development calculations

DID YOU KNOW?

Countries with an HDI of more than 0.9 are classified as very high, those between 0.8 and 0.89 as high, between 0.5 and 0.79 as medium and under 0.5 as low.

Very high	HDI	High	HDI	Medium	HDI	Low	HDI
Norway (1)	0.971	Bahrain (39)	0.895	Thailand (87)	0.783	Malawi (160)	0.493
Australia (2)	0.970	Poland (41)	0.880	Iran (88)	0.782	Senegal (166)	0.464
New Zealand (3)	0.950	Argentina (49)	0.866	Maldives (95)	0.773	Burundi (174)	0.394
Singapore (23)	0.944	Cuba (51)	0.863	Jamaica (100)	0.766	Chad (175)	0.392
Barbados (37)	0.903	Mauritius (81)	0.804	Algeria (104)	0.754	Niger (182)	0.340

Source: United Nations, Human Development Indicators, 2009

> **ACTIVITY**
>
> Do some research to find where these countries are ranked and their HDI score: Greece, Argentina, Cuba, Zambia, Senegal, Brazil, Sri Lanka, Singapore, Kuwait, Mexico.

Criticisms of the HDI are that it fails to take into account the impact of economic growth on the environment. The economist Bryan Caplan has criticised the HDI as concentrating on too narrow a range of indicators. He says that the HDI is a measure of how *Scandinavian* your economy is because it focuses on areas such as education and health care, which countries like Norway and Sweden do particularly well.

In some countries HDI is also measured in areas of the country. In India HDI is measured for each of the country's states, and even for different districts within the states. This enables national and regional government to identify areas of great hardship and to use this as a basis for providing support. The Indian government also places particular emphasis on measuring infant mortality and this, rather than life expectancy at birth, is sometimes used as an indicator.

An alternative way of looking at development is the Human Poverty Index (HPI). This was created by the United Nations which regard it as a useful way of measuring human deprivation. It includes indicators such as the proportion of the population living below the poverty line and the rate of unemployment.

The HPI is often regarded as a more accurate measure of deprivation than the HDI in highly developed countries because it takes account of those living below the poverty line. For the purpose of the index, these are people whose incomes fall below half the average (median) disposable income in the country.

> **ACTIVITY**
>
> Find out where your country ranks in the HDI ranking this year. Is this higher or lower than each of the following: Australia, Barbados, Bahrain, Kenya, Syria, Peru, Nigeria, the US?

> **SUMMARY QUESTIONS**
>
> 1 Why does GDP only give a very rough measure of how well off people are in different countries?
>
> 2 What is the HDI and what does it measure?
>
> 3 If a country scores very high in the HDI, what does this tell you about the country?

> **EXAM TIP**
>
> The Human Development Index has recently been included in the syllabus, so you need to make sure that you are able to discuss this economic indicator as well as GDP per head.

> **KEY POINTS**
>
> 1 The standard of living measures access to levels of material comfort.
>
> 2 GDP is criticised as being too narrow a measure of broader quality of life.
>
> 3 The HDI has been developed as an alternative measure.
>
> 4 The HDI takes account of the standard of living, life expectancy and education.

> **DID YOU KNOW?**
>
> The infant mortality rate measures the number of deaths per 1,000 live births in one year of infants under one year old.

Unit 6 — Practice exam questions

SECTION 1: Multiple-choice questions

Each question has ONE correct answer.

1. Which of the following is NOT usually used as an indicator of the overall health of the whole economy?
   a. The level of unemployment
   b. The level of economic growth
   c. The level of retail sales
   d. The level of inflation

2. What is inflation?
   a. An increase in the population of a country
   b. An increase in the value of a country's currency
   c. An increase in a country's interest rate
   d. An increase in a country's general level of prices

3. If the Retail Price Index at the start of 2006 is 100 and increases to 130 by the end of 2009, what is the average yearly inflation rate for the time period?
   a. 10 per cent
   b. 11 per cent
   c. 15 per cent
   d. 30 per cent

4. Which of the following may be an advantage of an increasing rate of inflation for the population of a country?
   a. People who borrow money find that the real value of repayments falls
   b. People on fixed incomes find that their spending power decreases
   c. Poor people must pay higher prices for basic foodstuffs
   d. People who save money find that the real value of their savings have fallen

5. Unemployment may cause a negative 'multiplier effect' because:
   a. People spend less so businesses close down
   b. People may claim welfare benefits
   c. People have out-of-date skills
   d. People suffer from low self-esteem

6. What does the participation rate for workers in an economy measure?
   a. The total number of people of working age
   b. The percentage of people of working age who are prepared to work
   c. The percentage of workers who are in full-time jobs
   d. The number of retired people who continue working

7. Which of the following works in a secondary industry?
   a. A school teacher
   b. A restaurant chef
   c. A car factory worker
   d. A mobile phone salesman

8. Which of the following is a disadvantage of increasing rates of employment for the population of a country?
   a. Rising prices for goods and services
   b. Rising wage rates
   c. Rising levels of income
   d. Falling level of benefit payments

9. Which economic indicator measures the total output of an economy?
   a. Gross Domestic Product
   b. Human Development Index
   c. Gross Domestic Product per head
   d. Retail Price Index

10. Which of the following is a problem with using GDP to measure the total output of a country?
    a. Workers' incomes are not equal
    b. Prices are different in different areas
    c. Some incomes are not reported
    d. Higher earners pay more income tax

SECTION 2: Structured questions

Country A is a developing nation, whose population, due to better health care, is now growing at 10 per cent per year. There are two major cities and several large towns, but the majority of the population live in rural areas and farm small areas of land. There is an increasing trend for people to move to the cities, but there are not enough jobs, so many people end up living in poverty. The increasing population is also putting pressure on resources. Gross Domestic Product (GDP) is only increasing at 2 per cent yearly, causing average prices to rise by an average of 12 per cent per year.

1. a Explain why 'better health care' may lead to an increase in population. (4)
   b Country A's government measures price changes using a Retail Price Index. Explain how this is constructed. (6)
   c Using the information given, explain how you would expect the measure of 'GDP per head' to have changed. (4)
   d Discuss whether GDP might be an accurate way to measure living standards in Country A. (6)

2. The government of Country A is worried about the rising prices. The Minister of Finance is quoted as saying '12 per cent inflation per year is far too high'.
   a Explain why the increasing population of Country A is causing prices to rise at 12 per cent per year. (A suitable diagram may be used here.) (4)
   b Why are some types of products, such as basic foodstuffs, given a 'prominent weighting' in the Retail Price Index in Country A? (4)
   c Explain the effects of 12 per cent inflation on the different population groups of Country A. (6)
   d Discuss why the RPI may not provide an accurate measure of the level of price rises suffered by all citizens in Country A. (6)

3. In the capital city of Country A, 30 per cent of people are estimated as being unemployed. There are increasing numbers of jobs in secondary employment in new factories, but people moving into the city do not have appropriate skills, as they only have experience in primary farming occupations.
   a Why might it be difficult to measure the unemployment rate in the capital city of Country A? (4)
   b Explain the economic causes of unemployment of the people moving into the capital city of Country A. (6)
   c Describe likely changes in the structure of industry and types of occupation that will be available to Country A's population as it becomes more developed. (4)
   d How might the government of Country A decrease the level of unemployment in its capital city? (6)

4. The President of Country A has been quoted as saying 'this increase in our population can only be good for living standards in the long run, as we will have more workers'.
   a Explain what is meant by 'living standards'. (3)
   b Explain the president's view that 'more workers will lead to better living standards'. (3)
   c Apart from using GDP to measure output, how might living standards in a country be measured? (6)
   d Discuss which will be the most important factors that will determine whether the President will be proved correct in his assumption. (8)

Total: 80 marks

SECTION 3: Analysis and critical evaluation

Country B is a developed nation, whose working population are mainly employed in jobs in the tertiary sector. The country has been suffering from an economic recession and the government has reported the following indicators for the third quarter (three-month period) of 2009:

- A fall in GDP of 0.2 per cent for this quarter, which is the sixth successive quarter of falling GDP.
- A population which has increased by 408,000 to 61,383,000 from the previous year. This is noted to be due to 'increase in births, decrease in deaths and changing patterns of international migration'.
- An unemployment rate of 7.8 per cent, having increased by 0.1 per cent over the quarter, indicating that unemployment is still increasing but at a slower rate than in previous quarters. However, there are 'over one million employed and self-employed people working part-time, as they are unable to find a full-time job'.
- An inflation rate of 0.3 per cent as measured by the Retail Price Index, or 1.9 per cent as measured by the Consumer Price Index, the government's preferred measure. It is noted that the largest upward pressure on inflation is due to the rising price of oil leading to increasing transport costs for businesses and individuals.

1 a Explain what 'A fall in GDP' means. (2)

   b Why might the government of Country B be worried by 'six successive quarters of falling GDP'? (2)

2 a 'Most of the working population in Country B are employed in the tertiary sector'. Give examples of one occupation in each of the industrial sectors. (2)

   b Explain ONE likely reason for the increase in employment in the tertiary sector. (2)

3 Discuss whether 'over one million people working part-time' may benefit the economy of Country B. (5)

4 a Explain what is measured by the 'HDI' or Human Development Index. (2)

   b Discuss the benefits to an economist of using the HDI to compare Country B with another country. (5)

5 Using a diagram and written explanation, show how 'the rising price of oil causes transport costs to increase'. (5)

6 Using all the information in the text, write an assessment of the health of the economy of Country B. (7)

Total: 32 marks

7 Developed and developing economies

Unit 7 explores themes and issues associated with the development of economies. The unit starts out by investigating some different views about development. The unit also explores the nature of poverty and some of the policies used by governments to combat it.

Population growth is closely associated with development. When a country's population is increasing at a fast rate it is difficult to provide an acceptable standard of living for all its citizens. The unit compares the structure of population in different types of economies and some of the effects of population growth. In some countries population growth is accelerating, in others it is slowing down; in some countries the population is falling. The unit therefore goes on to show that an ideal population size is one in which the number making up the working population is sufficiently large to combine effectively with other factors of production and to support the dependent population (mainly those who are too young or too old to work).

Finally, the unit looks at what is meant by the standard of living and how standards of living vary both within an economy and between economies.

LEARNING OUTCOMES

With regard to **development**, candidates should be able to:

- describe why some economies are classified as developed and some are not
- recognise and discuss policies to alleviate poverty.

With regard to **population growth**, candidates should be able to:

- describe factors that affect population growth
- discuss reasons for the different rates of growth in different countries
- analyse the problems and consequences of population change for countries at different stages of development
- describe the effects of changing size and structure of population on an economy.

With regard to **standards of living**, candidates should be able to:

- discuss differences in living standards within countries and between countries, both developed and developing.

7.1 What is development?

LEARNING OUTCOMES

Candidates should be able to:
- describe why some countries are classified as developed and others are not.

Economic development

For economists, **development** can mean different things. Most definitions relate to the ongoing raising of living standards (what a person can afford to buy) and the improved ability of a country, through its own efforts, to produce more goods and services over time. Definitions usually include improving medical and education services.

A key aspect of the development of any economy is the education of children. Enrolment in schools is a major development indicator

The World Bank defines countries as **low income**, **middle income** and **high income**. This helps it to make decisions about lending money and supporting development projects in specific countries. Lower-income countries can borrow more finance for development. The World Bank considers low- and middle-income countries to be 'developing'. High-income countries are regarded as 'developed'. Figure 7.1.1 shows a range of countries, from developed to developing.

Low GDP/head Developing						High GDP/head Developed
Afghanistan	Zambia	Bangladesh	Algeria	New Zealand	Italy	Singapore

Figure 7.1.1

DID YOU KNOW?

At an international level the World Bank plays a prominent role in coordinating development initiatives. It is not a bank in the normal sense of the word, but rather a specialised agency of the United Nations. One of its purposes is to transfer resources from rich countries to poor countries to support economic development. The World Bank has 184 member countries collectively funding development projects.

In Unit 6.8 we explored another view of development, in terms of Human Development Indicators. These indicators included three elements: standard of living, life expectancy at birth and education. Development is then measured by an index that includes each of these indicators (Figure 7.1.2).

Low human development	Medium human development	Very high human development
Low incomes, low life expectancy and low school enrolment		High incomes, high life expectancy and high school enrolment
Niger | Mozambique | Zambia	Vietnam | Jamaica | Thailand	Singapore | Italy | Norway

Figure 7.1.2 Measuring development

Some of the other characteristics of developing economies include high infant mortality, high rates of population growth, relatively poor levels of education and health care, poor infrastructure (such as roads and water supplies), sanitation and housing, an over-reliance on a small number of export industries, and low productivity in large parts of agriculture.

Development as freedom

Amartya Sen is a famous economist who has won the Nobel Prize for his work. He believes that development should be seen as a process of expanding *freedom*. Freedom (and hence development) requires the removal of poverty, tyranny, lack of economic opportunities, social deprivation and the neglect of public services. In his book *Development as Freedom* he showed that, contrary to accepted views, economic growth on its own does not bring about development. He showed that people in the relatively poor South Indian state of Kerala, in which there are plentiful public services (including a public distribution system providing subsidised food), had a higher **life expectancy** than African Americans living in poverty in the US, a country with a much higher GDP per head. Amartya Sen believes that by providing freedoms – that is, social opportunities, political freedom, economic opportunities and security – development is most likely to occur.

Inequality as uneven development

Differences in income can be measured by the Gini index. Zero represents an imaginary society with absolute income equality between households; 100 represents absolute *in*equality. Scandinavian countries and Japan have the lowest levels of inequality; the US has one of the highest. In 2009 this was 41, with the poorest 10 per cent of households only receiving 1.9 per cent of income, while the richest received 30 per cent. See if you can find the Gini score for your country and compare this with that of the US. Inequality can be seen as an indicator of uneven shares between the rich and the poor in terms of the rewards of development.

SUMMARY QUESTIONS

1. How does the World Bank classify the development of a country?
2. Why might the World Bank's classification not give a true reflection of development?
3. What types of freedom are associated with development?

ACTIVITY

Research one country on each of the continents of South America, North America, Asia and Africa. Find out whether these countries are considered by the World Bank to be low income, middle income or high income. Then, using the United Nation's Human Development Indicators, find out whether these countries are defined as having a high, medium or low development index.

EXAM TIP

You may be asked to consider why some countries are classified as developed and others are not; make sure that you can show an understanding of what is meant by 'developed'.

KEY POINTS

1. Development occurs when people are better off, not only with higher incomes, but also with access to benefits such as improved education and health.
2. International bodies, including the World Bank and the United Nations, have created classifications of development.
3. Amartya Sen believes that development requires freedom.

7.2 Policies to reduce poverty

LEARNING OUTCOMES

Candidates should be able to:
- recognise and discuss policies to alleviate poverty.

Brazil is a rapidly developing economy: 13.6 per cent of adults are still unable to read, so providing literacy classes is now a priority in the poorest communities

DID YOU KNOW?

From October 2010 the United Nations' Human Development Report will include a new measure of poverty. This measure is called the Multidimensional Poverty Index (MPI). The MPI assesses a range of 'deprivations' at household level: from education to health outcomes to assets and services. Taken together these provide a fuller picture of poverty than simple income measures. Half of the word's poor as measured by the MPI live in South Asia and one quarter in Africa – 93 per cent of the population of Niger is classified as poor using the MPI.

Defining poverty

Poverty can be defined as absolute or relative.

- **Absolute poverty** defines someone as poor by a particular standard. For example, a recent Indian government committee report (2009), led by the economist S.D. Tendulkar, defined being poor as not having enough to meet basic needs, including an adequate diet and access to education and health services. The committee estimated that about 38 per cent of India's population (400 million) is poor. The World Bank defines extreme poverty as living on less than US$1.25 per day (2010).

- **Relative poverty** involves making comparisons between poor and rich people in a society. In the UK, for example, a 'poor' household is one trying to live on less than 60 per cent of average income. Being poor usually means being deprived in many ways, so there may be high rates of infant deaths, low levels of literacy (reading and writing), poor health conditions and a lack of job opportunities.

Dealing with poverty

Policies that can help to reduce poverty include the economic growth of a society (this can lead to benefits for the poor), redistribution of income – for example, by taxation and benefits – or targeted policy measures designed to help poorer people – for example, by providing employment opportunities in rural and urban areas.

Sustained economic growth

Economic growth maintained over time leads to a rise in Gross Domestic Product (see Unit 6.7). In an ideal world everyone benefits. However, there is no guarantee that this will happen – the rich may simply become richer. Economic growth can be achieved if the government helps markets to work more smoothly by cutting out unnecessary regulation, or by providing subsidies and tax incentives to new growing industries. The government could also invest in new training and employment creation schemes (see Unit 5.5).

DID YOU KNOW?

An argument in favour of free market economies is that growth has a trickle-down effect. This means that people with high incomes are the most likely to benefit when the economy grows, but everyone is likely to benefit from greater spending and more job opportunities. How true do you think this theory is?

Redistribution of income

Income can be redistributed through raising taxes so that the rich pay more than the poor (**progressive taxes**). **Regressive taxes**, where the poor pay the highest percentage, can be lowered. However, critics of such a scheme argue that high taxes discourage effort. Businesses might also get around this by raising wages for better-paid workers and cutting wages for those on lower pay.

Measures to help poorer people

There are many measures that a government can use to help poorer people directly: public distribution schemes for subsidised food, means-tested benefits such as cash payments to low-income families, and subsidised or zero-cost housing and education. Minimum-wage legislation can also be implemented for low-paid workers.

In Brazil the Alfasol programme has been created to increase literacy rates for young people and adults. The programme concentrates on the poorest rural and urban communities.

> **EXAM TIP**
>
> You may be required to discuss policies to reduce poverty. As part of your discussion, you should be able to explain which policies you think will be more likely to be effective, and why.

CASE STUDY | Policies to alleviate poverty in India

Professor S. Subramanian, at the Madras Institute of Development Studies in Chennai, has suggested that India adopts the following policies:

1 Collect unpaid income and wealth taxes and use the proceeds to tackle poverty.
2 Create an additional element to income tax – a poverty surcharge to redistribute income from rich to poor.
3 Improve the public distribution system.
4 Draw up maps to identify poor districts – for example, those without access to drinking water, fuel for cooking, a school or other basic amenities – and then seek to improve these areas.
5 Extend free adult literacy schemes.
6 Improve social security schemes to provide better pensions for those who have had accidents or who are old.
7 Improve pro-growth policies to grow the whole economy – for example, by encouraging more foreign investment.

Questions

1 Which of the suggestions listed involve:
   a growing the economy as a whole
   b redistributing income
   c targeting initiatives at the poor?
2 Which of the policies do you think are likely to be particularly effective at tackling poverty?
3 Which of the policies are most similar to those that you have read about for your own country?

KEY POINTS

1 Relative poverty involves comparisons between richer and poorer members of society. Absolute poverty measures poverty against set poverty thresholds (e.g. US$2 per day).
2 Policies for combating poverty include redistributing income, economic growth and targeting benefits at the poor.

SUMMARY QUESTIONS

1 An individual earns US$10 per day. Why might they be classified as being poor?
2 An individual earns US$3 per day. Why might they be classified as not being poor?
3 State three policies that might be effective for reducing poverty.
4 How might the redistribution of income through progressive taxes benefit the poor?

7.3 Factors that affect population growth

LEARNING OUTCOMES

Candidates should be able to:
- describe the factors that affect population growth.

The main factors

The four key factors affecting population growth are the birth rate, death rate, fertility rate and net migration.

- The **birth (natality) rate** is the ratio of total live births to total population in an area in a particular time period. It is often expressed as the number of live births per 1,000 of the population per year.

The birth rate is the number of live births per 1,000 people

- The **death (mortality) rate** is the number of deaths per 1,000 of the population per year. Two important indicators in this context are the **infant mortality rate** (the number of children under one year dying divided by the number of live births that year) and the **maternal mortality rate** (the number of deaths of women related to childbearing divided by the total number of live births that year).
- The **general fertility rate** can be measured by the number of live births per 1,000 women between the ages of 15 and 44 years. It can also be measured by the number of children born to the average woman in her lifetime.
- **Net migration** measures the difference between *immigration* (that is, into) and *emigration* (from) of an area during a year. If the number of emigrants is greater than the number of immigrants, the net migration figure is negative.

DID YOU KNOW?

Every year over half a million women and girls die as a result of complications during pregnancy, childbirth or in the six weeks following delivery; 99 per cent of these deaths occur in developing countries.

EXAM TIP

In questions on population growth, candidates usually refer to the birth rate and the death rate, but you should also mention the impact of the net migration rate on the size of a country's population.

ACTIVITY

Find out the most recent figures available for birth rates, death rates and net migration in your country. What will be the impact on population growth? Make a poster or wall chart that displays your findings.

Population growth

To calculate annual **population growth** (or **fall**), subtract the population figure at the start of the year from the figure at the end. Divide this number by the figure at the start. Multiply this number by 100 to get a percentage figure for population growth (or decline).

Here is the calculation for a population increase from 50 million to 51 million over one year:

51 million − 50 million = 1 million

$$\frac{1}{50} \times \frac{100}{1} = 2 \text{ per cent population growth}$$

Factors affecting population growth

A number of factors affect population growth:

- **The birth rate**: more births per 1,000 lead to an increasing population. Birth rates are highest in developing countries, because people aim to have more children to counteract high infant mortality, and children can add to household earnings once they start work.
- **The death rate**: the under-fives mortality rate per 1,000 live births fell in sub-Saharan Africa between 1990 and 2007, leading to an increasing population. Better medical care, inoculation against diseases and better diet will cause a fall in death rates.
- **The relationship between the birth and the death rate**: in Brazil in 2009 the birth rate was about 18.5 per 1,000, compared with a death rate of 6.35 per 1,000. Thus there is a **natural increase** here, as is the case in many other developing economies.
- **The net migration rate**: the 2009 net migration rate in Brazil was −0.09. This helped to reduce the impact of the natural increase in population. **Economic migration** occurs when people come to, or leave a country in search of work. Relatively low wages in a country will lead to workers emigrating to areas where wages are higher.
- **The fertility rate** (children born per woman): Brazil had a relatively low 2009 fertility rate of 2.21.

Birth and fertility rates are affected by numbers of women of childbearing age, attitudes to having children and the extent to which contraception and other methods are used to limit the number of children per family (China has used a one-child-per-family policy to control the birth rate). The death rate is affected by the quantity and quality of food available and medical facilities. Net migration is determined by the ease with which people can move between countries, and whether they want to do so.

KEY POINTS

1. Falling infant mortality rates result from better medical care and nutrition.
2. Net migration also influences population growth, as does the fertility rate.

EXAM TIP

You will need to be able to discuss the possible reasons for different rates of population growth in different countries. This means that you will need to consider which reasons may be more important than others.

SUMMARY QUESTIONS

1. What would be the effect of a fall in the death rate on population growth?
2. Why might a population grow even though the death rate is higher than the birth rate?
3. How might a fall in birth rate affect the fertility rate in future years?

7.4 Reasons for different rates of population growth

LEARNING OUTCOMES

Candidates should be able to:

- discuss reasons for different rates of population growth in different countries.

Young people in Uganda: in some developing countries half the population is under 15

Pyramid A
Typical of developing countries
- high death rate
- high birth rate
- low life expectancy

Pyramid B
Typical of developed countries
- low death rate
- lower birth rate
- longer life expectancy

65 years
15 years

Figure 7.4.1 Population pyramids for a developing and a developed country

Population growth in developing and developed countries

- **Developing countries** have high death rates and birth rates, and low life expectancy. Higher death rates result from lower incomes, which in turn result in poor nutrition for the poorest. There are fewer doctors, nurses and hospitals per head of the population. There are fewer medicines and a much lower percentage of the population is inoculated against diseases. Malaria and HIV/AIDS are major causes of high mortality rates – the drugs to combat and treat them are very expensive.

- **Developed countries** have a low death rate, lower birth rate, and longer life expectancy. The low death rate results from better health care and relatively high incomes, enabling people to have a more nutritious diet. The average age at which women have their first child is higher. Most families choose to have fewer children so that they can enjoy a higher standard of living.

Population pyramids

A **population pyramid** compares the numbers of males and females in different age categories in a country or territory. Each bar in the pyramid represents five years and the length shows the population in that age category: the age distribution. The structure of the pyramid is determined by births, deaths and migration.

Figure 7.4.1 shows that the shape for the developing country is triangular, with a wide base and a narrow top. For the developed country it is more egg-shaped. It also shows that in the developing country a large proportion of the population is under 15 and very few live beyond the age of 65.

Population growth in Uganda and the UK

Figure 7.4.2 shows the numbers in the different age bands in the UK population (61.5 million in 2008). There are fairly even numbers of people in each age category up to the age of 60 when, as a result of old age, numbers start to decline. Children aged under 16 represent about one in five of the total population, around the same proportion as those of retirement age. The tapering of the pyramid for people aged 31 to 37 reflects low fertility rates in the 1970s as people chose to have smaller families. Low fertility occurred again in the late 1980s to early 2000s, but increased from 2003 onwards, broadening the base of the pyramid.

In 2009 the UK birth rate was about 10.7 per 1,000 and the death rate 10.1 per 1,000, with net migration +2.0. Net migration increased as a result of migrant workers, particularly from countries like Poland which became part of the European Union in 2004 (enabling them to live and work in EU countries).

The table shows how the population in Uganda in 2009 is rising at a very fast rate.

Population	33 million
Population growth	3.2 per cent per annum
Birth rate	48/1,000
Death rate	12/1,000
Infant mortality rate	65/1,000
Average fertility	6.5 per woman
Age distribution	50 per cent under 15
Population by 2050	100 million

So while Uganda has a rapidly growing population, there is also long-term poverty and poor health, particularly for children. Infant mortality is high because of a lack of trained midwives and medical clinics, particularly in rural areas. The birth rate is high because of a lack of availability of family planning advice, and because children are seen as providing hope for the future.

Some developed countries like Japan have a falling population. The birth rate is lower than the death rate as Japanese families choose to have fewer children. The table below shows birth and death rates in Japan, 2008–10.

	Birth rate (births/1,000)	Death rate (deaths/1,000)
2008	7.87	9.26
2009	8.10	8.98
2010	8.37	8.92

Figure 7.4.2 UK population distribution by age and sex, 2008
Source: Office for National Statistics

Figure 7.4.3 Uganda population distribution by age and sex, 2010

ACTIVITY

Is population rising quickly, slowly or declining in your country? What are the latest figures for birth rate, death rate and net migration? Draw a population pyramid.

KEY POINTS

1. Developed countries have stable or declining populations as a result of low birth and death rates and as a consequence of higher standards of living and better medical facilities.

2. Developing countries have high death rates, including high infant mortality rates. Health facilities are poor, particularly in rural areas.

3. Developing countries have high birth rates, often as a result of a lack of availability of family planning education and resources, and choosing to have more children.

SUMMARY QUESTIONS

1. Why is the shape of the population pyramid different in developing and developed economies?

2. Why is population rising in many developing countries and falling in some developed countries?

3. Why might the growth of population of a country speed up or slow down?

7.5 Problems of population change

> **LEARNING OUTCOMES**
>
> Candidates should be able to:
>
> - analyse the problems and consequences of population changes for countries at different stages of development.

Demographic transition

Demography is the study of population features, such as size, growth and distribution in different age groups.

Demographic transition describes the process of a society moving from high to low mortality and fertility rates. As societies become more prosperous – that is, developed – average incomes rise, along with higher literacy rates and improvements in diet, access to clean water, health care and sanitation. As societies develop, mortality rates typically start to fall before birth rates, leading initially to an increase in population. Once the birth rate starts to fall, the rate of increase of population will slow down. The table indicates different stages of demographic transition.

Low development ⟶ High development

Stage 1: High mortality and fertility rates	Stage 2: Falling mortality combined with high fertility rates	Stage 3: Low mortality and low fertility rates
Problems: low life expectancy, poor health and sanitation conditions, high birth rate	Rising life expectancy leads to rapid increases in the population because birth rate is still high	Rising standards of living but problems may arise from falling population
Current example: Afghanistan, with high infant and maternal mortality rates	Current example: Uganda, with high birth rate and falling mortality rate	Current example: Japan, with falling mortality, fertility and birth rates

Demographic transition varies from one part of a country to another. For example, in a number of southern Indian states fertility rates are low, while in northern India the rates, while falling, are still quite high.

Consequences of population change for developing countries

The following table shows recent United Nations population predictions. The figures make it possible to calculate how much population will increase in different countries between 2010 and 2020.

Name of country	Start-date population 2010 (millions)	End-date population 2020 (millions)
Afghanistan	29,117	39,585
Uganda	33,796	46,319

Within 10 years the populations of these countries are estimated to increase by between 30 and 40 per cent.

The following table compares aspects of development in these countries in 2009.

A primary school class in Afghanistan. Improvements in health care and a rise in the number of trained midwives are helping the national population figure to rise

Indicator	Afghanistan	Uganda
Average income per head	US$335	US$300
People not meeting daily food needs	40 per cent	31 per cent
Women dying in childbirth	1,800/per 100,000 live births	435/100,000
Children dying before the age of 5	191/per 1,000 live births	137/1,000
Children receiving primary school education	37 per cent (2004)	52 per cent

Rising population growth has a dramatic effect on economies where resources are already stretched. In Uganda problems are made worse by the **HIV/AIDS pandemic** and many children are being brought up in orphanages.

If the population grows in a poor country, there is less to go round. Problems include threats of famine, the rapid spread of disease, overcrowding and lack of employment opportunities. There is unsustainable use of natural resources if forests are cut down for firewood and land is overused for agriculture and the soil quality falls. The movement of people into towns and cities creates further problems of overcrowding and lack of access to basic amenities.

Consequences of population change for developed countries

Developed countries are more likely to face problems of falling population. As shown in Unit 7.4, Japan has a declining population: between 2010 and 2020 the population will fall from about 127 million to about 124 million. Couples are marrying later and more women prefer to work longer before starting a family. Many young couples no longer live with their parents, thus fewer people to look after children.

In a number of countries there are not enough people of working age. In parts of Germany migrant workers from Turkey have for many years provided extra labour in car factories and other industries. To counteract a falling population in France, the government provides generous state benefits for parents who have more than two children. This has helped to counteract the fall in the birth rate, and after a time lag is leading to increases in numbers of younger workers.

With longer lifespans in developed countries there is more pressure on those in work to pay taxes to provide the pensions for those who are retired. Lower fertility results in a smaller working population and a larger **dependent population** – the young and the old depend on those in work.

EXAM TIP

You need to show in the examination that you are aware of the problems that can be caused in a country by a rapidly rising population.

ACTIVITY

Search the UN online World Population Prospects database (http://esa.un.org/unpp/) to find three other countries where population is increasing rapidly. Are these developing or developed countries? Set out a table like the one for Afghanistan and Uganda, comparing these countries.

SUMMARY QUESTIONS

1 What is demographic transition? How might a society benefit from demographic transition?

2 Describe three problems that may be caused by rapid increases in population in developing economies.

3 What problems result from a falling population in developed economies?

KEY POINTS

1 A feature of many developing countries is rapid population growth.

2 Resources are stretched by population growth, leading to pressures on health, education and other services and an inability to meet the basic needs of people.

3 Developed economies are more likely to suffer from population shortages.

7.6 The effect of changing size of population on an economy

LEARNING OUTCOMES

Candidates should be able to:
- describe the effects of the changing size of population on an economy.

Uruguay has an ageing population. It has the lowest birth rate in South America and average life expectancy is just under 80

ACTIVITY

Discuss with your classmates how a country could be 'overpopulated' with a relatively small population, and 'underpopulated' with a relatively large population.

EXAM TIP

Whether a country is regarded as underpopulated or overpopulated depends on the availability of its resources to support the population; you must be able to show that you understand this.

The optimum population

Most countries are either **underpopulated** or **overpopulated**: they have too few people to work efficiently with other resources available (or not enough people with the required skills), or they have too many people for the resources available. For economists the **optimum** – that is, ideal or best – **population** size has the best ratio of people to other resources. The optimum population depends on the availability of other resources. Some countries are underpopulated – they do not have enough people to use existing land, capital and other resources efficiently.

CASE STUDY: Underpopulation in Canada

Canada is one of the largest land masses in the world, with an abundance of raw materials – for example, coal, iron ore and oil reserves (although many of these are buried beneath frozen ice sheets for much of the year). The table shows changes in the population of Canada in 2009.

a Births	100,953
b Deaths	57,910
c Natural increase (a – b)	43,043
d Net international migration	+90,455
e Total growth (a + c – b)	133,498

Source: based on figures from Statistics Canada, 2009

Canada recruits migrants from a range of countries, but they are required to have the skills needed to support the development of the Canadian economy – for example, IT professionals, doctors and nurses.

Questions

1. How did the population of Canada grow in 2009? What was the major source of growth?
2. Why do you think it makes economic sense for Canada to focus on encouraging certain types of economic immigration?
3. What is likely to be the effect of immigration on productivity in Canada?

Overpopulation

The world's population is growing (in 2009 it was about 7 billion and growing by 265 per minute) and this raises questions as to whether the planet as a whole will be able to support growing numbers in the future. The threat of overpopulation is very real.

176

Some economists suggest that areas of land have a carrying capacity – that is, an optimum number of people for sustainable economic development. If a population is greater than this carrying capacity, the water tables may be lowered, leading eventually to drought, overuse of land so that soil capacity deteriorates, increased pollution from human activity, and other non-sustainable effects.

Areas most in danger of overpopulation include:

- small island economies with large populations (e.g. Haiti)
- landlocked economies with no access to ports (e.g. Chad, Central African Republic)
- parts of **megacities** where there are large numbers of people overstretching facilities such as sanitation and water (e.g. the slum area of Dharavi in Mumbai, India, and Kibera in Nairobi, Kenya).

Ageing populations

An **ageing population** occurs when the average age in a region or country increases. This is currently happening in almost every country in the world. For example, in Uruguay improvements in sanitation, quality of drinking water, vaccinations and other public goods have raised life expectancy so that a newborn girl can now expect to live to 78 years. Now, too, 17.3 per cent of the population is over 60. The economic effects are:

- an increase in the dependency ratio – there are fewer people working and paying taxes, and they must support more older people who may be receiving state pensions, so there is increased government spending on health care and pensions
- higher taxes for those in work, which could discourage them from working so hard
- a shortage of workers, which could push up wages, leading to wage inflation.

In Germany in 2010 there were four workers supporting each retired person. By 2030 the ratio could be down to 2:1.

Ageing populations push an economy towards overpopulation by putting more pressure on the working population. However, older people can be an economic asset because of their greater experience and willingness to work hard and take on more responsibility. Governments can raise the retirement age, making it illegal for employers to discriminate against older workers, and making it compulsory for employees to contribute towards paying part or all of their pension.

KEY POINTS

1. The optimum population is a state where a population is combined most efficiently with the resources available to that population.
2. Some countries are underpopulated and some are overpopulated.
3. The ageing of the population often pushes an economy away from the optimum position.

DID YOU KNOW?

According to a report by the Worldwide Fund for Nature in 2006, in order for all humans to live with a high degree of luxury, we would be spending three times more than the planet could supply. However, some people criticise this view, saying that it does not differentiate between sustainable (e.g. spending on bread) and unsustainable (e.g. spending on oil) consumption.

EXAM TIP

You will need to be able to discuss the effect of an ageing population. For example, you should be able to consider the consequences for a country and what the government might do to reduce the impact of an ageing population.

SUMMARY QUESTIONS

1. How might a small country be underpopulated and a large one overpopulated?
2. What is the relationship between carrying capacity and optimum population?
3. What are the main economic problems associated with an ageing population?

7.7 Changes in population structure and its effect on an economy

LEARNING OUTCOMES

Candidates should be able to:

- describe the effect of the changing structure of the population on the economy.

Recent years have seen large-scale migration to megacities like Mumbai (14 million people in 2010)

EXAM TIP

You will need to be able to show a clear understanding of the effects of a changing structure of population on an economy. You can include examples from your own country.

DID YOU KNOW?

A major change taking place in India is that women are having fewer children and more are joining the paid labour force for longer periods. How will this be a demographic bonus for India?

The structure of the population

The structure of the population is the way that the total population can be divided into distinct groupings:

- **Age structure** – grouping people according to age.
- **Occupational structure** – grouping people by their jobs or employment sector.
- **Urban/rural divide** – grouping people according to where they live (that is, in towns and cities or in villages).

Age structure

Economists make a distinction between the working population and the dependent population. The working population is those people who are old enough to work and under retirement age. Dependants are those who, for various reasons, such as age or condition, are not in paid work.

The table shows the age groups in India. Since the 1970s the fertility rate in India has been falling, leading to fewer dependants in the young age group; this will continue until 2025–30. This decline means that the number in the working population, compared with the dependent population, is increasing. It is expected to peak by 2025.

Young (0–14)	Together with the elderly group, the young are most dependent on the working population for services such as education, health, accommodation, food
Youth (15–24)	Working or studying
Young working age (25–49)	With dependants, will not be able to save much
Mature working age (50–64)	Higher incomes and work experience; group most likely to be able to save
Elderly (65+)	Similar requirements to 0–14 group

The mature working population is currently increasing. There is a great opportunity therefore for India to increase productivity of labour and to save and invest more in the economy. However, after 2025 there will be more in the elderly age group. This will lead to an increasing burden on health care and social security.

ACTIVITY

Investigate the changing structure of your own population. Set this out in the form of a newspaper article outlining problems resulting from changes in the age structure, occupational structure and rural/urban structure of the population.

Occupational structure

There are three main occupational sectors: agriculture and extraction of raw materials; manufacturing and construction; and service occupations.

In most economies there has been a change in the occupational structure of employment. To continue with the example of India, in 1972 the proportion of employment in agriculture was about 75 per cent. Many farm labourers however, are, able to earn barely enough for subsistence and in 2010 the figure was about 50 per cent. During the same period the percentage involved in industry increased from 11.5 per cent to almost 20 per cent. However, the biggest growth area has been in services, which now account for almost 30 per cent of jobs.

There has been rapid growth in service sector employment, in software and IT services, as well as banking and communication. The growth in numbers working in manufacturing and services in India has led to rising living standards for an increasing percentage of the population. Economic growth has also benefited rural populations as more roads, schools and clinics are built.

Urban/rural divide

The UN forecasts that by 2030 three out of five people worldwide will live in cities. Poor agricultural workers seek better opportunities in cities so that they can send money home to their families. An important economic effect is that as younger workers leave rural areas, these areas become increasingly dependent on an ageing (less efficient) workforce. Rural incomes fall, leading to a deterioration in rural services.

One effect on cities is to increase overcrowding. Overcrowding makes it difficult to provide suitable sanitation, water and electricity. In the highly populated Dharavi area of Mumbai (with a population of nearly one million) it is estimated that there is only one toilet per 1,500 residents. In other overcrowded cities some areas are characterised by high levels of unemployment and high crime rates.

In other countries underpopulation is the problem in urban areas. For example, Hoyerswerda in eastern Germany has become almost a ghost town as its population has moved to western areas of Germany seeking employment. Depopulation often leads to a deterioration of local services because there are not enough people to pay for them.

KEY POINTS

1. A key feature of the age structure of the population is the relationship between the working and dependent populations.
2. The service sector is the fastest-growing part of the occupational structure.
3. Large-scale migrations are taking place from rural areas to cities.

DID YOU KNOW?

The US, Germany and Japan have ageing populations. The average age of the population is increasing and there are more people of retirement age. One effect is a 'pension timebomb': it will be increasingly difficult for the working population to pay enough taxes to provide for pensions of retired people.

ACTIVITY

Investigate the changing structure of your own population. Set this out in the form of a newspaper article outlining problems resulting from changes in the age structure, occupational structure and rural/urban structure of the population.

SUMMARY QUESTIONS

1. How can a decline in the fertility rate of a population provide an opportunity for economic development?
2. Give three examples of occupations that are employing increasing numbers in service industries worldwide.
3. Describe two problems associated with the rapid growth of cities.

7.8 Living standards

LEARNING OUTCOMES

Candidates should be able to:
- discuss differences in living standards within countries.

Some members of an economy have access to a large basket of goods (their standard of living), while others have access to a much smaller basket

Living standards

The **living standard** is the level of material comfort that is available to an individual or group, as measured by the goods, services and luxuries that they have. A person's living standard can be thought of as a basket of goods and services they need in order to live their day-to-day lives. The imaginary basket does not just contain goods that you can buy in shops, but also access to clean water supplies, health services, education and other requirements for a good life. Some people have access to more goods and better services than others.

Differences in living standards within countries

Within countries there are considerable differences in living standards. These differences arise for the following economic reasons:

- Some people have inherited wealth which is handed down from family and friends.
- Some people earn a higher income because of the type of work they do. Those with scarce skills, such as doctors and lawyers, will receive a much higher income than unskilled workers.
- Some people own their own business, or have a shareholding in businesses. These people take a risk in running an enterprise. The rewards in the form of profit may be high.
- Some people prosper because they work harder than others (or because they are lucky to be doing the right job at the right time).

DID YOU KNOW?

Mexico has the second highest income per head in Latin America after Brazil. Wages for farm workers may, however, be very low (particularly when people are working illegally). Human Development Indicator scores show 0.80 for northern states and 0.70 for some southern states. Wages for factory workers are higher than for other workers.

Figure 7.8.1 Different living standards are enjoyed by people within the same society

Differences in living standards between countries

There are many indicators that can be considered in comparing living standards between countries.

Living standards will depend on how effective an economy is in producing goods and services – that is, the productivity of its industries. Productive industries enable employees to achieve high living standards and they also contribute benefits to everyone in the economy – for example, through higher taxes. Living standards also depend on the provision of health and educational facilities within countries. For example, Norway, Sweden and Denmark invest heavily in education and health care.

Typically citizens of more developed countries have access to bigger baskets of goods and welfare services. However, the relationship between development and well-being is not a straightforward one – for example, some countries with relatively high GDP per head do not always come out on top in terms of other indicators of well-being.

Living standards and quality of life

What is 'beneficial' depends on personal judgement. For example, while some people may want to own a car, others may consider cars to be harmful in terms of the pollution they create, road accidents and other negative impacts. Access to the internet may be regarded by some as beneficial, while others may see it as an intrusion on privacy.

While living standards may be useful for making comparisons in terms of access to goods and services, they may not be so useful at measuring **quality of life**. For example, the greater the volume of goods that a society creates, the greater the potential to create pollution and negative externalities. Quality of life is difficult to measure, but it is more concerned with providing individuals with what they value – this might include access to fresh water and clear unpolluted air. When we look at other indexes of well-being, it is possible to question how closely living standards represent quality of life. For example, indicators of life expectancy give a different perspective on the growth of a society.

You might expect the US to feature higher in such a table. However, just as poor countries have illnesses associated with poverty, rich countries like the US have illnesses associated with wealth, such as obesity and its links to diabetes and heart disease. Also, as we saw on the last two pages, national indicators for GDP per head often hide inequalities within a society.

New Zealand citizens benefit from high quality health care and schooling. GDP per head (US$25,334 in 2009) is lower than that of Spain (US$31,142), but in HDI scores New Zealand scores 9.50 compared with 0.855 in Spain

ACTIVITY

Carry out some research to find out the HDI, GDP per head and car ownership per 1,000 people in one other country in each of the seven continents. How similar are the figures to those of the countries shown in the table above? Set out your findings in a chart.

Country	Life expectancy at birth (years)
Spain	80.9
New Zealand	80.2
US	78.2
Saudi Arabia	76.3
Jamaica	72.6
India	64.7
Uganda	51.5

KEY POINTS

1 Standards of living vary between rural and urban areas, regions of a country and different income earners.
2 Inequalities exist within countries and between countries.
3 Some people feel that living standards fail to measure quality of life.

SUMMARY QUESTIONS

1 What are the main differences in living standards within a country? Use your country as an example.
2 What are the main differences in living standards between countries? Compare your country with another country.

Unit 7 — Practice exam questions

SECTION 1: Multiple-choice questions

Each question has ONE correct answer.

1. Which of the following would NOT be a sign of economic development in a low-income country?
   a. Decreasing death rate
   b. Increasing literacy rate
   c. Increasing access to medical care
   d. Decreasing GDP per head

2. What does the Gini index measure?
   a. The average level of income in a country
   b. The difference between the highest and lowest incomes in a country
   c. How equally income is distributed in a country
   d. The average level of direct taxation in a country

3. Which is NOT a feature of absolute poverty?
   a. Inability to afford basic housing
   b. Inability to afford a television
   c. Inability to afford food
   d. Inability to access any income

4. Which of the following is more likely to lead to a falling population?
   a. Negative net migration and a falling birth rate
   b. A falling death rate and a static birth rate
   c. Negative net migration and a falling fertility rate
   d. Rising fertility rate and positive net migration

5. Which of the following is a threat of high population growth in a developing country?
   a. Increasing birth rate
   b. Increasing education provision
   c. Increasing workforce
   d. Increasing need to support dependants

6. Which of the following is a possible problem of a below-optimum population?
   a. GDP per head is low
   b. Factors of production are left unused
   c. Unemployment is high
   d. Poverty is increasing

7. Which is NOT a government policy to try to reduce poverty?
   a. Paying welfare benefits
   b. Subsidies on food
   c. Regressive taxation
   d. Provision of schooling

8. Which of the following is a change to the occupational structure of a population?
   a. Rising average incomes in the population
   b. Increasing numbers of the population employed in service industry jobs
   c. Increasingly unequal distribution of income among the population
   d. Increasing unemployment among young people in the population

9. Which of the following is NOT included in the Human Development Index?
   a. Level of income
   b. Access to education
   c. Life expectancy
   d. Access to new technology

10. One advantage of rural–urban migration to the government of a developing country may be:
    a. Increasing pressure on city infrastructure
    b. Decreasing population in rural villages
    c. Increasing skills of workforce
    d. Decreasing reliance on family structures

SECTION 2: Structured questions

Country A is a developing nation, whose government faces major economic and social challenges over the next few years. The country's wealth in the past relied on mineral and metal ore mining, but the prices and demand in this sector have been falling, which has led to considerable deprivation in areas that were previously wealthy. The government has a declared objective to eliminate absolute poverty. GDP is increasing slowly, but the gap between higher-income households and those living in poverty has widened. Average life expectancy is around 53 years of age, higher in urban areas.

Urbanisation has been a big factor in changes in population in recent years – more people now live in the towns and cities and the countryside is increasingly seen as a 'poor' place to live. In the bigger towns and capital city, new western-style shopping centres are being built and more people are gaining access to technology in the form of mobile phones and the internet. These are particularly popular with the young, who are keen to embrace all aspects of western culture.

Charities and NGOs (non-government organisations) are very active in the country, concentrating on provision of facilities in poor rural areas and education, particularly for girls, which is seen to be the key to lifting many families out of poverty. Diseases such as HIV/AIDS and malaria still take a heavy toll on the population, but education and funding has led to better health care and better family planning support.

1 a Identify and explain TWO likely features of a developing nation. *(4)*

b Explain, with the use of a diagram, the likely shape of the population pyramid for Country A. *(6)*

c Explain what is meant by *average life expectancy* and comment on this for Country A. *(4)*

d Suggest TWO policies the government of Country A may implement to try to increase the average life expectancy in rural areas. *(6)*

2 a Explain what is meant by the *occupational structure* of a population. *(4)*

b Using information from the text, comment on the likely changes in the occupational structure of the population in recent years. *(4)*

c Explain what is meant by *fertility rate*, *birth rate* and *death rate* for a country's population. *(6)*

d Discuss the impact that *better education and health care* may have on the urban population in Country A. *(6)*

3 a The government of Country A would like to 'eliminate absolute poverty'. Explain what is meant by this term. *(4)*

b Discuss TWO ways in which the government of Country A may try to achieve this objective. *(6)*

c The government of Country A would also like to make the 'distribution of income more fair'. Suggest ONE policy that could work towards this aim. *(4)*

d Discuss the extent to which the use of new technologies, as described in the text, may help to increase incomes in Country A. *(6)*

4 a Explain what is meant by *economic development* in a country such as Country A. *(3)*

b Explain why rising GDP may not lead to economic development. *(3)*

c Suggest TWO ways in which the work of charities and NGOs may lead to economic development in Country A. *(6)*

d Considering the case study information and economic objectives of Country A, discuss the view that 'education will be better than aid' in improving the standard of living. *(8)*

Total: 80 marks

SECTION 3: Analysis and critical evaluation

Country B is a small developed country, whose population is increasing fast due to positive net migration, an increasing birth rate and an ageing population. The capital city has a large population, whose numbers are boosted by tourism as it is a popular destination for visitors from abroad. Property prices and rents are extremely high and there is increasing pressure on services such as doctors and schools as more and more people move in. In contrast, rural villages are sparsely populated and the pace of life is slow. Most people are involved in agriculture, growing mainly food crops and flowers to satisfy the demand from the city and overseas markets.

The Morelle family live on their flower farm in a rural village and live well on their small income from agriculture. Their daughter, who trained and works as a highly paid lawyer, has married and moved to the capital city. The family have frequent discussions comparing the quality of life in their chosen locations.

1 a Explain what is meant by *positive net migration*. (2)
   b Explain how an increasing birth rate may continue to affect the population of Country B. (2)

2 a Explain what is meant by an *ageing population*. (2)
   b What might be the effect of an ageing population on demand for services in Country B? (2)

3 Discuss why the population of Country B's capital city might be described as *greater than optimum*. (5)

4 a Explain what is meant by the measurement GDP per head. (2)
   b Explain why the GDP of Country B may be rising, but GDP per head may fall. (5)

5 Discuss the view that 'GDP per head does not necessarily give a full picture of the quality of life enjoyed by all citizens in Country B'. (5)

6 Using information from the text, discuss the Morelle family's argument about where the quality of life is better. Which members of the family do you think have a better quality of life? Justify your conclusion. (7)

Total: 32 marks

8 International aspects

This unit introduces international aspects of economics. The world economy is more closely linked now than at any other stage in history. This provides potential benefits to people and communities across the globe. The unit explains how regions and countries are able to specialise, and the effect that this can have in terms of benefits to the country itself, but also on its relations with trading partners.

The unit also introduces and explains the structure of the current account of the balance of payments, the financial record of trade between countries. The material shows how the current account records the overall value of trading between a country and the rest of the world and provides a useful picture for governments and economists of how competitive an economy is, particularly in its ability to sell goods and services to foreigners.

Finally the unit examines the nature of exchange rates, how one international currency can be traded against another. It is explained how rates fluctuate over time, and the effect of this on international markets. The need for protection for industries in a domestic economy is introduced and the different ways countries can achieve this, ending with a comparison of the merits of free trade with those of protection.

LEARNING OUTCOMES

With regard to **international aspects of economics**, candidates should be able to:

- describe the benefits and disadvantages of specialisation at regional and national levels
- describe the structure of the current account of the balance of payments
- define exchange rates
- discuss the causes and consequences of exchange rate fluctuations
- describe methods of protection
- discuss the merits of free trade and protection.

8.1 Benefits and disadvantages of specialisation

LEARNING OUTCOMES

Candidates should be able to:
- describe the benefits and disadvantages of specialisation at regional and national levels.

Regional specialisation

Countries and regions concentrate on producing things that they are best at rather than wasting resources on products that they make less efficiently.

The climate of a country is obviously a major factor affecting what a country produces. Italy shows how a country can have distinct **regional specialisations**: in the north, the cooler climate is suitable for producing grains, meat and fruits like pears and apples. The region is also industrialised, with large car factories and banks. In the warmer south, citrus fruits (oranges and lemons), oils and vegetables are produced and there is a stronger focus on agriculture and tourism. This pattern of regional specialisation has led to more skilled workers in the north, and less availability of capital and skilled workers in the south – southern Italy has about 40 per cent of Italy's population, but only earns 25 per cent of the GDP.

Southern Italy specialises in producing citrus fruit because its resources, including land and climate, give it an advantage in this line of production

International specialisation

The table shows national specialisation that has resulted from superior factor endowments (the qualities of production factors that make them particularly efficient at doing certain things).

Country	Main product and factor endowment
Saudi Arabia	World's leading producer of oil: it has the most plentiful oil reserves in the world, and the technology to extract it
Japan	World's leading producers of cars: new technologies have been used to develop efficient manufacturing systems
Guinea	Has the world's largest reserves of bauxite lying close to the earth's surface; this is extracted by large earth-movers and then refined to make aluminium
New Zealand	A cool, damp climate and pastures have led to the country becoming a leading producer of lamb and wool
UK	Major publisher of books, based on its history of developing expertise in this industry over time

ACTIVITY

What products does your country specialise in producing? Why does your country specialise in making these products? Keep notes of your findings to use for the Activity in Unit 8.2.

How does specialisation occur?

Countries specialise in lines where they have superior factor endowments. There are several reasons for doing this:

- The country has the resources required to produce certain goods. For example, the geology of South Africa has created the rock formations in which diamonds are found.

- The country has abundant resources of the right kind. Some resources, such as oil reserves, occur naturally; others, such as Japan's investment in automated car manufacturing technology, are developed over time.
- By **trading**, countries may be able to acquire certain goods more cheaply than they can produce them domestically. For example, people in the UK can buy T-shirts made in Pakistan for the equivalent of just three or four US dollars. It would cost at least twice as much to make a similar T-shirt in a British factory.

The table shows some of the advantages and disadvantages of specialisation.

Advantages	Disadvantages
Enables increased output: Mexico, for example, uses large areas of land for onion growing; large-scale farming yields large low-cost outputs.	A country can be vulnerable if it has to rely on imports to meet its needs. For example, if a country fails to invest in its own domestic energy industries, it will have to import energy from overseas.
Consumers have access to a greater variety of higher-quality products from across the world.	A country may be vulnerable if the specialised products can be replaced by alternatives. For example, Malaysia produced large quantities of rubber from rubber plantations for the automobile industry – today most of the rubber is produced synthetically.
Specialisation and international trade increase the size of the market, enabling economies of scale.	Jobs in areas such as production may be vulnerable if cheaper labour is available elsewhere. Too much specialisation can result in inflexibility in the economy.
Leads to greater efficiency which in turn leads to production being carried out by the most efficient producers/countries.	A country becomes very vulnerable to changes in exchange rates and also world economic conditions.

KEY POINTS

1. Specialisation involves concentration on what a country does most efficiently.
2. Regional specialisation often results from differences in climate, geography or skills of the local population. People in these areas develop skills based on the specialisation.
3. International specialisation increases world production and provides consumers with greater variety and choice. Resources are used more efficiently, but risks are involved.

SUMMARY QUESTIONS

1. What is international specialisation? Give one example of a country that specialises in:
   a a primary product
   b a secondary product
   c a tertiary service.
2. Explain the difference between regional and international specialisation.
3. What arguments would you put forward to encourage a country to increase its specialisation in products that it makes well?

EXAM TIP

Specialisation is an important concept in economics. You should be able to explain what it means and how it comes about, and to discuss its various advantages and disadvantages. It is always useful to support the points you are making with appropriate examples.

8.2 The current account of the balance of payments

LEARNING OUTCOMES

Candidates should be able to:

- describe the structure of the current account of the balance of payments.

Oil is Saudi Arabia's largest export by value. It appears as a visible export in Saudi's current account of the balance of payments

ACTIVITY

Find out the top 10 imports and exports of your country. Using this information, and material gathered from the Activity in Unit 8.1, create a poster to display this information.

Figure 8.2.1 New Zealand's top 10 imports and exports include cars and butter

The current account

The **current account** of the balance of payments shows the income earned by a country and the expenditure it makes in dealings with other countries. It consists of four elements:

1. Trade in goods (visibles)
2. Trade in services (invisibles)
3. Income flows
4. Current transfers.

The balance of trade in goods and services

The **balance of trade in goods and services account** shows the flows of money coming into and going out of a country as a result of trading.

- **Trade in goods – visible items**: these are literally items that you can see, physical goods that a country trades. For example, in 2009 New Zealand's top 10 exports were all visible products: milk powder, crude oil, meat (lamb), butter, frozen beef, cheese, aluminium, coal, kiwi fruit and wine.
  – Visible exports are goods sold by New Zealand to foreign countries bringing revenue into New Zealand.
  – Visible imports are purchases by New Zealanders of goods from other countries.
- **Trade in services – invisible items** are non-physical traded items. The UK's main invisibles include banking, insurance and transporting goods.
  – Invisible exports consist of services sold to foreigners, bringing revenue into the UK. For example, when a UK bank lends money to a foreigner it will charge interest on the loan.
  – Invisible imports consist of expenditures on services bought from outside a country. For example, when a UK company hires an overseas shipping company to transport goods for it, the payment is counted as an invisible import.
- **Exports** – lead to inflows of money.
- **Imports** – lead to outflows of money.

The balance of trade in goods and services account can therefore be set out as shown in the box opposite.

Debits represent payments to countries where goods and services are imported from. **Credits** represent receipts from sales of exports.

To calculate the balance of trade in goods and services:

1. Find the visible balance. In the illustration the visible balance is US$10 million.

	Credits (US$ million)	Debits (US$ million)	Net difference (US$ million)
Visibles			
Food, beverages, tobacco	100	40	60
Oil and fuel	0	100	−100
Manufactured goods	400	350	50
Total goods	500	490	**Visible balance 10**
Invisible services			
Transport	200	100	100
Financial services	300	100	200
			Invisible balance 300
Current total			**Current balance 310**

> **EXAM TIP**
>
> You only need to know about the current account of the balance of payments, but you should have a clear understanding of the four elements in the current account.

2 Find the invisible balance. In the illustration the invisible balance is US$300 million.

3 Find the balance of trade by combining the totals from the visible and invisible balance. In the illustration the country has a surplus on both visible and invisible trading, giving it a positive current balance. The current balance is US$310 million.

$$\text{Visible balance} = \text{US\$10 million}$$
$$\text{Invisible balance} = \text{US\$300 million}$$
$$\text{Current balance} = \text{US\$310 million}$$

The economy of the country would benefit from exporting more goods and services than it imports.

Income flows

The current account also records two other types of income flows between a country and the rest of the world. Taking the example of Germany:

1 Add wages, salaries and other benefits received by Germany's residents who are working abroad. Deduct wages, salaries and earnings of foreign nationals working in Germany.

2 Add investment income earned by Germans from overseas investment (e.g. profits). Deduct investment income paid to overseas citizens with investments in Germany.

Current transfers

These are transfers of money, goods or services that are not part of a trading process – for example, the sending of presents and gifts, donations to charities. The current account shows these four types of movements of money for trading (1 and 2) and other current types of movement of money (3 and 4).

> **KEY POINTS**
>
> 1 The balance of trade in goods and services account shows the visible and invisible trade of a country.
>
> 2 Imports appear as debit items in the account. Exports appear as credit items.
>
> 3 Also included in the current account are movements of money resulting from income payments and current transfers.

> **SUMMARY QUESTIONS**
>
> 1 Classify the following items as visibles or invisibles: transport, insurance, motor vehicles, banking, chemicals, engineering products, steel, coal, postal services.
>
> 2 A country's exports of goods in July were US$60.5 billion and its imports were US$105.8 billion. Exports of services were US$24 billion and imports of services US$20.7 billion. Calculate the balance of trade in goods and services.
>
> 3 A country typically imports more than it exports, but receives large sums in charitable donations. How would these movements of money affect the current account balance?

8.3 Exchange rates

LEARNING OUTCOMES

Candidates should be able to:
- define exchange rates.

The exchange rate

When you buy T-shirts or other items of clothing produced in China you will want to pay for them in the currency of your own country (unless of course you live in China). The T-shirts will most likely have been imported into your country by a specialist importer or by a large retailer. The Chinese manufacturer that made the T-shirts may not want to be paid by the importer in the currency of your country. This is because the Chinese manufacturer will need to pay its own workers and suppliers of cotton in the currency of China, the yuan. The importer will therefore need to purchase yuan to pay the Chinese manufacturer. Foreign currency can be bought and sold in the foreign exchange market (or forex). This market specialises in exchanging dollars, yuan, rupees and other currencies.

The exchange rate between the US dollar and the Indian rupee is determined by demand and supply in international currency markets

The **exchange rate** between two currencies is determined by demand and supply. If the demand for US dollars by Indians (to buy American goods) rises quickly while the demand for rupees by Americans (to buy Indian goods) remains steady, then the value of the dollar will rise against the rupee – for example, from US$1 = 45 rupees to US$1 = 47 rupees.

You can see from this analysis that a major determinant of the value of a currency is how popular the currency is – that is, the strength of demand for it. One of the major factors influencing demand is the extent to which foreigners want to buy goods from that country. For example, the Singapore dollar tends to be a relatively strong currency because many foreigners buy goods from Singaporean companies.

Another factor strengthening a currency is its use for international trading. For example, the US dollar has for many years been used

ACTIVITY

Find out the current exchange rate of your currency against the euro, US dollar, yuan and Indian rupee. After two weeks, check the exchange rates again. How have they altered? What explanations can you provide for this? Produce a graph or chart that shows the rates over six weeks.

by countries for trading because it tends to keep its value over time. It is therefore both a means of exchange and a store of value (see Unit 3.1).

Multiple exchange rates

There is not just one exchange rate for a currency: it can often be exchanged for the currencies of many other countries – for example, the yuan against the dollar, the yuan against the euro, the yuan against the rupee. This means that there can be multiple exchange rates.

Exchange rate systems

A country's government must decide how to manage (influence) the exchange rate. There are two main approaches:

- **Fixed exchange rates**: the value of the currency is fixed against another currency or group of currencies. This fixed rate is maintained by the government. For example, the government could set the exchange rate such that two dollars of your currency might be exchanged for one US dollar. This helps to make the currency stable. However, it may make it difficult for the country to sell its goods on international markets if the exchange rate is set at too high a level for exporters to be competitive. A disadvantage of having a fixed rate is that the government has to support the existing rate even when the rate makes it difficult for exporters to sell their goods competitively.
- **Floating exchange rates**: the value of your currency changes from day to day according to the demand and supply for it. If we are finding it difficult to sell exports the currency will fall in price (as demand falls). Lowering the price of the exports makes them more competitive – and hopefully sales will improve.

CASE STUDY | The Eurozone

Most of the countries in the European Union have a shared currency, the euro. These countries include France and Germany, and smaller economies such as Luxembourg and Greece. An advantage of having a common currency is that there is no need for the paperwork and costs involved in exchanging money. This makes trade within the Eurozone more efficient. Management of the euro is carried out by the European Central Bank in Frankfurt. The euro has become an important international exchange currency. Exporters from smaller countries are happy to be paid in euros or US dollars, knowing that these currencies are likely to retain their value.

Questions

1 What benefits would there be to an individual country from being part of a common currency zone?
2 Why might German manufacturers be pleased that their country is part of the Eurozone?

EXAM TIP

You should be able to demonstrate in the examination an understanding of the various advantages and disadvantages of these two types of exchange rate system.

KEY POINTS

1 The exchange rate is the rate at which one currency exchanges for others.
2 A country's currency will have multiple exchange rates.
3 Exchange rates can be fixed against other currencies or be free to float according to the laws of supply and demand.

SUMMARY QUESTIONS

1 Define the term *exchange rate*.
2 What factors determine the exchange rate of one currency against another?
3 What are the benefits to producers of having a freely floating exchange rate rather than a fixed one?

8.4 Causes of exchange rate fluctuations

LEARNING OUTCOMES

Candidates should be able to:
- discuss the causes of exchange rate fluctuations.

The US dollar is used widely as a generally acceptable international exchange currency

DID YOU KNOW?

A destabilising effect on currencies can be caused by speculators – people who make money from trading in currencies. Sometimes they will sell a country's currency, and others rush to do the same. The speculator might then buy the currency back at a much lower price and gamble that it will rise again.

Appreciation and depreciation

Another way of looking at the exchange rate is as the price of buying the currency of one country with that of another country. Like other prices, the exchange rate will then be determined by the demand for and supply of it.

If more people in India want to buy US dollars, the demand curve will shift to the right and the price of dollars will increase when bought with rupees. This may be because more Indians want to import goods from the US. Figure 8.4.1 shows this change. It is referred to as an **appreciation** in the price of the dollar. (In contrast, if Indians want to buy fewer goods from the US, this leads to a fall in demand for dollars and a fall in value – that is, **depreciation** – of the dollar.)

Figure 8.4.1 An appreciation of the dollar against the rupee

Figure 8.4.2 A depreciation of the dollar against the euro

The price of a currency may fall as a result of an increase in the supply of that currency – for example, as a result of citizens of that country using their domestic currency to buy more imports. An example of this is that the US dollar is accepted widely as an international trading currency and more and more dollars have been entering the international exchange market. The increase in supply of dollars over time (see Figure 8.4.2) leads to its depreciation against other currencies, such as the European Union's euro. For the last 20 years the US has been running large current account deficits with the rest of the world. This has helped the world economy because US dollars are widely accepted as a means of international exchange.

Under a system of freely floating exchange rates the value of currencies will appreciate and depreciate continually, in line with changes in demand for and supply of currencies for international exchange.

Foreign exchange is bought and sold for trading purposes and also for investment, such as buying shares in companies in other countries. Some people also buy currency in order to speculate – for example, to buy at a low price and sell when prices rise.

> **DID YOU KNOW?**
>
> Currency price can also be affected by the interest rate in one country compared with interest rates in other countries. Investors want to invest where interest rates are higher: raising the rates can encourage an inflow of capital, increasing demand for the currency and leading to a rise in its exchange value.

> **DID YOU KNOW?**
>
> Devaluation is a serious step to take – before it takes place, foreign exchange dealers lose confidence in a currency and try to sell it, often leading to a greater fall in the currency than the government devaluing their currency would wish.

Devaluation and revaluation

Revaluation of a currency occurs when its value is adjusted. For example, the rate of exchange between a country's currency and the US dollar was previously 10 units to one US dollar. Now the government changes the rate to 5 units equal to one US dollar. This would make the dollars half as expensive to people wanting to buy them with the revalued currency.

In a system where exchange rates are fixed against other currencies, they may become overvalued over time. For example, a country might find that at the existing exchange rate it is difficult for exporters to compete with cheaper (or better-quality) products from rival countries. The government may then have to act and **devalue** the currency – that is, force the exchange rate down. The central bank would be instructed to supply an increased quantity of the currency onto international markets. This would reduce its price and bring about **devaluation** (see Figure 8.4.3), and at the same time make imports more expensive. These two effects would help to improve the current account balance (see Unit 8.2).

Figure 8.4.3 Devaluing a currency by increasing its supply

> **KEY POINTS**
>
> 1 Fluctuations in exchange rates are caused by changes in the supply and demand of international currencies.
>
> 2 Changes in demand and supply for currencies results from the demand and supply of currencies for trade purposes, and for capital flows.
>
> 3 Speculation can lead to unsettling changes in the price of foreign exchange.

> **EXAM TIP**
>
> Make sure that you understand the difference between an <u>appreciation</u> and a <u>revaluation</u>, and a <u>depreciation</u> and a <u>devaluation</u> of a currency.

> **SUMMARY QUESTIONS**
>
> 1 How might a change in the demand for the Indian rupee, by people in the Eurozone buying more Indian goods, lead to a change in the exchange rate of the rupee against the euro?
>
> 2 How might a change in the supply of the New Zealand dollar lead to a change in its exchange rate against other currencies?
>
> 3 Explain the difference between:
>   a depreciation and devaluation
>   b appreciation and revaluation.

8.5 Consequences of exchange rate fluctuations

LEARNING OUTCOMES

Candidates should be able to:
- discuss the consequences of exchange rate fluctuations.

Fluctuating exchange rates

Changing exchange rates affect those most concerned with the trading process – exporters and importers. They also have knock-on impacts on the economy – for example, price changes for consumers (of imported goods), and for producers whose inputs have an imported component, such as the cost of raw materials, including energy costs.

The table below shows the effect of rises and falls in the value of a currency.

Home currency appreciates (gets stronger); external value of the currency goes up.	Exports from home country become more expensive to customers from mother countries, therefore more difficult to sell. Exporters will sell less/make less profit. Value of exports decreases.	Imports from other countries become cheaper, including raw materials and finished goods. Importers will find goods from other countries cheaper to buy, so they can sell more in the home country, enabling them to make more profit. Value of imports increases.
Home currency depreciates (gets weaker); external value of the currency goes down.	Exports from home country become less expensive to customers from other countries, therefore easier to sell. Exporters will sell more/make more profit. Value of exports increases.	Imports from other countries become more expensive, including raw materials and finished goods. Importers will find goods from other countries more expensive to buy, so they can sell less in the home country/make less profit. Value of imports increases.

Strong demand for Australian coal in 2009–10 was one factor leading to an increase in demand and hence the price of the Australian dollar – increasing profits in Australian mining

EXAM TIP

Make sure that you can show an understanding of both the causes and the consequences of exchange rate fluctuations.

CASE STUDY — Australia: 'the lucky economy'

In 2010 a number of Australian economists predicted that the Australian dollar was moving towards parity with the US dollar (that is, US$1 = 1 Australian dollar). In 2008 the Australian dollar had only been worth US$0.600. However, by 2010 it had risen to more than US$0.923.

Australia is a major producer of mineral products such as copper, iron and coal. These products are in high demand in rapidly growing markets in Asia, particularly China. When interest rates were low in the US and Western Europe (1–2 per cent), Australian interest rates were relatively high, at about 3 per cent. Many investors put their money into Australia because of the higher interest rates there, and because the economy was doing well and the currency was rising in value. The country has been called 'the lucky economy' because it missed the global recession in 2008–9. As a result of the appreciation of the currency, Australian exports are now more expensive and imports are cheaper.

Questions

1 Why did the price of the Australian dollar increase against the US dollar in 2010?

2 What is the likely effect on the price and quantity sold of Australian exports, and the price and quantity bought of Australian imports?

3 Does it benefit Australia for its imports to be cheaper and exports more expensive?

ACTIVITY

Search newspapers and the internet to find a country whose exchange rate has been rising and a country where it has been falling. Create a short newspaper report highlighting the reasons for the change in the value of the currencies in question.

Price elasticity of demand for exports and imports

The consequences of exchange rate fluctuations depend on the price elasticity of demand for traded goods. In 2010 the Australian dollar appreciated because more people wanted to buy Australian goods. Demand for these goods was relatively inelastic. The demand for Australian dollars was also relatively inelastic. The table shows the effect of this.

Australian exporters	exporting goods with an inelastic demand benefited from higher sales revenues. (Other exporters selling goods with elastic demand were not able to benefit.)
Australian importers	were able to import goods more cheaply, leading to increasing profit margins.
Australian consumers	benefited from cheaper prices of imported goods.
Australian importers	benefited from cheaper fuel, raw materials and part-finished goods.
Australian government	benefited from a healthy economy with a strong foreign trade sector.

The consequences of a depreciating currency

There are also advantages to the depreciation of a country's currency. In 2010 the British pound depreciated against the euro because of the weakness of the UK economy in the 2008–9 recession. This fall in the value of the pound sterling was a major factor in helping to pull Britain out of the recession in 2010. In 2010 UK manufacturers reported increases in exports, particularly of modern engineering products, because their goods were less expensive for foreign buyers.

The effect of a depreciating currency depends on the price elasticity of demand for exports and imports. If demand for exports is elastic, a fall in the currency will lead to a greater than proportional increase in sales of exports. If the demand for imports is also elastic, a depreciating currency could lead to a more than proportional fall in imports.

KEY POINTS

1 Changes in the exchange rate influence five major groups.

2 An appreciating currency can help most groups in a 'strong' economy.

3 A depreciating currency can help exporters to sell more, while leading to a fall in imports.

SUMMARY QUESTIONS

1 What impact is an appreciating domestic currency likely to have on
   a exporters
   b importers?

2 Why is it important to consider the price elasticity of demand for exports when discussing the impact of a depreciation of a currency?

3 How might consumers in a particular country be affected by the appreciation of their currency?

8.6 Methods of protection

LEARNING OUTCOMES

Candidates should be able to:
- discuss methods of protection.

What is protection?

Trade **protection** is restricting the entry of foreign goods into a domestic market, or imposing a tax to raise the price of imports.

Limiting numbers or prices

To protect domestic industries, a government can restrict the number of imports allowed into its country. It can make imports more expensive by taxing them. Another way of restricting imports is to limit the availability of foreign exchange required to purchase them.

Types of trade protection

The following are the main types of protection:

- **Import tariffs**: taxes on types of imports – for example, in 2009 the US imposed a tariff on imported car tyres to protects its own tyre industry against cheaper imports – or from certain groups of countries. Tariffs increase the cost of importing and increase the price of the imported goods in domestic markets. (Tariffs can also be imposed on exports. However, they are unlikely to be used, as this would have a negative effect on domestic industries.)

- **Import quotas**: quotas set a physical limit on the number of imports – for example, the number of Japanese cars entering the European Union in a given year. Restricting quantities in this way is also likely to make them more expensive.

- **Import licensing**: governments can grant licences for the import of certain goods. Not granting a licence is a type of protection.

- **Administrative complexity**: the government may require importers to fill in time-consuming paperwork. This creates a burden that can be seen as a cost and therefore a discouragement for importers.

- **Subsidies**: payments to a domestic producer. The effect is to make domestic goods cheaper to produce, often enabling them to be sold at lower prices than imports. The subsidy may take the form of a lump sum or a cheap loan to a domestic business. Export subsidies are the opposite of tariffs. They involve a direct payment to an exporter (the US government provides a number of agricultural subsidies, including those to cotton farmers).

- **Exchange control**: governments preventing or limiting the amount of foreign exchange to which importers have access – for example, if Indian importers are not allowed to buy dollars, they may not be able to buy goods from the US.

- **Exchange rate manipulation**: the government can buy or sell its own currency in order to alter the exchange rate – for example, it could sell its own currency in order to reduce the exchange rate and make exports cheaper.

- **Embargo**: a complete ban on the import of certain types of goods, or goods from specified countries.

In 2009 Ecuador imposed import tariffs on over 600 goods, including pasta, an important part of the diet for Ecuadoreans

ACTIVITY

Carry out some research to find examples of goods that are protected in your country against foreign imports by the use of:

a import quotas

b import tariffs

c the requirement for importers to have an import licence.

Report your findings to your class and explain how these different methods of protection help domestic industries.

CASE STUDY: Ecuador's protectionist measures

Ecuador is a small South American economy with a population of 14 million people. The economy's main export is oil. As a result of the world recession in 2009, the price of oil on world markets fell from US$120 a barrel in June 2008 to US$40 a barrel six months later. The country's currency is the US dollar. With the recession the country was suddenly exposed to very high import costs compared with exports – leading to a huge deficit on the current account. The government imposed tariffs on 627 products, including furniture, phones, shoes and pasta, intended to halve the imports to the country. The Ecuadorean government argued that without these measures the country would have rapidly run out of money. These measures have been successful in protecting Ecuadorean industries and in keeping the economy running in difficult times.

Questions

1. Why did Ecuador decide to impose tariffs on so many goods? What criteria might they have selected in choosing goods to protect?
2. What would be the impact if many other countries decided to act in the same way as Ecuador?
3. Who would have benefited most from Ecuador's actions?

EXAM TIP

You need to be able to discuss the various types of protection that could be used. This means that you need to consider their relative advantages and disadvantages.

DID YOU KNOW?

In 2000 Ecuador adopted the US dollar as its currency. Up to that point the country had been characterised by instability and high levels of inflation. Introducing the US dollar was designed to create price stability. A small number of other countries use the US dollar as their currency. See if you can find out which they are.

KEY POINTS

1. Protectionism is the means by which a government 'protects' its economy.
2. The main methods of protecting domestic industries are through tariffs and quotas.
3. Countries may use protectionist measures to improve their current account balances.

ACTIVITY

Carry out some research to identify five protectionist measures that have each been used recently by a country to protect its domestic industries. Explain why the country used this measure and outline the advantages and disadvantages of using each one. Produce a leaflet of your findings to compare with others in your group.

SUMMARY QUESTIONS

1. Divide the following according to whether they predominantly affect the price or the quantity of imports:

    tariffs   embargoes   quotas   import licences

2. What would be the impact on the quantity of exports of introducing an export subsidy?
3. How can governments make it more difficult for importers to import goods?

8.7 The merits of free trade

LEARNING OUTCOMES

Candidates should be able to:
- discuss the merits of free trade.

The ASEAN–China free trade area is the largest in the world in terms of population

The case for free trade

Free trade is trading without hindrance in the form of barriers such as import tariffs.

Free trade enables countries to specialise in what they do most efficiently and then trade with others to buy – at less cost than manufacturing itself – what other countries produce.

Free trade can make people more prosperous. If countries specialise in their best lines of production, the global output of goods and services is increased. Along with economies of scale, more will be produced at lower cost per unit and of better quality.

Comparative advantage

Brazil is the world's leading exporter of sugar, coffee, beef and orange juice. Soyabeans are its most rapidly increasing export, mainly to China. Other major exports include aircraft, vehicles, iron ore, steel, textiles and footwear. If it wished, Brazil could also be self-sufficient in making all its own clothes (using its existing land and labour), but to understand why the country concentrates instead on the other products you need to be familiar with the theory of **comparative advantage**.

An important economic principle is that of **specialisation according to comparative advantage**. This states that a country should concentrate on the lines at which it is relatively most efficient. For example, Pakistan and Bangladesh are both very efficient textile producers. This is because they have access to the raw materials such as silk, cotton and wool. They also have a highly skilled labour force and many factories equipped with modern machinery. It therefore makes sense for these countries to produce textiles.

ACTIVITY

Make a list of all the food and drink that you have consumed today. Discuss with your classmates which of these items are likely to have been produced in your own country or imported. Now list the white goods (e.g. refrigerators, washing machines) that you have in your home. Find out the make of these goods and whether they are likely to be imports.

EXAM TIP

There are clearly a number of potential advantages of free trade: make sure that you are able to discuss these various benefits.

The UK, and other European countries, import textiles from Pakistan and Bangladesh. This does not mean that the UK cannot produce textiles – indeed it has a number of textile manufacturers, particularly of woollen garments. However, many businesses that produced textiles in the UK closed down (particularly between 1970 and 2000) because they could not compete with the textile industry in Eastern Europe, Pakistan, Bangladesh and elsewhere. Instead of producing textiles the UK therefore concentrates on products in which it has a comparative advantage, in this case pharmaceutical products, among others.

Other benefits of free trade

- Free trade enables people to sell their products to those who are willing to pay the highest price for them. This means that the producer is able to capture a larger proportion of the value of the product.
- Free trade increases the range of products available, giving consumers more choice.
- Free trade enables consumers to buy better-quality imports from other countries.
- Free trade enhances the spread of new ideas, new lifestyles and new products.
- New job opportunities result from the growth of production.

The World Trade Organisation

The **World Trade Organisation (WTO)** was set up in 1995. Its purpose is to open up trade for the benefit of all, achieved by rules and agreements set out for trading between nations. Its main principles are:

- to pursue open borders – that is, free trade
- the most favoured nation principle: if a country reduces tariffs to another country it will do so to all the other members of the WTO.

WTO agreements are followed by most of the world's trading nations. Through the organisation, trade ministers come together to make agreements and to settle trading disputes. The main activities are negotiating a reduction or elimination of import tariffs and other barriers to trade, and agreeing rules on the conduct of trade – for example, rules relating to dumping of waste.

Free trade areas

There are a number of **free trade areas**. These include:

- European Union (EU), consisting of 27 countries including Germany, France and the UK
- North American Free Trade Area (NAFTA): US, Canada and Mexico (NAFTA)
- Asia-Pacific Cooperation, consisting of over 20 countries, including the US, Japan, Russia and China
- Association of South East Asian Nations (ASEAN)
- South American Free Trade Area (SAFTA).

ACTIVITY

Mexico is a major producer of agricultural products. It is the world's largest producer of avocados, onions, limes, lemons and sunflower seeds. Produce a poster that explains how Mexico benefits from concentrating on these agricultural products.

KEY POINTS

1 Free trade leads to specialisation and the possibility of increased production of goods at lower cost.

2 With free trade countries can specialise in lines where they have the greatest comparative advantage.

3 There are a number of free trade areas in the world, the largest of which is ASEAN–China.

SUMMARY QUESTIONS

1 Explain how your country benefits from advantages resulting from free trade.

2 Explain why your country imports a particular product that it could produce domestically, but chooses not to.

3 How does the WTO contribute to creating free trade?

8.8 The merits of protection

LEARNING OUTCOMES

Candidates should be able to:
- describe the merits of protection.

DID YOU KNOW?

An infant industry may need some trade protection as it develops in an economy. India and Pakistan have developed their pharmaceutical industries in the last 25 years – initially they needed protection against European and US imports. Today companies from India and Pakistan are world leaders in the industry.

Most countries subsidise wind energy – because it is an infant industry and part of a strategic industry

Reasons for protection

In Unit 8.6 we saw how countries can take measures to protect domestic industries. Here we look at the purposes of these measures:

- To help a new industry to grow: for example, a country trying to develop its own biofuels industry might find it difficult to compete with other large countries that have already developed their own large-scale biofuels industry, such as Brazil or the US. There is a good case for protecting new **infant industries** until they are strong enough to be competitive. The government can then gradually reduce the protective measures.

- To protect small industries that are important to an economy: for example, **small island economies** (e.g. Mauritius) will not be able to produce agricultural goods, such as sugar cane, or manufacture products, such as packet sugar, on the same scale as large countries. However, the country may want to develop the sugar industry because the climate and conditions in the country are favourable for sugar production.

- To protect local jobs against cheap imports from large countries: many people in a country might depend on, for example, work in the textile industry. A strong argument for protection is to protect domestic industries against dumping (selling at a price that is below the cost – technically the marginal cost – of producing a product). This occurs when a business takes advantage of different

EXAM TIP

In the examination you might be asked to discuss protectionism. You will need to be able to consider both its advantages and disadvantages and come to a reasoned conclusion. A one-sided answer will limit the number of marks you can be awarded.

price elasticity of demand in two markets. It may sell mass-produced goods at a relatively high price at home, but the goods will also be exported and sold at a very low cost overseas.

- To protect the current account of the balance of payments: the case study in Unit 8.6 showed how Ecuador has imposed tariffs on over 600 products to reduce imports and prevent the country getting into debt.
- To protect domestic industries from cheap subsidised imports: dairy farmers in the EU received export subsidies for butter, cheese, milk and skimmed milk powder which drove down prices of these agricultural goods in importing countries. In 2009 many farmers in developing countries complained and the countries retaliated by subsidising their own farmers.
- To protect strategic industries: for example, electricity, gas, nuclear, wind and solar energy. Without steady energy supplies a country's industries could be forced to shut down. Governments try to make sure that a large percentage of energy is supplied within the domestic economy. In the UK the government has been subsidising the development of wind, wave and nuclear energy, as well as low carbon-emitting coal-fired power stations.
- To encourage green and environmentally friendly technologies: the government may subsidise these technologies within the domestic economy. Industries that are less cost-efficient but more environmentally efficient are protected against lower-cost but less environmentally efficient imports.
- To protect intellectual property rights (IPRs): for example, the formula for a new medicine or scientific invention. It may take years of research to develop these and it may be argued that individuals, businesses and countries should be able to protect them against copying.

Protectionism is everywhere

We have seen how all countries protect their industries in some way. Even countries that appear to be strongly in favour of free trade may be **protectionist** when it suits them. During the recession of 2008–9 the US government initially set out a requirement for US firms to use domestic steel and manufacturing projects as part of a package of measures designed to pull the country out of recession. At the same time governments in North America, the EU and Japan paid out subsidies worth billions of dollars of to protect their automobile industries.

SUMMARY QUESTIONS

1 Set out three arguments for protectionism that you feel are valid.
2 Identify two arguments for protectionism that you feel have less merit.
3 In what situations are all countries likely to protect their industries?

ACTIVITY

Find a story in the national press about the protection of a national industry. Then produce a balanced editorial article, setting out details of the protective measure and why it has been introduced. Present arguments in your editorial for and against the protective measure from the perspective of the home economy.

DID YOU KNOW?

Some Americans argued that the US should not join NAFTA. They argued that American jobs would be lost to Mexican workers who would be willing to work for lower wages. It was also argued that Mexico's lower environmental standards would give Mexican firms an unfair comparative advantage.

KEY POINTS

1 Protectionism can be used to support infant industries and strategic industries.
2 Protectionism helps against the effects of dumping and against imports from countries with a poor environmental record.
3 All countries protect their industries in some ways.

Unit 8 — Practice exam questions

SECTION 1: Multiple-choice questions

Each question has ONE correct answer.

1. Which of the following may be a disadvantage of specialisation and trade for a country?
   a. Less choice of goods for consumers
   b. Increasing reliance on income from one product
   c. Lower production costs
   d. Less efficient use of factors of production

2. Which of the following is NOT included in the balance of payments current account?
   a. The value of goods exported
   b. The value of incomes from abroad
   c. The value of money transfers out of the country
   d. The value of import taxes

3. Which is an example of an invisible export for a country?
   a. Tourists from abroad spending on hotels
   b. Tourists from the country spending in other countries
   c. Businesses from the country using another country's banking services
   d. Businesses from the country selling goods abroad

4. What is meant by a *floating exchange rate*?
   a. The price of a currency is fixed against one other currency
   b. The price of a currency fluctuates due to supply and demand
   c. The government controls the price of a currency
   d. Prices of exports and imports are stable

5. In the year 2009, the UK pound (£) was worth US$1.50. If the UK pound appreciates by 10 per cent, the new exchange rate will be:
   a. UK£1 = US$1.35
   b. UK£1 = US$1.40
   c. UK£1 = US$1.65
   d. UK£1 = US$1.55

6. Which of the following is the most likely effect of speculators moving money out of a country?
   a. The country's government needs to increase spending
   b. The value of the country's currency goes up
   c. Interest rates in the country go down
   d. The value of the country's currency goes down

7. What might be the effect of government monetary policy on a country's rate of exchange?
   a. Tariffs increasing import prices and higher exchange rate
   b. Subsidies decreasing export prices and lower exchange rate
   c. Increased interest rates leading to higher exchange rate
   d. Increased interest rates leading to lower exchange rate

8. Assuming that the price elasticity of demand for a country's exports is inelastic and for imports is elastic, what may be the effect of an exchange rate rise of 10 per cent?
   a. Imports rising by less than 10 per cent and exports rising by more than 10 per cent
   b. Imports rising by more than 10 per cent and exports falling by less than 10 per cent
   c. Imports falling by more than 10 per cent and exports falling by more than 10 per cent
   d. Imports falling by less than 10 per cent and exports rising by less than 10 per cent

9. Which of the following is NOT a method of trade protectionism?
   a. An embargo
   b. An import quota
   c. A sales tax
   d. An export subsidy

SECTION 2: Structured questions

Country A is a developing nation, whose economy has made great progress in recent years. This sustained growth has transformed the nation from one that was in receipt of food and development aid from international institutions to a self-sufficient net exporter. The government of Country A has recently decided to fix the value of its currency to the US dollar, to allow for more stability in trade.

Manufacturing has modernised and diversified, with traditional industries such as textiles being joined by highly automated car production plants and an infant computer production industry. These products are generally aimed at the cheaper end of the market and are starting to be demanded worldwide.

Service industries have also been a large area of growth; in particular, new technology has allowed multinational financial organisations to base their service and call centres in the country.

As the economy grows, however, consumers are becoming increasingly wealthy and demanding high-value imported products. Tourists from Country A are also increasingly able to afford to travel abroad for holidays, with the US a popular destination. The government of Country A is concerned that this may lead to a balance of payments current account deficit in the near future.

1 a Explain what economists mean by *sustained growth* for a country. (4)
  b Describe TWO ways in which food and development aid may have helped Country A become self-sufficient. (6)
  c Explain what is meant by *net exporter* and comment on this for Country A. (4)
  d Suggest TWO reasons why fixing the currency against the US dollar may lead to *trade stability*. (6)

2 a Explain, in the context of balance of payments, what is meant by the *income and transfers*. (4)
  b Using information from the text, give ONE example of each of the following: invisible imports and exports, visible imports and exports. (4)
  c Explain what will happen to the price of Country A's exports and imports if the price of the US dollar appreciates against other major trading currencies. (6)
  d Discuss the view that 'a floating exchange rate may be better for trade' in a developing country. (6)

3 a Explain how the operation of services such as call centres for international banks may contribute to the balance of payments current account of Country A. (4)
  b Discuss TWO ways in which the government of Country A may support the fixed exchange rate of the currency against the US dollar. (6)
  c The government of Country A believes that its producers have a *comparative advantage* in the production of cars. Explain what this means. (4)
  d Discuss the extent to which the use of protectionist trade policies by other countries may affect Country A's ability to benefit from comparative advantage. (6)

4 a Explain what is meant by *free trade* as an objective of the World Trade Organisation. (3)
  b Explain what is meant by an 'infant computer production industry'. (3)
  c State TWO reasons why the government of Country A may wish to support any infant industry in the short term. (6)
  d Considering the case study information and your economic knowledge, discuss the view that 'free trade will be more beneficial than protection in the long run' for developing countries. (8)

Total: 80 marks

SECTION 3: Analysis and critical evaluation

Mr Patel owns a new private limited computer production company in Country A. The company, Web Tech Ltd, makes a range of low-priced equipment, including laptop and desktop computers, printers, scanners and associated products. The company's unique selling point is its low prices, especially for the latest laptop, which the company sells at a wholesale price of US$200. Web Tech's prices are highly competitive on the domestic and international markets. All of the company's products are assembled in the main factory, which is situated in a rural area. The employees live near the factory in accommodation provided by the company and the low wages are one reason for Web Tech's low unit production costs. The company's growing output also means that it benefits increasingly from further economies of scale, especially in the bulk purchase of imported components.

Web Tech has high hopes for the export market and orders are very encouraging. However, there is potential competition from a very large company in a neighbouring country, which has recently started a strong marketing campaign. Mr Patel would like the government to impose a tariff on imported computers. He is also concerned at the recent appreciation in the exchange rate of the dollar, to which the currency of Country A is fixed, against other major currencies.

1 a Explain what is meant by *private limited company*. (2)
  b Suggest ONE likely business objective of Web Tech Ltd. (2)

2 a Explain what is meant by *low unit production costs*. (2)
  b Give ONE other example of a possible *economy of scale* for Web Tech Ltd. (2)

3 Discuss whether the company's unique selling point of low prices will guarantee success on the export market for laptop computers. (5)

4 a Explain what is meant by an *appreciation in the exchange rate*. (2)
  b Explain how an appreciation of the dollar exchange rate may affect Web Tech's exports of computers and its imports of components. (5)

5 Discuss the view that free trade and specialisation between countries benefits developing countries such as Country A. (5)

6 Using your economic knowledge and information from the text, discuss how the government of Country A may help Web Tech Ltd get established in the domestic and export markets. (7)

Total: 32 marks

Glossary

A

Absolute poverty a measure of the number of people with income below a certain figure, often UN figure of US$1.25 per day.

***Ad valorem* tax** a tax levied as a percentage of the value of the item it is imposed on (e.g. value added tax and many import taxes).

Ageing population a population with increasing average age, usually resulting in increased proportion of older to younger people.

Appreciation of currency rise in the value of the currency in terms of other currencies for which it can be exchanged.

Average fixed cost (AFC) total fixed cost of a business divided by the number of units produced or sold.

Average revenue (AR) average receipt to a business from the number of units sold.

Average total cost (ATC) total cost of production of any given output divided by the number of units sold; also referred to as average cost (AC).

B

Balance of payments account setting out financial flows resulting from a country's trading and financial exchanges with other countries.

Barter exchange of one good for another; relies on a double coincidence of wants (i.e. that two people each require what is offering the other).

Base year a year used as a basis for comparison when creating an index. The base year is given a figure of 100. Comparisons can then be made against the base year (e.g. 110 would represent a figure 10 per cent higher than the base figure).

Budget plan for the future set out in numbers. A national budget sets out government spending and expected tax and other revenues in the period ahead (often one year).

C

Capital refers to items that go into further production (e.g. machines, factory buildings). Can also be used to refer to the finance acquired by a business to pay for its activities.

Capital employed relates to financial definition of capital: total amount of finance used by a business to support its activities.

Central bank a country's main monetary authority (e.g. the United States Federal Reserve) controlling the supply of money and supervising other banks).

Choice opportunity to select from alternative end products and between alternative actions.

Company a business that is recognised in law as being separate from its owners, who are its shareholders.

Comparative advantage being relatively more efficient at certain activities compared with others that can be carried out using the same resources.

Complements goods demanded for use together (e.g. laptop computers and the computer software that can be installed on them).

Consumer Price Index (CPI) measure of the change over time in the cost of a fixed basket of goods and services, including food, housing, transport and electricity.

Contraction in supply/demand a decrease in quantity demanded or supplied resulting solely from a change in the price.

Cooperative organisation set up by a group to further their mutual interests (e.g. farmers for joint marketing of their crops).

Core worker full-time, relatively well-paid employees typically working on long-term employment contracts.

Cost-push inflation general rise in prices resulting from increases in production costs, such as an increase in the price of imported raw materials or energy.

Credit card used for making purchases; the user pays for items by a stipulated later date. A set credit limit determines how much can be spent in this way. The amount of interest charged depends on the length of the credit period.

Current account a bank account enabling an account holder to deposit and withdraw sums and make payments using their bank card. The account holder pays interest on negative balances.

Current account balance the part of the balance of payments that sets out exports and imports of goods to and from a country in a specific period of time.

Cyclical unemployment unemployment resulting from downturns in the trade cycle (i.e. when there is a general fall in demand in an economy).

D

Debit card enables the holder to make payments and to withdraw cash from their current account. The money is deducted immediately (compare credit card).

Deflation a general fall in the level of prices in a country.

Demand the quantity of a good or service that will be purchased at a particular price. Effective demand describes the desire to purchase goods backed up by the money to pay for them.

Demand-pull inflation general rise in prices resulting from a general increase in the demand for goods in an economy.

Demographic transition stages in the development of population structures from low life expectancy, with high birth and death rates, to longer life expectancy, with falling birth and death rates.

Depreciation of currency fall in the value of an international currency on international exchange markets.

Derived demand demand for a product or service resulting from its use in producing some other demanded good or service.

Glossary

Devaluation fall in the value of a currency, usually brought about by the central bank. Action is taken, such as selling the domestic currency to lower its price and make a country's goods more competitive.

Developed country country characterised by relatively high GDP per head and HDI indicators, low birth and death rates, allowing 'all … citizens to enjoy a free and healthy life in a safe environment' (Kofi Annan, former Secretary General of the UN).

Developing country low- or middle-income country, characterised by lower levels of GDP per head and industrialisation, with higher birth and death rates than developed countries (World Bank definition).

Direct tax a tax that has to be paid directly (e.g. by the income earner (income tax) or the householder (government rates)) (compare indirect tax).

Discrimination favouring or showing preferential treatment to one group or individual over others.

Diseconomies of scale the result of a firm becoming too large, when inefficiencies occur, leading to rising costs.

Disposable income money available for spending after tax and other compulsory deductions.

Division of labour concentration of workers on specific specialist work tasks.

Dumping increasing sales by exporting goods into a foreign market at lower prices than the goods cost to make in the domestic market.

E

Economic growth the increased efficiency of an economy to produce goods over time, measured by rising GDP.

Economic indicators measures used to record changes in economic performance (e.g. GDP per head in 2010 compared with 2011).

Economic problems issues that arise from balancing uses of scarce resources and goods. An opportunity cost is involved.

Economies of scale the advantages of a larger firm over a smaller one, enabling it to produce larger outputs at lower unit cost.

Equilibrium price the price at which quantity demanded equals quantity supplied to a market, and at which demanders and suppliers are content.

Equity shares in a business.

Euro international currency of most of the countries in the European Union.

Eurozone area in which the euro is the generally accepted currency (e.g. France, Germany, Belgium, Netherlands, Italy, Spain, Ireland). There are currently 16 countries in the Eurozone.

Exchange control limiting the quantity of foreign currency available to the general public and to business, as well as controlling the purposes for which foreign currency can be used.

Exchange rate amount at which one country's currency can be bought with another's (e.g. the Mexican peso against the US dollar).

Extension in supply/demand an increase in the quantity demanded or supplied resulting solely from the change in the price of that good.

Externalities effects resulting from a particular activity, such as pollution caused by a production process. Externalities can be positive or negative.

F

Factors of production resources used in production: land, labour, capital and enterprise.

Fiscal policy deliberately adjusting the relationship between government taxes and spending in order to achieve government policy objectives.

Fixed costs any costs that do not vary with the level of output (e.g. rent and rates).

Fixed exchange rate established rates at which one currency will exchange for another. The government can fix the exchange rate between its currency and one or more other currencies; difficult to maintain over time.

Fixed incomes incomes not related to the rate of inflation in a country, and tend to remain stable because the earners have little bargaining power (e.g. pensions of older people).

Floating exchange rate an exchange rate between one currency and others determined by their relative demand and supply; changes from day to day.

Free trade carrying out trade without tariffs, quotas or other restrictions on trading.

Free trade area region in which there are no restrictions on importing and exporting (e.g. North American Free Trade Area (NAFTA)).

Frictional unemployment employment resulting from a lack of smoothness in demand and supply adjustments. Tends to be of a relatively short duration.

Fringe benefits non-monetary work-related advantages, such as subsidised travel or low-price company canteen meals.

G

Government interference government actions to regulate and control market forces (e.g. through taxing and subsidising business activity).

Gross Domestic Product (GDP) the value of the output of an economy in a given period. Also the value of all earning and spending in an economy within a time period.

Gross Domestic Product per head the value of total output of the economy in a given period, divided by the population.

H

HIV/AIDS Acquired Immune Deficiency Syndrome (AIDS) is an infectious disease caused by the Human Immunodeficiency Virus (HIV).

Human Development Index (HDI) an index used to measure human well-being. It is made up of three elements of human development: life expectancy, education and standard of living.

Glossary

I

Incidence of tax the burden of a tax: the extent to which the burden falls on the end consumer or the business selling to the end consumer.

Indirect tax a tax that is paid by an intermediary who then passes the tax on to an end payer (e.g. taxes on the purchase of goods are first paid by a business, which then passes some or all of the tax on to the purchaser/consumer).

Inelastic demand demand that changes by a smaller proportion than the change in price that instigated demand to change.

Inequality differences in income and living standards between members of a society.

Infant industry an industry that is in its earliest stages of development in a particular country.

Inflation a general increase in the level of prices in a country over time.

Integration the bringing together of businesses and their operations (e.g. through merger and takeover). Vertical integration involves taking over an earlier or later stage of production. Horizontal integration involves the joining together of businesses at the same stage of production.

Interest rate the price charged for borrowing money.

International Monetary Fund (IMF) an international body set up to provide finance for countries that need relatively short-term financial support (e.g. because they are not able to meet international debts in the short term).

International specialisation countries focusing on lines of production at which they are relatively efficient.

Invisible trade trade in services (e.g. banking, insurance, transport).

J

Joint supply two or more goods that are produced as part of the same production process (e.g. by-products created in the production of sugar from sugar cane can be used as fuel for sugar mills).

Joint venture an organisation jointly set up by two organisations; frequently set up when one international company wants to enter a new market.

L

Labour the human resource enabling both physical work and intellectual work.

Land a general term used to describe the gifts of nature. It not only includes farmland, but also other gifts of nature, such as oil contained in an oilfield.

Legal tender currency that is recognised in law as suitable payment in a given country.

Life expectancy the average age that a person can expect to live to in a particular area.

Limited liability the greatest amount that a company's owners might have to pay out to meet debts, the maxium being the sum that they invested in the business.

Loan a sum of money advanced to a borrower, usually in return for a payment of interest as well as the repayment of the loan.

Loan capital that part of the finance of a business that is borrowed rather than raised by the owners from their own resources.

M

Market any situation where buyers and sellers come into contact.

Market capitalisation the value of all the shares of a company on a particular day.

Market clearing price the price at which the quantity supplied to the market will be bought in its entirety (with no unsatisfied demand).

Market demand the total value of the demand in the market arrived at by adding together the individual demands of all buyers.

Market economy an economy in which most economic decisions are made freely by private citizens, with only a limited amount of government interference.

Market failure inefficient allocation of resources by the market such that another outcome would have led to participants in the market being better off.

Megacity a city with over 10 million inhabitants.

Merger an agreement between two businesses to join together to create a single enterprise.

Merit good a good that it is judged an individual should have on the basis of need (e.g. food provided to the poor through a public distribution system).

Microbusiness a business that employs fewer than five people.

Mixed economy an economy in which decisions are made through a combination of buyers and sellers deciding what to buy, produce and sell, coupled with some government interference, such as taxing or subsidising the production of some goods.

Monetary policy regulations created by the government and monetary authorities to control the supply of money in an economy and the level of interest rates.

Monopoly existence of only one firm in an industry. Businesses with monopoly powers are able to exercise some control over the supply to the market and the prices charged.

Mortgage borrowing to purchase land or property that is secured against the land or property.

Multinational a business that operates in two or more countries. Most large multinationals have a presence in several countries across the globe.

Multiplier effect the ripple of ongoing spending that results from an initial increase in spending in an economy.

N

NAIRU the Non-Accelerating Inflation Rate of Unemployment: defines a level of unemployment below which there is an increase in inflation.

Glossary

National debt the sum of money owed by the government as a result of borrowing, usually through the issue of government bills and bonds (promises on paper to repay in the future coupled with additional interest payments).

Natural increase in population increase in population resulting from the birth rate exceeding the death rate.

Natural monopoly a monopoly resulting from natural factors (e.g. minerals being found only in a certain region).

NICs (newly industrialised countries) countries such as Brazil, Russia, India and China that are experiencing rapid industrial growth.

O

Opportunity cost the next best alternative that is given up when a decision is made.

Optimum population the most efficient size of population in terms of combining the other resources in the economy with the number of people.

Overpopulation in a country, too many people relative to the availability of other resources, leading to an inefficient use of resources.

P

Participation rates number of people who are prepared to work; number of people within working age range.

Partnership a business owned by two or more people, often carrying out professional work or a business service on a local scale.

Perfect competition a situation in which there are many buyers and sellers in a market, each of whom has knowledge of all of the prices being offered in the market. Their products are identical. New firms can readily enter or leave the market.

Population pyramid a diagram indicating the numbers of people in a country, by age and gender groups.

Price competition situation in which businesses seek to sell at lower prices than rivals.

Price elasticity the responsiveness of quantity demanded of a product to changes in price.

Price elasticity of demand the responsiveness of quantity demanded to a change in the price of a specific item.

Price elasticity of supply the responsiveness of quantity supplied to a change in the price of a specific item.

Price maker a firm that is able to decide what price it will charge for goods and services.

Prices and incomes policy a government-imposed limit on wage increases and prices that businesses can charge.

Price stability a situation in which prices stay more or less the same over a period.

Price taker a business that can only sell at the market price (i.e. a firm in a perfectly competitive market).

Primary industry the first stage in a production process that uses natural resources (e.g. land for farming).

Private benefits advantages to an individual or group resulting from their economic actions.

Private costs the disadvantages to an individual or group resulting from carrying out an economic action.

Private sector the part of the economy owned by private individuals and organisations, not the government.

Privatisation the transfer of a business from government to private ownership.

Profit the reward for risk taking; the sum that remains after all costs have been subtracted from revenues.

Profit maximising point the production or sales level at which there is the greatest difference between total revenue and total cost.

Progressive tax a tax by which richer people pay a higher proportion of their income than poorer people.

Protection measures to limit import quantities, or to raise the price, in order to give domestic industries an increased advantage.

Public corporation government-owned firm, such as the public railway network or a state-owned airline. Senior government-appointed officials manage the firm on a day-to-day basis. Government approval is required for major expenditure decisions.

Public expenditure government spending.

Public good a product (e.g. street lighting), consumption of which by one person does not reduce the possibility of someone else consuming it (referred to as non-rivalry), and where no one can be excluded from consuming the good.

Public sector part of the economy run and managed by the government.

Q

Quality of life measurement of the benefits to living, such as the built environment, health and leisure activities, not just material goods or income.

Quota limitation on the numbers of items that can be exchanged between countries.

R

Rate of unemployment percentage of the working population who are unemployed.

Real GDP the real value of national income (or national output) when inflation is taken into consideration.

Recession two or more consecutive quarters (three-month periods) in which there is a fall in GDP.

Regional specialisation the focus of a geographical area on certain lines of production.

Regressive tax a tax by which poorer people pay a higher proportion of their income than richer people.

Regulations rules and laws.

Relative poverty state of being poor resulting from one individual or group receiving relatively less than others (e.g. less than half the average national earnings).

Glossary

Revaluation an increase in the value of a currency usually resulting from deliberate actions by government and/or monetary authorities (e.g. through the purchasing of the currency in international exchange markets).

Revenue the value of total sales made by a business within a period, usually a year.

S

Savings income that is set aside for a purpose.

Savings account a bank account designed to encourage regular savings. The interest rate is higher than for a current account.

Scarce a resource or good in limited supply compared with the demand to use it.

Secondary industry the stage in the production of goods concerned with making or using raw materials from primary industry.

Shift in demand/supply curve the effect of a change in factors other than the price of a good (e.g. a demand curve will shift to the right if a good becomes more popular, or if consumers' incomes rise; a supply curve will shift to the right if technological improvements make it easier to produce that good).

Social benefits the advantages of a particular activity to members of a society.

Social costs the negative effects to members of a community resulting from a particular activity or production of a good or service.

Specialisation concentrating on one or a small range of activities.

Specific tax a tax levied at a fixed rate per unit of output regardless of its price.

Standard for deferred payments a measure for making payments in the future.

Standard of living the basket of goods and services that an individual is able to purchase and enjoy with their income (including access to health and education services).

Stock exchange a building in which stocks and shares are traded by dealers.

Structural unemployment unemployment resulting from a major restructuring of industries in an economy (e.g. from the shift from labour-intensive agriculture to capital-intensive manufacturing).

Subsidies money granted by the state to keep down the price of goods and maintain the supply.

Substitutes alternatives that can replace others (e.g. travelling by bus instead of by car).

Supply the quantity of a good that will be produced or sold at a particular price.

Sustainable economic growth ongoing increases in GDP or living standards over time.

T

Takeover the acquisition of 51 per cent or more of the shares of another business in order to take over control of that business.

Tariff a sum of money that an importer or exporter has to pay to trade goods across borders.

Technological unemployment unemployment resulting from new developments in technology (e.g. automatic machinery replacing human labour for certain tasks).

Tertiary industry service industries that provide value for people (e.g. postal services, insurance and banking services, leisure industries).

Total cost the sum of all the fixed and variable costs at a given level of output.

Total revenue the average revenue multiplied by the number of units sold. The total receipts of a business from selling activities.

Total variable cost the sum of all the variable costs at a given level of output.

Trade cycle increasing and falling levels of economic activity over time. After four or five years of upswing (increasing production), there may be a downturn.

Trader buyer and seller of commodities and paper assets such as shares; buyers and sellers on Stock Exchanges and other financial exchanges (e.g. a trader in foreign exchange).

Trade union body, recognised in law, of employees with a common work interest who seek to further this through bargaining with employers.

U

Underpopulation too few people in a country to make efficient use of the resources available.

Unit of account one of the functions of money; money can be divided into separate units (e.g. dollars and cents), which can be used to record the value of transactions, loans and other financial deals.

V

Variable costs expenses that vary with the level of output (e.g. fuel costs, raw material costs).

Virtual monopoly an organisation, though not an absolute monopoly, able to exert considerable monopoly powers in terms of setting prices or the quantity supplied to the market.

Visible trade exports and imports of physical goods.

W

Wage gap difference in money earned by sectors of the workforce (e.g. male and female earnings).

Weighted price index a way of calculating price changes. Items on which more of a typical person's income is spent are given the greatest weighting in the index. The index is thus weighted to give greater consideration to relatively important items of expenditure.

Weighting importance attached to items appearing in an index; the greater the weight, the more account is given to a particular factor that appears in an index.

World Trade Organisation (WTO) international body supervising international trading. It actively seeks to encourage the removal of tariffs and quotas and to create regulations governing fair trading between nations.

Index

Key terms are in **bold** and are also listed in the glossary

A
absolute poverty 122, 168
acquisitions 105
ad valorem **tax 128**
age distribution of population 23, 172
ageing populations 177
appreciation of currency 192, 194
apprenticeships 54
auditors 51
average fixed cost (AFC) 88, 90, 93
average revenue (AR) 94–5, 99
average total cost (ATC) 90, 93, 99
average variable cost (AVC) 89, 90, 93

B
balance of payments 124–5, 188–9
banker's drafts 47
banks 46–7, 48–9
barter 44
base year 141, 143
birth rates 170, 171, 174
board of directors 74–5
bonuses 52
borrowing 46, 64, 65
budget 118
businesses
　competition 98–9
　costs 88–93
　economies and diseconomies of scale 106–7
　factors of production 86–7
　goals 96, 97
　growth 84–5
　inflation and 147
　integration 104–5
　monopolies 100–1, 108–9
　profits 96–7
　revenue 94–5
　sizes of 102–3
　types of 72–81

C
capital 4, 38–9
capital employed 87, 102
carrying capacity (population) 177
central banks 48–9
cheques 47
choices 2, 3

　the market and 33
　opportunity cost 6–9
commercial banks 46–7
commission 52
companies 74
　multinational 78–9
　private 75
　public 76–7
　see also businesses
comparative advantage 198–9
competition 98–9
complements (complementary goods) 22, 23
conglomerates 105
conservation 38
construction industries 150
consumer durables 64
Consumer Price Index (CPI) 118, 140–1
consumers 8
contraception 171
contractions in supply/demand 19
cooperatives 80–1
core workers 149
corporation tax 134
cost-push inflation 144–5
costs
　fixed and variable 88–9
　and inflation 144–5
　and output 92–3
　production 24
　total and average 90–1
cowrie shells 44
credit cards 46
current accounts 46
current account (balance of payments) 123–4, 188–9
cyclical unemployment 153, 154

D
death rates 170, 171, 174
debit cards 46
deflation 146, 147
demand 16–17
　causes of change in 22–3
　effective 32
　equilibrium price and 20–1
　monopolies and 100–1
　price elasticity of 26–7, 30–1, 134–5, 195
　resource allocation and 32
demand-pull inflation 145
demographic transition 174

demography 174
　see also population
depreciation of currency 192, 194, 195
derived demand 59, 86
devaluation 193
developed countries 166, 172, 175
developing countries 166, 172, 174–5
development, economic 166–7
direct taxes 128
directors, company 74
disciplinary procedures 61
discrimination 58
diseconomies of scale 107
disposable income 23
dividends 51, 74
division of labour 62–3
dumping (of goods) 200–1

E
earnings 52–3
　changes in over time 54–5
　different occupations 56–9
　trade unions and 60, 61
economic growth 120–1, 168
economic indicators 139
　employment/unemployment 148–55
　Gross Domestic Product 156–7
　inflation 141, 144–7
　living standards 158–61
　price indexes 140–3
economic problems 2–3
economies of scale 106–7, 108
effective demand 16, 32
embargoes 196
employees
　changes in earnings 54–5
　choice of occupation 52–3
　earnings in different occupations 56–9
　government 115
　specialisation 62–3
　trade unions 60–1
employment 148
　government policies 116–17
　patterns and levels of 148–51
　unemployment 152–5
enterprise 4
equilibrium price 20–1
equity 75
euro 195

210

Index

Eurozone 195
exchange control 196
exchange rates 190–1
   fluctuations 145, 192–5
   manipulation 196
expenditure
   patterns of 66–7
   public versus private 39
exports 124, 188, 195
extensions in supply/demand 19, 28
externalities 37
extractive industries 150

F
factors of production 4–5, 86–7
fertility rates 170, 171, 174
firms *see* businesses
fiscal policy 119
fixed costs 88, 90
fixed exchange rates 191
fixed incomes 147
floating exchange rates 191, 192
foreign exchange market 190
free trade 198–9
free trade areas 199
freedom and development 167
frictional unemployment 153
Friedman, Milton 39
fringe benefits 52
full employment 116

G
Gini index 167
goals, business 96, 97
government interference 14
governments
   balance of payments 124–5
   central banks and 48–9
   conflicting aims 126–7
   and economic decision-making 14
   and economic growth 120–1
   as employers 115
   and employment/unemployment 116–17, 155
   and opportunity cost 9
   poverty reduction 168–9
   and price stability 118–19
   as producers 114–15
   public corporations 82–3
   redistribution of income 122–3, 169
   regulations 130–1
   subsidies 132–3

   taxation 128–9, 134–5
Gross Domestic Product (GDP) 120, 156–7, 158–60
Gross Domestic Product per head 120, 157

H
HIV/AIDS 34, 175
Human Development Index (HDI) 160–1
Human Poverty Index (HPI) 161

I
imports 124, 188, 195
   trade protection 128, 196
incidence of tax 135
income
   disposable 23
   fixed 147
   low, middle and high income countries 166
   patterns of 66–7
   redistribution 122–3, 169
   taxes on 129
indirect taxes 128, 135
inelastic demand 27, 31, 134, 135
inequality 122, 167
infant industries 200
inflation 118, 141, 142
   causes of 144–5
   consequences of 146–7
integration 104–5
intellectual property rights (IPRs) 201
interest 46
interest rates 48, 64
International Monetary Fund (IMF) 49
international specialisation 186
invisible trade 188

J
job satisfaction 52
joint supply 25
joint ventures 105

L
labour 4, 116
   demand for 56, 59
   division of 62–3
   see also employees
land 4, 144–5
legal tender 48
life expectancy 167
limited liability 51, 74
living standards 158–61, 180–1

loan capital 75
loans 46

M
manufacturing industries 150
market 32
   and economic decision-making 14–15
   merits of market system 32–3
market capitalisation 102
market clearing price 21
market demand 17, 22–3
market economy 14
market failure 34–5
market share 102
medium of exchange, money as 45
megacities 177
mergers 104, 105
merit goods 35, 115
microbusinesses 52
migration rates 170, 171
mixed economy 15, 39
monetary policy 48
money
   banks and 46–7
   functions of 44–5
   spending, saving and borrowing 64–5
monopolies 100–1, 108–9, 115
mortality rates 170, 171, 174
mortgages 46
multinationals 78–9, 102
multiplier effect (spending) 155

N
NAIRU 126
national debt 49
nationalisation 83
natural increase in population 171
natural monopolies 115
NICs (Newly Industrialised Countries) 150

O
occupations
   choice of 52–3
   earnings and 56–9
OPEC 82
opportunity cost 3, 6–9
optimum population 176
overdrafts 46
overpopulation 176–7, 179
overtime 52

211

Index

P

participation rates (employment) 149
partnerships 72–3, 84
patents 31
pay *see* wages
perfect competition 98–9
population
　change 174–5
　factors affecting growth 170–1
　rates of growth 172–3
　size 176–7
　structure 23, 178–9
population pyramids 172
poverty 122–3, 161, 168–9
price competition 98
price elasticity 26
price elasticity of demand 26–7
　for exports and imports 195
　and taxation 134–5
　usefulness of 30–1
price elasticity of supply 28–9
price indexes 140–3
price makers 99, 100
price stability 118–19
price takers 99
prices
　competition and 33, 98–9
　equilibrium price 20–1
　governments and 118–19
　inflation 144–7
　market economy and 14–15
　monopolies and 100
　and substitutes 23, 31
　and supply 24, 25
prices and incomes policies 119
primary industries 150
private companies 75
private costs and benefits 36
private expenditure 39
private sector 57, 77, 83
　see also businesses
privatisation 83
producers
　decisions made by 9
　government influence on 130–5
production
　costs 24
　factors of 4–5, 86–7
profit 96–7, 101
profit maximising point 96
progressive taxes 128–9, 169
proportional taxes 129
protection, trade 196–7, 200–1
public companies 76–7, 85

public corporations 82–3
public expenditure 39
public goods 34, 115
public sector 57, 83, 115

Q

quality of life 160, 181
quotas, import 196

R

rate of unemployment 116
real GDP 157
recession 48, 121
redistribution of income 122–3, 169
regional specialisation 186
Registrar of Companies 75, 77
regressive taxes 129, 169
regulations 48, 130–1
relative poverty 122, 168
resources 2
　allocating 14–15, 32
　conserving versus using 38–9
Retail Price Index (RPI) 140–3
revaluation 193
revenue 30, 94–5

S

salaries *see* wages
sales taxes 134–5
savings 64–5, 66, 147
savings accounts 46
scarce resources 2
seasonal unemployment 153
secondary industries 150
Sen, Amartya 167
service industries 150
shareholders 51, 74, 75, 77, 96
shares 50, 51, 76–7
shifts in demand/supply curve 22, 24
Smith, Adam 15
social costs and benefits 37
sole traders 72, 84
specialisation 62–3, 186–7, 198
specific tax 128
stakeholders 38
standard for deferred payments, money as 128
standards of living 158–61, 180–1
stock exchanges 50–1, 76
strategic industries 201
structural unemployment 153
subsidies 25, 123, 132–3, 196, 201
substitutes 23, 31
suppliers 14, 18

supply 18–19
　causes of change in 24–5
　equilibrium price and 20–1
　price elasticity of 28–9
　subsidies and 133
sustainable economic growth 121

T

takeovers 104, 105
tariffs 128, 196
taxation 128
　and goods 31, 134–5
　and redistribution of income 123
　and supply 25
　types of 128–9
technological unemployment 153
tertiary industries 150
total cost 90, 93, 96, 97
total fixed cost 93
total revenue 94, 95, 96
total variable cost 93
trade
　balance of 188–9
　merits of free trade 198–9
　protection 196–7, 200–1
trade cycle 121
trade offs, government 126
trade unions 57, 60–1
traders 50

U

underpopulation 176, 179
unemployment 116, 152
　causes of 152–3
　consequences of 154–5
　dealing with 117, 153
unit of account, money as 45
urban/rural divide 178–9

V

value added tax 129
variable costs 88, 89, 90
virtual monopoly 100, 108
visible trade 188

W

wage gap 57, 58
wages 52, 53
　changes in over time 54–5
　different occupations 56–9
　and inflation 144
　trade unions and 60, 61
weighted price index 142
weighting (in price indexes) 141
World Bank 166
World Trade Organisation (WTO) 199

212